Two men

A former urban cop contending
and a seeker of solace and adv
the deserts of the American Sou

A harrowing trek

With as much food and gear as they can carry, and little else but their wiles to help them traverse an inhospitable, unmappable labyrinth of canyons near the Arizona-Utah border, the two men undertake a fortnight's journey, assuming the life-or-death challenge of exploring this land — and of then finding a way out.

A spellbinding chronicle

"That it's gritty and riveting is not just a testament to the inherent drama of the story but to Childs's successful effort to challenge himself as a writer. He's moved beyond describing rock formations and cloud patterns into deeper, more dangerous terrain and found a way to make a straightforward narrative about a tough two-week hike into something much more complex and meaningful. . . . Childs's fearlessness is infectious, and his skill and absolute sincerity make him a vital companion on an exploration of the desert or the meaning of life."

— Jeff Baker, *Portland Oregonian*

THE WAY OUT

THE WAY OUT

A TRUE STORY OF RUIN AND SURVIVAL

CRAIG CHILDS

BACK BAY BOOKS
Little, Brown and Company
NEW YORK • BOSTON

Back Bay Books / Little, Brown and Company
Time Warner Book Group
1271 Avenue of the Americas, New York, NY 10020
Visit our Web site at www.twbookmark.com

Originally published in hardcover by Little, Brown and Company, January 2005
First Back Bay paperback edition, March 2006

Copyright acknowledgments appear on page 271.

Library of Congress Cataloging-in-Publication Data

Childs, Craig Leland.
    The way out : a true story of ruin and survival / Craig Childs. — 1st ed.
        p. cm.
    ISBN 0-316-61066-6 (hc) / 0-316-10703-4 (pb)
    1. Southwest, New — Description and travel. 2. Childs, Craig Leland — Travel —
Southwest, New. 3. Deserts — Southwest, New. 4. Canyons — Southwest, New.
5. Wilderness survival — Southwest, New. I. Title.

F787.C49 2004
917.9 — dc22   2004006759

10 9 8 7 6 5 4 3 2 1

Q-FF

Book design by Fearn Cutler de Vicq

Printed in the United States of America

This book is dedicated to Laura Slavik, the indomitable.

Dirk: *Highland Scottish;* A double-edged fighting knife worn close to the body, often fashioned from a broken sword.

Craig: *Gaelic;* Of rocks and crags.

CONTENTS

THE WAY OUT

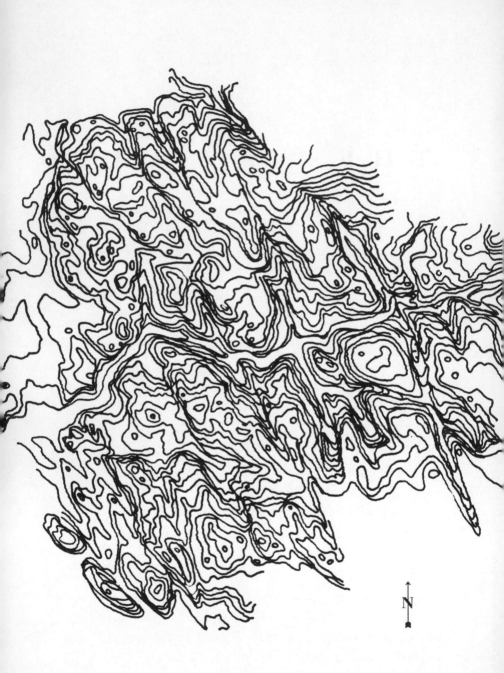

N

PROLOGUE

There is a dead man in the desert. His eye sockets are jeweled with broken stones that have randomly fallen from above. He lies curled on his side, the long bones of his legs pulled toward his chest as if he had fallen asleep in a clamshell. He is my barren saint, my man of patience waiting out the epochs in a dust-dry natural rock shelter. How he died? Impossible to tell and irrelevant. It is how he lived that brings me here. How these bones carried a man in this land.

I have walked to the skeleton before, kneeling beside his intricately derailed spine. I have touched his bare forehead, imagining his life in this same land. There are patterns I have recognized on his teeth, a certain smoothness to the wear that names him as a hunter-gatherer, a person who lived here seven hundred years ago, a thousand maybe.

Not far from him now, I am traveling across a bizarrely eroded tableland. I have come alone. In the white, tasteless heat of August in southern Utah, the dead man's bones are a point on the compass that I move toward. I carry very few belongings: no stove and no map. Water bottles are mostly empty. There is a bag of nondescript nuts and dried fruit. For sleeping I carry a threadbare serape. My pack is light.

I know other people who travel this way. They are companions of mine, itinerants roving the landscape, engrossed in a world beyond civilization. We keep boats hidden near rivers to use as ferries. Our food caches wait buried in sand so that we can eat chocolate and rice in the weeks and months of our walking.

I pause to scan the terrain ahead, considering the choices. I can walk among lopsided boulders or cut in and out of shallow canyons. A sand wash looks as though it eventually pours down the throat of a cliff . . . better not to go that way.

This is my life. It is what I do. I am a navigator. Any work I have ever taken — researching obscure fields, occasionally guiding extended tours on the pale and sandy rivers that sweep this desert — has kept me close to this place. Between jobs I survive by drinking from water holes in the far country, mapping canyons and routes for my own curiosity. Passages appear between staggering cliffs, and I follow them. I vanish layer after layer into shadow and sunlight. After weeks of walking in this kind of territory, there is no doubt about my place in the world. I am here.

One of these other travelers should be coming into view soon, walking toward me from the south. I lift a pair of binoculars and try to sight any movement in the distance, an off color in the blush of desert, a moving shadow. He is a close friend. We had planned on meeting at the skeleton, spending a couple of nights together, then continuing on our separate ways.

I do not see him out there, so I move over a ridge, into the shade of an alcove. With my pack resting behind me, I sit in red sand that is as fine as flour. My hand flattens to hold my body. When I lift it, there is a perfect print, revealing even the lines of my palms. The dust adheres to my skin. I am marked by this place, as if by birth. My life holds the reflection of this desert as much as I bear my father's eyes and my grandfather's lips. Each of us is born to a particular place, a landscape that lies in our oldest memories. Some of us remain in our places, while others flee. I am one who remained.

Looking out from this curve-ceilinged shelter, I am surrounded by a terrain worn back to its primary shapes, one geologic moment away from eroding into nothing. The wind has left globes of stone, a landscape of moons lying about, some of them weatherworn into crescents and some left whole and round. Nothing is hidden. Every fault and fracture is revealed. I am sitting in some geological notion, a weakness in the stone that the wind has gotten to, hollowed out so that a space remains.

Blocks of dark rock stand on the farthest horizon, forty, fifty miles away. I know each of them by shape, split-topped buttes two or three weeks of walking from here. Between here and the buttes I see the dark teardrop of an alcove no larger than a poppy seed in the distance. I remember its floor: pieces of pre-Columbian pottery painted with black designs on white-slipped clay, and tiny flowers of mouse prints in the blow sand. Beyond this distant alcove, I see broken cliffs. They hold a thousand-year-old ambush site where stone weapons lie derelict on the ground. Bighorn sheep still use this old hunting route, stepping into its high passages, shattering purple knife blades and crystal-white arrowheads under their hooves. Not far beyond that is the place where I once carried a handful of my father's ashes for twenty-six days and finally let them go. It is also where my friend, who is walking from the south to meet me, came after he killed a man.

This is a storytelling landscape. There is no way to move in complete silence. Shadows shift. Eroded towers of maroon and rust stand around in conversation. Up close: a tale of four boulders, four that were once one; an overhead wedge of sandstone fallen and toppled into pieces like building blocks. My boot prints come around these four boulders and lead to me, a man in a rock shelter. I turn my head to look south, toward the skeleton. Invisible to me, my friend is out there at this moment, moving through the heat.

We have traveled many times together, this friend and I, clothed in thirst, our fingertips raw among rocks. We have come here hoping for moments of exquisite beauty, for the shuddering sensation of extremity. We have pushed with our backs against the door of the land, opening it slightly more each time to let the wind, the light, the strange shadows fall onto our arms and our feet. This shifting landscape compels us in one direction and the other, wearing us down to our essence as we move.

We carry our memories into this place as if cupping water in our palms, guarding them as we walk. When we stop to rest, we open our palms and drink. We share stories, and our words are worn down by the wind and by the desolate matrix of cliffs and canyons. The stories erode into their finest grains, and then we can pick through what is left of ourselves. We come to this place to understand what has become of us.

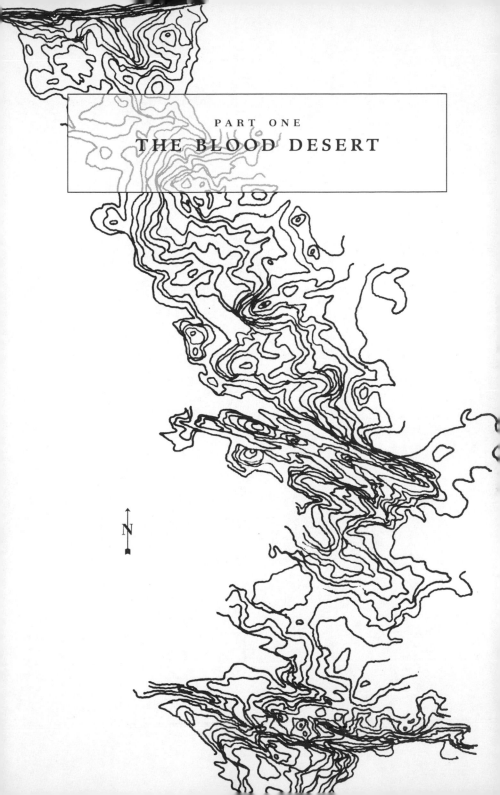

PART ONE

THE BLOOD DESERT

N

Now at Earth's lips,
Now at my lips.

— *Diné Blessingway ceremony*

DAY ONE

Winter, now. The desert races past.

Driving is a blessing of speed you don't get from walking. I lean into the seat with my boots against the dashboard and watch this oceanic country of southern Utah surge and collapse around us. Canyons fall away, inhaled by red earth. Dirk Vaughan's hand drapes the steering wheel, his fifteen-year-old Bronco moaning to the road. He drives like an old street cop, body hanging relaxed on its skeleton as if loosely prepared for impact, his eyes scanning easily, seeing everything. We pass a semi painted in the highway grime of snowmelt, nipples of soiled icicles hanging from its frame. Dirk's posture does not change as we speed around it, the signal flicked on, wheel nudged, accelerator touched, signal flicked the other way. He has been in sixteen car accidents in the forty-five years of his life: a reckless teenage rollover, numerous impacts maneuvered in close quarters with a patrol car, and high-speed collisions that left cars welded together. I have never felt safer in a vehicle with anyone.

The stereo is rattling badly. Rap music he brought along. I listen to the rainfall percussion of words. It's Dirk's Bronco. He can play whatever he wants.

Outside the window is the wilderness. It is the place beyond the road where a raven hangs tethered in the wind, its talons bunched into fists over red dirt and villages of blue-green sagebrush. For ten years Dirk and I have been walking this country together. He often talks about traveling in this place as if it were a sex act. He speaks of fluids and the enchanting touch of skin, making love with a woman of solid earth, drinking out of the belly curves of her water holes, sinking into her flood-carved folds of canyons.

I treat my travels in the same way I did when I was a child, walking with my cigar box of pencils and erasers and paper out the school door at lunch, past the tetherball and four-square games, past the blacktop to a patch of unmanicured dirt where I could alone pursue the inquiries of ants. I think of this land where I travel not as a woman, but as a moment, an instant in which a breath is drawn, a still point that ends only when forgotten.

In this place, Dirk and I have reached for each other across wind-spanned cliff faces, shouldering the weight of the other up to safe ledges. If it were not for Dirk, I imagine nothing would be left of me but a cautionary tale, a boy who learned to fly and then tumbled helplessly out of the sky. And if not for me, Dirk would still be living like a cop, a man clutched hungrily over his retired badge, alone in the wilderness.

We are driving now toward a sanctum of desert canyons in the south. It is territory foreign to us. From the air, from the maps, this unfamiliar region looks like the miscellany of a plumber's yard — a geological mess of standpipes, tubs, sink traps, and spouts trash-heaped all over one another. I have imagined for years what this far place, a cavernous domain of sandstone, might look like from the ground. Natural bridges and barren holes and shafts of shadow played against sunlight in the deep canyons. This is what I envision ahead of us. Usually Dirk and I are in a specific part of the desert, a few thousand square miles in Utah where we have named the canyons and mesas for ourselves. This will be different.

Snow as dry as sawdust tumbles at the windshield. A squall briefly passes the highway. The road swings around cliff heads, beyond the brief tempest, taking us down a canyon, through a small town where I've stopped numerous times for Navajo tacos, the restaurant and the gas station owned by the same man, whose face is always waiting in the window. Many of my memories lie along this road. I used to drive here at the beginning and end of each work season, back when I earned a living guiding on rivers to the south. I once drove out alone to spend an entire winter in that nation of salmon-colored mesas to the west, walking the cold desert as if I were a long-distance trader, my wares banging against my back. When I was younger, there were journeys along this road with my father, his truck loaded with guns and whiskey bottles clacking in a box like explosives, a boot-battered copy of *Walden* on the floorboard.

Past the town, barbed wire goes by, gates rigged shut. Faint two-track roads stab away, overgrown with smoky-green rabbitbrush. I know where the roads go: That one bucks over groves of bedrock; the next leads down a canyon to a wall of nine-hundred-year-old rock carvings of bighorn sheep and spirals and humans with spears.

Music scratches out of Dirk's tinny speakers. He sings along only to the lyrics he most wants me to hear. His fingers work a rhythm over the steering wheel. I see him glance my way, and he says, "People in the city just don't see the minutiae the way we do."

He waits, and when I say nothing in response, he continues, his steering-wheel hand flashing as he talks. "Wilderness. You need to be fucking awake out there. It's truly too much god-damned work for people. To go out and survive. To truly live and not get killed. Too much work."

His voice jousts around as if he is in a knife fight. I don't bother arguing with him. Not now. We will be on foot soon enough, and I will be on my own home ground.

"Wilderness teaches you to see this" — he gestures at the road, at the burgundy streaks of sand wind-pushed across asphalt, canyons carved out of plateaus in the distance. "It requires that you be awake."

But I cannot listen quietly to him. I shake my head.

"I don't think it's so different for people in the city," I tell him. "Some see the minutiae, some don't."

"There you go with that magnanimous Buddhist bullshit of yours," he says over the music. "All the same . . . the world is one."

I half shrug. "I don't think it's that. Everything is different."

"There it is again. It's all the same . . . it's all different."

All I can do is look through the window. Dirk is not ready for convincing. There is a commotion ahead, birds on the side of the road, something dead. A hawk is guarding a road-killed animal. Three ravens challenge it, hopping and calling with flushed throat feathers. Suddenly the ravens are in the air, black capes sweeping away from the Bronco's speeding grille. The hawk sees us, eyes besieged, thinking us the next threat. It opens its ivory-banded wings, its beak wide with a screech we cannot hear. It does not fly off. We speed past it.

"Too close," Dirk complains. "It's gonna get hit." He puts on his signal.

I say, "I'll get it."

Dirk pulls over on the shoulder, his body still relaxed, unmoved, hand circling the wheel. We sweep into a U-turn, and the hawk lifts away, driven by us from the kill. I jump out and move toward the lump of a dead prairie dog, its stomach opened from the impact of a car tire. The air is winter cold with wind, its light stretched into ocher. A sandstorm is coming.

Dirk steps out. He is a white man, his beard gray in patches. The wind picks up blond-brown hair, and he reaches up with a hand the way women often do, tucking it behind his ears with the comb of a finger. A single green bead hangs at his throat on a strip of leather, and a simply curved earring is drilled into his left earlobe. His clothing is practical, forty dollars invested in a pair of softened canvas pants that he has been wearing for years, any repairs cleanly stitched by his wife. His frame is average like mine, but ten years older, body sturdy from working as a wilderness outfitter in southeast Utah, from hefting boats and field equipment onto his shoulders along the desert-rimmed Colorado River.

While I fetch the dead prairie dog, Dirk looks up at the ravens spiraling over his head. The hawk circles among them in the opposite direction, turning Dirk's sky into a clockwork of rival orbits. He thinks that even in the city, even when he was a cop, he would have noticed such a thing. He would have stopped on the street, eavesdropping on the birds, wondering why a hawk is flying among three ravens. The ravens, he thinks, are nothing but smart, cackling jesters. The hawk, on the other hand, is a pure, voiceless spear thrown through the air. The ravens will find their food anywhere. They'll steal who knows what from trash bins. They'll shamelessly tug at plump weeks-rotted carcasses. They'll fashion fishing hooks out of gutter metal. Meanwhile, the hawk knows only the bright flash of blood and the kicking of death. No doubt it was called in by the skitter of a car-struck rodent, came down and clipped its spine, fixing the prairie dog's life with a kind of precision that the laughing ravens do not know. This is what these turning shapes in the sky tell him.

I carry the prairie dog by its hind legs, its body going long, its wet gray intestines unwinding toward the ground. Along a barbed-wire fence off from the highway, I glance up at the ravens who are watching me and imagining my next move. They have their choreography well prepared, reviewing my motions on the ground while one by one cutting off and confounding the hawk. The hawk seems baffled inasmuch as a hawk can seem baffled.

I lay the prairie dog down gently so its body is elongated on the ground. I can feel its bones, the slender, miniature toes in my hand, the brads of knuckles. My thumb rubs between them, and they slide back and forth, sheets of muscle still free. It has been dead no more than half an hour. I apologize to it for the clumsy speeds at which we drive, bullets hurtling blindly down the highway.

I come back around to the Bronco, and Dirk is squinting upward. Without looking away from the movements overhead, he says, "Gray hawk. North for its range. But I'm pretty sure."

I have no idea. "Hawk," I confirm.

We get back in the Bronco and leave the bird scene behind. Dirk asks if he has ever told me his story about the horse on the side of the road, and even though he has, I say no. I've heard most of his tales many times. He is my storyteller, the man who carries me along the roofs of buildings, through gunfire, into places I would never travel on my own. I'll hear this story again.

He talks like a theater performer, hands slicing at the air, different voices assumed to tell different parts of his tales, a Southern accent called up for his *ain't*s, street smack for his *motherfuckers*.

He tells me about a horse. He gives me the introduction, how people kept horses in Denver in pockets of semirural land swallowed by the city. These animals were obsessively brushed and washed like beloved poodles, but they were horses none-theless, large, easily frightened beasts that should never face the roadside horrors of humanity.

"So the thing gets out," he says. "Who the fuck knows how. Someone left a gate open. It's running around at night terrified, headlights coming at it. *Pow!* Nailed broadside by a sedan, clipped right at the legs. Its back end was hamburger."

Every word has an exponent attached, charged and thrown. I do not listen so much to Dirk's exact words as to the way he threads them, how he pulls on some and pushes on others. His hands play off the steering wheel, air puppets to go with his story. He evokes every detail of the night, how cars stopped at odd angles and people stood horrified, helpless, while the side-walk horse thrashed on splintered legs.

Driving street by street in his patrol car, Dirk came upon the scene. Another patrol car was there, but the man in uniform was a rookie, a first-year cop. The rookie stood dismayed, not knowing whether he should contact animal control or the fire department.

Dirk slowed, studying the way people were positioned, their bodies drawn back in disbelief and fear. He looked at their faces and their relief upon seeing him. *Finally, help is here.* He pulled near and sighted the horse. His heart immediately fled his body like a faltered breath. He knew that there was no motive here, no evidence to gather, only this: An animal had stumbled into the carnage of his city. He slipped the patrol car into park. What mistake had been made? Who allowed this creature into our barren and cruel hands? Humans are all guilty, he answered himself as he opened the door, each of us condemned to this madhouse we have built. But the wild, commanding innocence of animals should never be laid open here.

Dirk could not tolerate being a passive witness to such suffering. He stepped out of the car, his body strained with resolve. He pushed a gap between the people. Their faces were glad for the relief, their questions dashing out: *How can we get this animal to the vet? Is there something you can do for the pain?* He did not return their deluded optimism, thinking, You all know what needs to be done. The first cop looked at him, same expression, *What do we do here?* Dirk slid by him.

He paced directly up to the dashing form of the horse and pulled a six-shot .357 revolver from his holster, steadying the barrel inches from the horse's head. He fired five of his six bullets.

Dirk mimics every shot across the steering wheel, his head cocked to the recoil, *pow, pow, pow, pow, pow!*

When he turned away from the executed horse, he faced the witnesses. A woman sputtered and cried through the spiderweb of her hands. A pair clung together, their eyes scandalized. A man's unbelieving face stared at him. He looked at each of their expressions in a single sweep, saying nothing. He walked past these bystanders toward his patrol car to make his calls. If they did not understand, he had no business explaining it to them. Everyone here will find a way to cope, he figured. We all have our illusions.

As Dirk drives, I think back to the way he fired his gun over the steering wheel beside me, the bravado of his recoil. I say, "You enjoyed it after a few shots."

He glances across his arm at me. "The killing? It's an abstraction at that point. Sure, there's a perverse pleasure. Otherwise, what are you going to do? You gonna hate yourself for doing what is right? For making the one move that no one else is willing to make? Of course, I didn't have to fire those last three shots with those badass hollow-point bullets blowing open its brains, but I was already there. The animal was going down."

"You adored the killing as much as you hated it."

"You, young brother, would be in an insane asylum if you had to do the shit I did."

"I've belonged in an insane asylum all my life."

Dirk laughs, shaking his head. "It's no contest of comparison, Opie, but the polarity between the two sides of my coin is more than a match for your crooked genes."

I unraveled his words in my mind, as if picking apart a code. *The two sides of my coin:* on one side is his human-stained memory of cophood and on the other his current life of drifting through the wilderness. *Your crooked genes:* a family of alcoholic men who died suddenly and early.

I look at Dirk. How dare he. He cannot claim one of us as crazier or more sane than the other. We are the yin and the yang wrapped around each other. He knows this, only he forgets in the boldness of his stories sometimes, imagining one of us as more glorious or more wretched. He will remember once we are out there, on foot.

I glance out the window to my side, a finger habitually running across a sickle of carved greenstone that hangs from my neck. Its edge is polished from years of my touching. Instead of pursuing an argument, I scan the comb of a distant ridge and follow it until I lose sight of it.

Shooting the Storm Drain

I was thirty-two years old. My father's wife called me at home. Her words came like a letter slipped quickly from its envelope, handed over: "Your father is dead."

I sat on the floor with the phone. I laid a hand down.

"He had a heart attack," she said. "I found him in the kitchen."

The first words to come out of my mouth were whispered, and I could not stop them. "You are free now."

There was silence. Slowly, she said, "You are free, too."

I almost laughed, but that would have broken me just then. I returned the phone to its cradle. I let my mind be quiet for a moment. I breathed in, holding myself still. The breath felt like one taken before a dive, its air treasured.

He is dead, I thought. Then I was gone.

The flight to the funeral carried me over the desert, a small commuter plane out of Colorado in the middle of July. Summer storms had broken their way into the deeper southwest. Fists of clouds lifted 45,000 feet above Arizona. The plane's wings plunged sideways in the turbulence, the body suddenly kicking forward. Poltergeists of luggage leaped from under the seats. As the six other passengers clutched seat backs and armrests, I stared out the window, watching the landscape that held my life.

We flew down off the sheer rock of the canyon lands into the cracks and cliffs that tumbled downward toward the southern desert, the dry, hot, rock-broken country where there is no rounded sandstone, no sheer cliffs, no green-topped mesas, only rags and breaks of cactus-studded mountains. The land I watched was filled with my father, memories of him taking me out, nights when he told me about the stars, his truck breaking down in far desert places where we shot rabbits and quail for supper.

This was the Sonoran Desert, my first home. No longer the erotic reds of Utah and northern Arizona, this was splintered earth, jags of dead volcanoes lying about, the Desert of the Fist, where I was born. I saw block-edged canyons opening like heel cracks. One night, my father plunged his truck off the edge of one of these canyons. The thing I remembered about his accident, even though I was not there, is a tow chain that came loose as the truck rolled. It snapped like a bullwhip, busting out the windshield. I imagine loose handgun bullets falling like snow through the cab as it tumbled. A fishing knife, spare keys, the diamond shards of a whiskey bottle, binoculars, a book on stargazing, pocket change. The truck rolled eight times before slamming against a boulder, stopping there. The bed tore off and continued on its own like a barrel thrust loose on a ship's deck. My father's wristwatch landed a hundred feet downslope.

He found himself trapped on the floorboard, bleeding. The roof of the cab was crushed to the seat. Gas dribbled onto his forehead like gutter rain. There was no moon that night. He could see nothing.

My father and I traveled to the site of this wreck many times. I was maybe ten years old the first time we went, seeing him only by visitation negotiated with my mother, who begrudgingly thought it important that I have experiences with a father figure. We found bits of his life scattered in the canyon — a matchbook, a writing pen, a 1976 Arizona fishing license. For years we kept finding things.

Every time we went to this place, he told me that devils had been there the night of the accident. He said that he had felt evil predators lurking around, sniffing him out. When he said this his voice curled with fear, the only time he ever showed such an emotion to me. He said he had been able to hear them and smell them as he shivered in the cold, upside down, his hair wet with gasoline. He reached around for a weapon, for anything. He had been drinking. Maybe it was the gas fumes. He was sure that these beasts wanted nothing more than to tear his heart from his chest.

For the first time, then, I knew that he would die. It would happen the same way his father died, the same way his father's father had died. It would be his heart.

The afternoon after his death, the commuter plane deposited me in Phoenix, and I caught a ride to his house on the north side of the city. There were quiet voices in the living room, gentle words about my father from friends and family. I stormed in. I told them, enough quietness. I would not stand to have his memory marred by sweet stories. *He was a sonofabitch,* I told them.

I left for the backyard, escaping the swelling tears and blank stares in the house. Like Sumo wrestlers bounding their stomachs and huge arms against each other, summer storms collided overhead, mooring together with straps of lightning. Rain sheeted down all at once. Flood rain. I could feel it — not the pounding of just a hard rain, but a blinding rip and a voice screaming out of the torrent: *Flood!* I did not move. I wore no coat, no hat. Neighbors' houses disappeared into the storm, the palm trees in their yards bending in silver strokes of rain. My clothes whipped like a flag, then sagged with water, tugging and slapping.

My father had known somehow of his impending death. There had been no diagnosis since he'd refused to consult medical doctors, but he knew anyway. He had gone to all the people in his life and made his peace with them. He went to my mother to say he would never see her again, when he had not seen her for many years as it was. High school friends he had not spoken with since graduation thirty-five years earlier were subject to eerie good-byes. For the first time, he confessed his fears and regrets to an old friend. The only one left was me. He did not tell me good-bye. Our last conversation had been a typically strained five minutes on the phone: awkward inquiries and irrelevant, wary answers.

I was now his unfinished business.

I lifted a hand to break the welting needles from my face. Lightning struck ground. The earth shivered, and then came the terrible crash of air. The wind turned hurricane. It threw water off the roof behind me, creating a jet of horizontal mist. It was the kind of storm that would be gone in an hour, leaving only water and busted tree limbs. A summer storm in the low desert.

To the west of the house ran a cement ditch maybe twenty feet wide. A flash flood quickly shouldered into this minor canal, propelled out of new subdivisions to the south, former desert land where my father and I used to walk. It burst through my father's fence and swept my boots. Crosscurrents took the trunk of a nearby telephone pole. Delicate and furious tendrils shot in all directions.

My father and I had stood in this spot a number of times before, admiring this very kind of event, the city's drain network unable to handle the suddenness of such thunderstorms. He asked me what I saw in the dark, swift water, in its surface of whirling vortices. I said order working within chaos, laminar flows within turbulent ones, and he listened thoughtfully. I said that embedded in a world of entropy is an equal world of gestation. He hung his hands from the chain link and told me not to fool myself; entropy is not to be underestimated.

My father had a canoe. He had said that we would put it into one of these floods someday, to see where it went. I had scoffed. It was a low-walled lake canoe with negligible aluminum skin. A ridiculous Indian head had been stenciled onto its bow over the brand name: Sportspal. Since I had worked off and on as a river guide for a decade or so, I often ridiculed my father about this trifling, haphazardly built boat of his. He owned one short wooden paddle for it. He did not own a life vest. I told him it would sink.

I had long watched floods charge down remote canyons and spill along urban streets, fascinated by the roil of water. I had wondered where these floods went. If I could follow one, if I could not chase the water but actually go with it . . .

Now, looking through the rain, I saw the Sportspal leaning against the fence. Its body had been factory-camouflaged to look like birch bark and shredded cardboard. I walked to the canoe and jerked it over my head so that a thwart rested like a yoke across my shoulders. Rain screamed on its hull. The wind kited it into the air, and I yanked it back down to my shoulders. I reached with a free hand, grabbed the paddle from among drenched black widow webs, and pushed my way through the wind, out the backyard gate.

The canoe rolled off my shoulder. I lowered it into the chocolate-milk floodwater. The bow caught. The canoe moved. I jumped in.

For a moment the canoe spun while I situated myself, spreading my knees so that my body braced into it, becoming part of the vessel. The canoe was flimsy, easily swayed by the squirrelly currents. It made bending and popping sounds as I moved.

I tested the paddle by sweeping it into the water. Searching for permanence through the paddle and through my braced knees, I looked for the things in nature that do not change. I knew they were there, lurking in the flood, patterns and paths to follow. I had two seconds, three maybe. With a quick straightening of the canoe, I ducked under a metal barricade and slipped from the canal onto a residential street.

The street was a river. Water overflowed the sidewalks onto surrounding lawns. A lawn mower had been left out. Its handles jerked helplessly. At the first stop sign I back-paddled to the left, drifted sideways, and moved forward to cross the intersection, rainwater streaking down my face.

I had to paddle fast to maintain maneuverability through the turns, slipping around parked cars. Houses moved by on both sides, wind chimes jangling madly, little whirling lawn ornaments spinning as if about to burst. I paddled to the center to avoid the overturned trash bins that lurched down the street, their open mouths belching rubbish.

The flood took a right turn down Hillary Drive, where a steep pillow of water piled against a fire hydrant. The underside of the canoe struck the big yellow nut on top. Water sprang through a sudden crease in the hull. Houses kept slipping by, each tightly packed against the next. People came to their porches. They saw me and shouted. Maybe phone calls were being sent ahead — *You gotta see this guy, he's in a canoe!* They clapped and raised their fists in the air for solidarity. I was fulfilling some long-held desire of theirs. I was betraying the grids of this enclosing city. Maybe I would be arrested. Maybe I would drown like people do every year in Phoenix floods. Regardless of outcome, I was a momentary hero.

These people have no idea, I thought as I paddled down their streets, turning their corners. My father's neighbors knew what it was like to live beside someone who did not obey the city's grids. They listened to gunfire the night he took a shotgun and a revolver out to demolish the shed in his backyard. They slammed their windows to the wail of his stereo at three in the morning, a bang-and-clash Mussorgsky symphony impaling the neighborhood, phone ringing unanswered.

I tempered this riverside applause with memories. I thought, You do not want me living next door. I do not even belong in this city, an unshaven nomad from the wilderness, living in a Colorado cabin with no indoor plumbing. I will satisfy your longings, but do not invite me into your homes. Like my father, I will light fires on your lawn. I will play loud, unbearable music. I will not sleep at appropriate hours. I will take your canoe and throw it into a flood, never to be seen again.

I floated across Greenway Road, toward a private retirement community where a sign lifted from the water, shivering against the current:

PRIVATE

STREET

NO

TRESPASSING

ARS 13-1502-A

I entered their private street. Other streets introduced more water, and I swept into a long, graceful curve around a park and community center.

The street turned right. The water continued straight, aiming directly into a cinder-block wall with a rectangular chute at its base. The flood funneled to a swift, smooth cord. Water always goes somewhere, I knew. I could get out now, but water is something to be followed. It knows the way. If I continued, eventually I would meet with the underworld of the city's storm drain. I would find the other side of this impulsive journey.

I came hastily into the low portal, lying back, gathering my body beneath the gunwales. The canoe and I slipped through the chute in the cinder-block wall. I sat up on the other side. I was out of the neighborhoods now, and there were no more onlookers to support me. The water felt different. Its voice deepened. It constricted, its surface no longer smooth. I traveled behind people's houses, hidden from them by their back walls.

Empty milk jugs and crushed aluminum cans banged against the canoe, their pitches shooting through my knees. I dropped the paddle deeper, working the current with more care and muscle, feeling the canoe no longer confirming my orders. I braced my knees tighter, lowering my shoulders.

I took the next plunge, striking off the edge of a four-foot waterfall. I stood half out, a boot sole landing on a concrete piling for stability, the other foot balancing the boat. It was a habitual maneuver, going through a river rapid of tight boulders, a quick push off and then back in. The bottom of the canoe screamed against concrete, dropping me into a much larger canal as I jumped back in. I threw my weight to keep from swamping, and nearly lost the paddle. The canoe swung backward. I worked it straight again, throwing my shoulders, digging the paddle until its shaft and my hands arced below the water's surface.

A busy street ran above and beside me, twenty feet over my head. I tried to keep out of sight of the cars whenever I came into view. I did not want to be rescued. I did not want to find myself on the cover of the paper the next morning, joining the usual suspects who drive into floods and have to be helicoptered off their car roofs, the teenagers who find themselves direly stranded against the pier of an overpass, floating in black inner tubes. I did not want a reporter going over the police record to reduce my life to a photo caption: *A moment of despair upon the death of his father.* They would not understand. I was not in this flood out of rage or blind anguish. I came because the water was moving, because it fell from hole to hole down the storm drains, leading to some point that I would reach only if I continued.

Waterfalls poured from all sides, from storm drains opening above. A shopping cart tumbled by, smashing into me. The gunwales dipped, took on water, and I pitched my weight. The channel banked into a long curve, its surface churning and foam-covered. Made of broken rock penned tightly with chain link, the canal walls had no steps or ladders leading out. They forced the water down the middle as if the place were a constricted bedrock canyon, leaving no escape. Unable to pause, breathe, or eddy, this water coiled into knots full of debris. I searched for the order, for the customary patterns I would expect in a wilderness flood. There were none. *Entropy is not to be underestimated.*

I sped through the first underground passage, a dark corridor, the flood loud and sloshing. Out the other side, I paddled hard around an incoming waterfall of trash and mud. There is a way out of here, I thought. Always a way. If there was not, I would die. Far better to die in this canal, the suddenness igniting my soul, than to waste away in a deepening hall of mirrors as my father had.

The Sixteenth Street Bridge came into view. A logjam of trapped branches and garbage bucked around its piers. The water boiled, allowing no breathing room between the debris and the underside of the bridge. Foam slapped onto the overpass sidewalk. I ruddered the paddle along the right side, slipping the canoe's body diagonal to the current. I studied the path between here and there.

The outcome was clear. There was no way to pass beneath this bridge. There was no way to stop before getting there. The canoe would be taken under. My body, I imagined, would be found hanging from racks of shopping carts and soaked tree trimmings.

But there must be another way through here, another outcome. There had to be. It was the solidity I sought in nature, the path within the ferment. I searched for it, back-paddling from one side to the next. A deep strain of fear took me. *I don't like this part, the* not finding.

A predator was sprinting one swipe behind my legs. I had thought that it was my father all along, that he was the one I feared. But he was gone now. The equation, flavored in adrenaline, ran quickly through my head. I realized that something was truly hunting me. It tasted like sweat. I felt it needling at my chest.

Don't let me die, Father. Not here. Not today.

I drove the paddle into the water on my left side, swinging the bow straight upstream, fighting the current, slowing just a bit more, with all of my strength. But not enough. The bridge was approaching.

My river instincts failed me. I looked for the slightest eddy, some twist of current I could grab. There was nothing. This was not a river. My customary escape routes did not exist here. I purposefully leaned my body too far upstream.

Water rushed the gunwales.

The canoe flipped.

I jumped clear, landing in the water.

Arms and legs instantly wrapped around me. A frenzy of wild children snatched and pulled. The canoe was gone. A sudden taste of dog urine and motor oil filled my mouth. I tried to sputter it out, but I was underwater. My paddle stayed in my right hand — a river rule that I refused even now to ignore: Never let go of the paddle, *never.* I thrust and parried with it, using it for leverage against the flow, but there was no flow to negotiate. The canal was filled with madness.

I could not swim this. I could not reach the surface. Swift

vortices played at my back. A hollow gulp of water drew me to the floor as if a whale had swept beneath me, pulling me down.

I stabbed the paddle upstream like a wand. It sent word through its shaft, into my hand, telling me of the shape of this water, its speeds and trajectories. I became aware that I was listening to the paddle faster than I could possibly think. My body was responding, shooting commands through me. Time changed. The distance between events widened. Whirlpools touched me from above and below, and I followed them away, feeling their spinning nets of turbulence.

My conscious mind remained aware of the quickness at hand. I was in a sandstorm, an avalanche, a flood. My landscape was nothing but squalls and convulsions, my lungs empty. I swirled and pushed, feeling the grate of the wall against my back. I swung the paddle into the wall, snapping and seizing with my free hand and my feet. A muscle tore in my ankle. I felt a fingernail splinter all the way to its root.

I grabbed between currents and chain-link metal, slowing myself. Finally, I found a solid grip. A bulwark of water instantly gathered against me. The water sent the rest of my body down-stream as my hand held the fence wire. I was stretched tight, body to hand to wall. I worked back upstream until both of my hands and feet were secure in the steel mesh, the paddle wedged between hand and wire. Climbing up far enough, I cleared my neck and head. Floodwater sped over my shoulders. I lifted my mouth and gasped at the air.

I looked downstream. I seemed no closer to the bridge now than when I had jumped. The canoe was still in view, rolling like a log. How long had I been in? It could not have been more than six or seven seconds, judging by the distance. But it had been a few minutes at least judging by memory. I had been stretched and re-formed, and now I was back, clinging like a barnacle to the side of this storm drain.

The canoe gathered speed into the bridge. It lifted onto a crest. Then it struck the entangled bridge debris. The stern rolled and jerked underwater, causing the bow suddenly to stand. The canoe fell back on itself and vanished beneath the surface.

I looked at my hand clinging to the wall, the other one free with the paddle, at the watercolor drain of blood from cuts and the snare of a fingernail. The blood told me that this time I had barely slipped the trap. I had been made by my father into a runner, someone clever and quick, and this time I had narrowly made my escape. My body was not pressed dead around a bridge piling right now. I had found my way through the chaos.

I climbed to the street. Cars sprayed arcs of rainwater as they passed. With a limp I crossed at the Sixteenth Street intersection when the white OK-to-cross light came on. I walked a couple of blocks, clothes torn and soaked, one hand dripping blood, one holding a wooden paddle.

At a corner gas station I found a pay phone and made a collect call home. They were beginning to wonder where I had gone. No one had noticed the missing canoe. I did not explain. I asked if someone could come with a car because I was a few miles away. And a towel, please, one that won't mind the stain of blood.

DAY TWO

Sunrise. Sitting in the cab of the Bronco, Dirk and I exhale thin, faint cirrus clouds of breath. We are parked in front of a general store at the meeting of roads on an Arizona Indian reservation, one belonging to the Diné. The building has no sign out front, just a dirt parking lot. It is known among people here as the Crossroads, dropped onto the countryside as if out of an airplane, a lone building that unfolded into place as soon as it hit the ground. Everything else is horizons of sparse juniper trees and the endless red of the earth. Good country for nomads, open range where winter-rugged livestock grazes the roadside, where a person can start walking and stop only when it is time. Luckily, the Diné had settled a piece of land barren enough not to interest the U.S. government or its homesteaders. After the deathly 1800s busywork of marching tribes here and there across the continent, the Diné were finally given back their land, as if handed some bitter, useless artifact no one was willing to steal.

Last night we slept off a side road on the reservation, Dirk in the back of the Bronco and me on the ground under the joined arms of a juniper copse. My water bottle froze all the way through. I should have known better and kept it warm with my body through the night. I keep it on the dashboard now so it can thaw.

The inside of the cab softens with the volcanic light of early morning. I shield my eyes with the lowered brim of my hat. Dirk looks like an odd wizard. He wears an expertly machined pair of sunglasses and a pointy wool cap from his wife's recent trek to the Andes.

We wait in the increasing light, watching for a blue Chevy

truck. The truck will be driven by a Diné man. This man will lead us down one of these unmarked roads to the home of his grandfather, an old sheepherder who still sings the original ceremonies. He is called a singer, a healer, a shaman. His permission is required for walking across a certain stretch of desert, ground considered sacred to the Diné. We need to talk with him.

Trucks are parked along the building front in a horse-tether row. I tell Dirk that I am going to pick up a sack of flour, and I leave him, moving into the cut-dry air, the barren warmth of sunrise. Inside the store are aisles of canned food, and my eyes have to adjust to the assault of colors and brand names. Faces of Diné men and women seem bored and busy with their first tasks of the day, their skin the russet of polished saddle leather. Coffee is sipped, ranch jackets worn thin.

When I lift a cotton sack of Bluebird flour onto my shoulder, a woman bundled warm smiles and says it looks like I'm going to be making some fry bread. I tell her that it's a gift for a sheepherder who lives north of here. Maybe she knows him, a man who still sings the Protectionway ceremony. She nods, having heard of him. She does not bother asking why I am bringing flour to him. People go to the Protectionway for their own reasons.

Outside I drop the flour into a box in back, adding it to the other dry goods we have brought: pistachios and pinto beans and coffee. Kept in an ice chest so it would not freeze is a stock of fruits and vegetables. I look through them, opening the chest, pulling bags from the box, wondering if these gifts are adequate. This is our offering to the singer for his blessing. It feels like a bribe.

I shovel myself into the front seat. Dirk has opened his jacket to accept some of the warmth from the rising sun. I mention that everyone in line at the counter drank coffee and smelled of livestock. Sheepherding country, I say.

Dirk responds that he hates the way we all wait in lines. Such a ludicrous fascination of ours, waiting one behind the next for some dangling carrot. I can tell by his tone that he is about to start into one of his stories, by the way his body turns slightly toward me, an exaggerated pause of contemplation. I brace myself. We are about to go somewhere, a sixty-second journey through Dirk's mind. I know better than to say anything.

"I had to get this backcountry permit at some visitors' center," he says. "There were these other people in line ahead of me, and I had to listen as one by one they stepped to the ranger desk, explaining that they had only a certain amount of time, asking which trail was nicer, which had the most scenic viewpoints, which had toilets, wooden steps, shade, cell phone reception."

Here comes the kicker; I hear it. The anger in his voice, the obvious flaws of human nature that he wants to expose as if he were a fire hose blasting away at civilization.

"What the fuck? Cell phone reception?" he complains, not to me, but to his pitted windshield. "All that shit has become normal. The ability to grab something and punch a button and *boom,* you're wired. You can get your stock reports. You can talk to any person in the world you want. You can get a weather report. You can summon the powers from above to your exact point on the map. We want to get back into nature? We want to experience the outdoors? We're so addicted to information and knowing everything a person can possibly know that we can't just say oh, here's a nature trail, let's go check it out."

His voice jumps a notch louder. *"It's a trail! There're no mines! There're no fucking lava pits!* You can walk on it for exactly the amount of time you want to walk on it. Which hike takes an hour? You can probably stay on that trail for three or four days, for half a goddamned year. I don't know, you gonna stop to fuck? Might take an hour and a half."

I imagine him standing in the visitors' center dismayed, hands in pockets, the people getting their permission and walking past him wondering why he is staring at them with those eyes, with that buzz of disturbance.

Now, the letdown part of his story. His body relaxes. He shakes his head, drawing his voice into a quiet tone. Now he sounds like a man explaining a bit of thoughtful philosophy.

"There are certain minds that just rail against that shit; then there are others that sink down into it like a cozy comforter. There're always going to be us crazy ones who don't want a railing to keep them from falling off the edge. Who don't want a trail to stare at like an amusement park ride. Who don't feel normal until they leave the road, pass through the air lock, escape quarantine, and go running naked."

I look over at his form, still heavy in cold-morning clothes. Traveling with Dirk is like standing in a public restroom, glancing up, and being stung by a curt and grossly relevant comment scrawled on the wall.

A blue Chevy truck pulls to our side. The bed is empty except for a battered red gas can and some old chains. A Diné man sits behind the wheel and looks at us. I step out and walk to him as he rolls down his window.

"*Yateh,*" I say, reaching out a hand.

"*Ya'at'eeh,*" he responds, shaking my hand in return. He glances slowly around, not really looking for anything. "Cold this morning."

"We slept up higher," I say. "There's still some snow."

He looks at Dirk's Bronco, seeing on its tires various ages of sprayed dog urine. His own tires have identical markings. Dirk comes around in his wizard outfit, the same thing that he will be wearing for the next few weeks, likely for the rest of the winter. He pulls off his sunglasses and shakes the man's hands.

The man says, "Why don't you follow me."

Dirk says, "We'll be right behind you."

We slip back into the Bronco. The blue Chevy leads us down a washboard road. A cattle guard buzzes under us. Barbs of elegant canyons spill off both sides of the road, multiplying into each other, cutting open a new landscape, which falls apart for the next landscape, and the next beyond that. Scarps of earth stand far off.

I can feel it here. The land is opening. The distant cliffs become more numerous, cracking away from each other. There are stands of wind-battered buttes farther off. I have never been down this road, but I have wondered what it would be like to walk out beyond it. For years I have hiked to the tops of buttes and peaks, looking south from Utah, seeing an emptiness on this horizon, only a few dark mulls of mountains as faint as mirages and nothing else. Thunderstorms rise from here in the summer.

The first time I saw this particular country was during the flight to my father's funeral. As it began I saw places below where I had slept and walked in my life. The larger space-bound features of the Earth became visible out of Colorado and into Utah, as if a fetus were kicking beneath the belly skin of the planet. There were no ant swarms of cities and in-between towns, only faintly cut dirt roads, and then none for a while; another plane a thousand feet higher, heading in the other direction; and the metal-rust and mustard colors of desert.

I remember staring out the airplane's tiny window, eyes soothed by the relentless thievery of desert erosion. Slender buttes and fins lifted from the ground as if a razor blade had been slipped around them. They were colored in Chablis, their hues bleaching into everything, reddening the mud-dark rivers that skimmed the surface and cut down through harder rock into obscure gorges. I saw the serpent curves of Utah cliffs, their embryonic hollows black in shadow. I saw exactly where I, as a teenager, had lain naked in a remote canyon, where I had walked in bare feet until blisters and gouges wore into hard soles. I had called this place the Blood Desert back then, red from the same minerals that darken my own blood, the pigments that give hematite its dusky shine, the color of iron hungrily burned by water and wind.

The Earth seemed even sharper to my eye now that I bore the weight of my father's death. I remember peering out the small oval window as if it were the only way to survive, knowing that the plane would eventually land in Phoenix and I would be mortal again. My father had taught me about the sky, going on about the movement of stars and the gravity of planets, waving his hand in the air around black holes and neutron stars. He found it curious that we believed we had conquered gravity when we built airplanes, as if we had not noticed that we are still held firmly to the Earth, that we keep dropping things and breaking them. He was the sort of man who once told me he watched ghosts dance in the desert. When I came to him with peculiar dreams, he would nod and say to me that he had seen the same thing. I believed he was a prophet. He said that we live within an invisible world, and sometimes our eyes are caught by what seems to be nothing, our heads turning to movement that is not there. He told me that I am supposed to live in both worlds, both the visible and invisible. *You will do both* was a mantra he chanted to me in my earliest memories, a command that lasted through even his most drunken decades, through his final years of violent thrashing while his wife waited in the bedroom, gun cocked and in her hand, waiting for the door to open, waiting to put a bullet through my father and end his madness.

While I watched out the window, I lost track, thinking of my father, eyes roaming the pale colors. Suddenly I could no longer identify the ridges, the plains of waterless sand. I had never walked in this place. Were we in Arizona or Utah? The window was not large enough for me to see the entire surrounding earth, so for that moment, I had no idea where we were. Somewhere south. We had yet to hit the thunderstorm clouds of the lower desert.

A gathering of canyons came into view, like the oblique sprawl of a city. I sat up. A maze formed beneath me as we flew, a landscape of incredible difficulty. My mind was immediately racing. It was indeed a city, skyscrapers and buttes of factories, house boulders and deep passageways into subterranean sewers. This city was made of stone. It was abandoned. If I were to walk there, I would be in Manhattan with no other living person anywhere, my footsteps echoing in the dark subway of canyons, climbing cliff-face stairways in unoccupied buildings.

So this is what lay on that empty horizon I had looked at so many times. It seemed remotely like some of the places I had traveled: a canyon-bound geography, barren bedrock composed of familiar, massive sandstone. But it appeared to be far more compressed and immense than any place I had visited. It looked like steroid-fed roots forced to grow in too small a pot. Canyons led impossibly back into themselves, confined and writhing like adders in a basket. Up-striking blades of rock just as suddenly inverted to shadow. I quickly gathered information, triangulating off distant landmarks so that I could later go to a map and pinpoint this exact location. I would have to find my way there.

Whom would I go with? Alone? No. This place below the plane looked too difficult. I would need a strong hand. Dirk came to mind. Besides his hands, he would guarantee a roller-coaster mental journey if I went down there with him. With his predatory tales, with his bloodstained memories, we would dive headlong together into the unknown. *Go, little mouse. There are riches you cannot imagine.*

Down this truck-rattling road, I am seeing the same landmarks in the distance as those I had figured from the plane on the way to my father's funeral. A mountain. A solitary plume of volcanic rock at the horizon. A high, juniper-covered mesa. We are getting closer.

Turns out that the land I saw from the plane is ceremonial country. It belongs to the Diné. A few months ago, Dirk and I sat down with a map and a man who used to live in this region. The man told us that he had never been beyond the far roads, but he knew of the place, a mythical labyrinth of canyons. He knew an old singer who had grown up traveling there. Sacred land. Taboos and offerings. An easy place to die, also. Cliffs and impenetrable canyons. Few people know the ceremony, the Protectionway, and few know how to get across the land claimed by this ceremony. We would have to talk with the singer. We would need his permission. Then we could go.

———

There is a house made of red mud. The old Diné singer lives here in the company of numerous cats, a radio tuned now and then to the half static of a Tuba City station, a wife who offers us fry bread and potatoes this morning, and several dogs who, as soon as they can, add their piss to the streaks on Dirk's tires. The ground is the soulful color of tomato soup, crumbling easily in the hand, thirsty.

The only entrance to this mud house is to the east, a wooden door with a strap of horse leather for a handle. Faint juniper smoke lifts from a rusted-thin stovepipe. Wind chases it off, as cold and barren as dry ice. Inside, the woodstove door leans open. Bronzed shadows lap against the corbel of a juniper-beam ceiling. Four of us gather at the stove, an oil drum cut in half and shoveled into the dirt floor.

Dirk and I lean into the warmth, reaching out occasionally to flick coals back into the fire with our fingers.

The man who showed us the way here, the singer's grandson, is standing in jeans and a coat.

The singer — he must be about eighty years old, his eyes milky but quick — sits sideways, grinning, in a chair made for schoolchildren. He wears a down jacket filthy from sheepherding.

For the moment, Dirk does the talking. His voice is usually charged, but this morning it is carefully drawn, spoken in soft church tones. He tells the old man that the two of us like moving across the land. We are hoping for permission to walk in this maze of canyons. He explains that we have a desire for the obscurities and irregularities of the ground. He says that we have a love for stone.

The singer nods and *hmms*. He does not speak any English.

The grandson examines Dirk, his eyes darkly calm, moving from point to point. He gathers his thoughts and translates Dirk's words into a different tongue. Voices change hands. The grandson's words are spoken in Athabascan, schoolbook artic-ulated. The grandfather speaks in return with subtle, watery vowels, his consonants cracking like small twigs. He is not a grim-faced, feather-laden wise man like those hung in art gal-leries. He is adorned only by the country, his fingernails dark at their edges, uneven from use, his teeth stained by coffee. He folds his hands and unfolds them as he talks, the skin creased light and dark like a paper grocery bag used too often. As soon as he is done with us this morning, he will return to his sheep.

I look over at Dirk, watching him watch the grandson speak to the grandfather. His elbows rest on his knees so that he leans toward the stove, a fire crouch. As the heat evenly coats his crotch, his chest, his knees, his face, he puzzles out the conver-sation, studying gestures between grandson and grandfather. Unable to understand their language, he investigates their bod-ies, focusing on their faces and hands.

The grandson finally turns to us and laughs at what he has to say, the guarded laugh of mixed company. "He says that you should herd sheep instead."

There is a short-lived silence; then we all step into the same laughter.

"You would make good sheepherders." He points at our boots, the leather scarred and thin on the insides. "The way you crouch like that on your haunches. Anyway, you guys are proba-bly looking for your umbilical cords, huh? That's why you go out and wander around?"

"Yes," I say, leaning forward, higher onto the balls of my feet.

But then I lean back. No. I do not want him thinking I am a fool itching at my navel, dumbly digging for the truth. I belong to this Blood Desert. I want to open my mouth and have sand spill onto the ground to explain myself. I give both the grandfather and grandson a pleading glance, wishing to explain that like them we have our own mysteries from the desert, that in the wilderness Dirk and I are like dogs feverishly rolling in something dead, coating our bodies in the toadstool stench of instinct. But all I say, quietly, is "We are dogs," and the grandson eyes my hands, my knees, my canvas work coat, deciding not to translate my comment to his grandfather.

"People come here looking for help," he says, the laughter shaken off now. "My grandpa knows the songs and the prayers, both ways, Earth and Sun. And the four sacred colors. Then there are offerings, which are very important, you know . . . at a little spring coming out of the ground, a little natural spring. You leave your offering. You ask for protection. You ask for prayers. Right there. That is how he goes about his life."

I am interested in this talk, but I feel a little as though I am eavesdropping. I do not want to horde information about ceremonies. I only want permission to go. I want to be in the canyons. Still, I am curious.

I lean forward, venturing, "These songs you mention, they're for the Protectionway ceremony?"

He looks at my shoulders and briefly passes my eyes, leaving nothing as he goes by. "Yes, Protectionway."

I take that in. I know of many Diné ceremonies from having spent most of my life not far from the reservation. The names are familiar: Evilway, Coyoteway, Beautyway, Red Antway.

The Protectionway is a regional ceremony, and I have heard that it is slowly being forgotten. It's a sanctuary ritual, something that men coming back from the Second World War and Vietnam went through, a rite that protects refugees and people being chased. Some time in the late 1800s it became popular around here. I imagine it was a response to devastating troop invasions by the United States, the sort of prayers and songs that people perform when pressed to the very edge.

The singer begins talking, and the grandson turns away from us, nodding receptively, saying "Ah, ah." He then translates back to us: "These canyons and certain features of rock inside of them, this is where the Protectionway songs come from, this is their origin, this place where you want to go."

The grandson tells us that when his grandfather was a child, other Diné children were being plucked by the Indian School, ridden south on horseback, and not returned to their families until a decade later. His parents sent him to hide in the same canyons where we want to carry our packs and ropes, a place where canyons lie within canyons within canyons. It is a place hard to imagine, so no one would ever dare go looking for him there. Each time the school patrols came through, he ran off alone into this farther desert. That, he says, is why his grandfather is this way now, why he knows so much about the land.

I imagine this old man as a child and the sound of his footsteps through sand in a canyon floor. He waited in a massive and revealing landscape. He walked through cathedral canyons carved one into the next, his voice carried into echoes as he prayed and sang and talked in his sleep. He found paths a thousand years old, small steps chiseled into cliffs where people had once traveled, people from long before the Diné. He slept in natural wind shelters so deeply eroded that he could not see the stars. I only know the place from maps and from looking down out of the airplane, but I know how to read and how to imagine.

There are more stories told at the fire, more wood added as we listen and ask questions. The singer draws objects from inside his coat one at a time, a polished leather pouch of corn pollen, a spear point made of a smooth stone, chert. Explaining that they are items of protection, the things he places in front of him for safe passage, he hands them around. Dirk and I admire them, turning them between our fingers, rubbing their polished surfaces.

The grandson speaks, and I look up.

"He says that you have what you came for. He has one more thing to show you." He gestures lightly toward the door, where we will leave to get the flour and vegetables and other offerings we have brought.

I pass the stone I'm holding to Dirk, who examines it and then returns it to the singer, who has stood and is bent. He places the rock back into his coat. We leave one at a time, out of the firelight and into the morning. As if emerging from a cave, we duck through the door, shielding our eyes from the eastern morning light. The wind has fallen away, but the air has not yet recovered from a night below 20 degrees. Still as loaves of bread, numerous cats sit on the red ground, eyes sleepy in the sun. Some rise and slip toward our legs, their tails grasping our calves.

The old man has a bundle in his hands. He unfolds its leather wings and draws out two long dowels draped in gray feathers. He lifts these, and the feathers slide out, catching on their leather cords, lolling like the heads of sleeping men.

"These are used in the ceremony," the grandson says as he takes them from his grandfather. "Very important. Grandpa is Salt Clan. He carries the medicine bundle."

The grandson does not hold these decorated rods tightly. He cradles them, the way a mother supports her baby's head, showing me how to do it as he passes them across. My hands come around them.

"Protectionway?" I ask.

"Yes."

They are light, fragile between my fingers, hardly thicker than pencils. They are rubbed into pearl by skin oils. Old scars in the wood have been sanded down by ceremony after ceremony, hand after hand. They are strung with beads, each dowel bearing a different set of colors. From what I know of Diné traditions, the color arrangements are male and female.

I see that beneath their dressings, these rods are actually arrows, broken so that the points are gone, the breaks cleanly bandaged in animal sinew. The wind- and dirt-chewed fletching along the tails has nearly disintegrated, touched by too many hands, the arrows fired too often.

I bring the ornamented pieces of wood up to one eye, as if checking a piece of lumber for warp, and I find them to be absolutely straight. Had these arrows been used for hunting or for killing men? I thought back to a flight the Diné had made into this territory more than a hundred years ago, when U.S. troops chased them into the canyons beyond here. Did they use these arrows then? How old are they? A hundred years, perhaps. Older, maybe.

"These are beautiful arrows," I say. "Can you tell me anything about their history?"

The grandson looks at me as if I have mistaken a raccoon for a car tire. "They aren't arrows."

"I mean, they were *once* arrows." I turn the butt ends toward him to show that I noticed the notches in back, each deeply worn, having been set numerous times into a bowstring and fired. "Here are their nocks."

He is still looking at me that way. I have misnamed them again.

"No, they are not arrows," he explains.

I dip my head in compliance. I realize that he speaks English only out of courtesy to us, replacing each Athabascan word on his tongue for the nearest English one. In his language these are, indeed, not arrows. In mine, we hold names from the past as if we would sink without them. My culture is different, and in this instant, I am glad; its intention does not mask the past. At the same time I am envious of the Diné's ability to move wholeheartedly ahead to where an object is purely what it is now, the past is tacitly understood, and the future is not even here yet.

I look to the singer for consent. He gestures *yes* toward Dirk. I pass on the two feathered pieces to Dirk, who turns them in his hands, checking their straightness, tenderly feeling for strength and weakness.

I think about something the grandson had translated to us, that the Protectionway stories are imparted by the shape of the landscape itself. Walking out there is the telling of the legend. Boulders appear in the path, and they already have names. Water holes are characters central to the story. Every object encountered has consequence. Nothing is formless. These arrows, I think, are the first tales of our own legend.

Dirk's hands ride over the broken weapons, fingers testing the skin-polished beads as if reading something about his own life. Like these objects, he is a weapon transformed, a cop snapped in half. He comes to the desert as a person of ceremony. He drapes himself in the feathers and beads of boulders and cliffs. I look at him. No matter how shiny his beads, he is still an arrow to this very day, sharp-tipped and seeking the kill. He is still a cop.

When Dirk is done, he passes these adorned rods of wood to the singer. The old man puts them back in their leather bundle. Dirk watches every move: the grandfather's hands closing the coverlets, the arrows leaving his sight. We now have permission to go.

Day in the Park

When Dirk was eighteen years old he owned a gun. He kept it in his bedroom. It was a heavy, chrome-plated handgun with a six-inch barrel, a .357 Magnum. He stored it on his shelf throughout his two years at the police academy, eager to slip on a uniform, hang this contrivance off his hip, and walk outside to command the world around him.

He was a teenager from a stable household, with a mother and father still married, two brothers, and a dog: a good home with an honest mortgage. Romancing the adrenaline of youth, he was a member of a boys' gang that perpetrated meaningless street crimes: blowing up mailboxes with small, illegal explo-

sives, hurling rocks through the windshields of parked cars —
the usual reckless thrills that serve as training for urban police
work.

After graduating from the academy, he moved onto the street
fully armed. His beloved .357 holstered for all to see. He also
wore a stainless-steel semiautomatic backup pistol in a holster
under his left armpit, something he could grab with his weaker
right hand in case of struggle. He carried sundry wooden batons
and canisters and artillery magazines on his belt, a double-
edged fighting knife on his calf, and an illegal lead-weighted
beaver-tail sap that waited in his back pocket like a flattened
sack of marbles, ready to snap a nose bone. He was twenty-one,
just old enough to drink.

The Denver police force he went to work for was notoriously
violent. During his rookie year, he testified against two fellow
officers, refuting claims on doctored paperwork. The next day,
his locker and the vents of his car were flooded with tear gas. At
headquarters his face was met with insults.

As a reprimand he was handed over to Buzz, a physically
brutal patrol partner in his fifties, a man who preyed on women
after the bars closed at 1:00 AM, inquiring out his patrol car window for sex or at least a feel. The women were always there.
Buzz knew the ones, those who would sit in the back letting
him paw their breasts. During these overtures, Dirk left the
patrol car and headed off with his radio to prowl the streets.
Buzz would announce himself over the air, talking in code to
alert Dirk when he was finished if it was an on-duty blow job.

When Dirk grimly turned a blind eye to Buzz's night games,
Buzz just shook his head. He thought Dirk was an oddity,
maybe gay.

Buzz hated gays. He hated Mexicans. He hated blacks. He

hated sloppily dressed, unshaven, or greasy-haired whites, which could mean that Buzz hated himself. He did not like to get out of his car, especially if he had to run, meaning Dirk chased down a lot of people himself, climbing fences, flashing into alleys among graffiti-lavished Dumpsters, sprinting through sidewalk crowds of people who despised cops, waving his baton to keep them from throwing concealed punches or trying to trip him.

Because Buzz hated Mexicans, he and Dirk were assigned to a city park that was becoming a popular weekend football and barbecue location for Hispanics. They were sent in to be a presence, to write petty tickets for busted taillights, open bottles of beer, or failing to use turn signals into the parking lot. Dirk and Buzz were thorns in the sides of several hundred people, from gang members to churchgoers.

One Sunday afternoon there was a car chase at the edge of the park. A banana-yellow late-model Trans Am with tires too big for its chassis took the corner with a chirp of tire rubber, Buzz's patrol car just behind, the cruiser's beacon lights spinning witlessly.

The Trans Am jumped the street onto the sidewalk, then sped across the park lawn. Grass mulched into the air around its tires as it swung past one of the barbecues, across a walkway, and onto the street on the other side, people peeling out of the way.

Buzz followed, aiming into the opening that the Trans Am had cleared, punching the accelerator. The patrol car struck the curb too hard. All four tires blew out at once. Pieces of black rubber flew through the air like meteorites.

The car plowed sideways. It came to a stop in the center of the park, in the midst of maybe three hundred people, barbecued chicken in hand, kids staring as if a woman had just stripped naked and was singing as loudly as possible right in front of them. But everything was absolutely quiet, the siren off, lights still spinning.

Buzz did not look at Dirk. "Just hold tight," he said. "Don't get out of the car."

Dirk held tight. He watched as the crowd closed around them like water moving in, shutting off any view to the outside. He watched every gesture out the windows and in the mirrors, mouths snarling to slur insults, hands on hips. Everyone was waiting for something to explode.

Then came the storm. At first there were only a couple of plinking sounds off the drum of the roof, like the first strikes of hail out of a thunderhead. A beer can crushed and thrown. A half-eaten chicken leg lobbed. The sounds multiplied, each slightly different in tone, one adding to the next until the hail poured down upon them, a steady, deafening roar from above. Glass bottles, forks, slices of tomato, handfuls of ice, a head of lettuce, a tennis shoe, pocket change.

Buzz clutched the microphone, demanding backup. A paper-plate Frisbee winged against Dirk's window, splattering the glass with Jackson Pollock ketchup and mayonnaise, a slice of bread sliding down, finally falling to the ground.

"Bullshit," Dirk shouted. He reached behind the seat for his riot helmet. "We're sitting here like fish in a fucking barrel!"

"Just hold tight, you hear?"

"Bullshit." He clapped, shoving the helmet onto his head, snapping the face shield into position. He reached beside him and jerked the seat-side shotgun from its hold.

The door flew open. The shotgun barrel lurched into position, as quick and wicked as a rattrap. Each cut of his posture announced the weapon, broadcasting his force clear across the park. He marched into the people, arcing his barrel from side to side, every arc sending a ripple of recoil into the crowd, wind touching grass.

"Which one of you motherfuckers wants to die today?" he bellowed. "Come on! Which one of you motherfuckers wants to die today?"

The crowd parted as sirens sounded in the distance. People turned and ran. They saw it in him, that he might just do it, that someone's chest might get shredded open. He was the man. He would kill.

The men with dark, netted hair, tattooed shoulders bare in the sun, staggered backward, trying to hold their ground against this sudden specter, jerking their heads back like startled horses. Even they fell away, cursing and thrusting their chins, eyes narrow with revulsion.

Soon there was no one, as if a drop of oil had hit water. The shotgun never went off. No one else drew a weapon or hysterically charged him. Dirk, twenty-one years old, stood alone as the last of the people swept to the edges of the park like wind-blown leaves. Nearby picnics were left abandoned, ice chests still open. He turned slowly. He felt the swift percussion of his heart, his eyes still training back and forth, the adrenaline high of inhuman, godlike strength racing through his mind.

So this is how it works, he thought.

He heard sirens even closer now, patrol cars turning corners at vengeful speeds. A web spread around him. Every thin strand of it was visible to him, every fleeing set of eyes, each car leading toward the axis. He was the center point standing in the park, shotgun in hand like a lightning rod. He felt his body charged, focused, full of force that could cut through any obstacle. He was a weapon, an arrow, the shaft hissing through the air in flight. He was the man.

DAY THREE

We float the smooth surface of a desert waterway, a river's gorge standing sheer around us. A dry and desolate cold pulls at the skin on our faces. As the bow of the boat nudges stone, Dirk jumps to the wall, landing on a ledge, the boat bucking behind him. His body is firm, well balanced as he moves. His hair is pulled back under his wool cap, tied above his shoulders. I throw him the bowline, and he swings it expertly around his wrist, securing it for an instant before reaching down with the loose end and sweeping it behind a few large rocks. The line goes taut. I situate myself with one foot on the bow, one on the ledge.

"Start with the packs," I say.

Two companions are on the boat moving gear toward us. After they get the two of us unloaded this afternoon, they will travel on their own downstream. Dirk and I will be left to walk from here into the singer's country. I heft the packs to Dirk, who rests them on the ledge.

"Whatever's left," I say. "The camera. That water. The rope over there."

Gear is stacked piece by piece on the ledge until room is hardly left for us to maneuver without pitching into the water.

It always seems this way before a long winter's foot trek, as if there is too much equipment and food and clothing, an infeasible weight to strap on to our backs. Fuel, water containers, folded tarps, food sacks heavy as cinder blocks, winter clothing, cooking gear, sleeping bags, pads, rain and snow gear. Small bags of ceaseless miscellany: lighters, love letters, sewing needles, pens, film, compass, headlamp, spoon, bandages, maps. Winter is the heavy time of year. Packs are never light.

We will sit on this ledge and deal with these things when our companions float away, arranging every last object by thrusting fistfuls into our packs. The two packs are slightly wider and taller than our torsos, made of heavy, dark Cordura and a festoon of straps and buckles.

The last item to come to the ledge is a book of poetry, a massive tome. I cringe; I'd hoped we'd forget it. Twelve chapters. Seven hundred fifty-eight pages. We don't truly know what kind of topography we are committing ourselves to, how much the smallest addition of weight will change our lives. It was Dirk's idea to bring this along. I look to Dirk, and he also draws his brow when he sees the book.

"I don't know," he says.

"We can trade it off every day," I offer, reaching out for it. Two hands are needed. I pass it to Dirk. He tests it by lifting it up, letting it drop, lifting it again. He glances up the gorge wall over our heads where this journey will begin, a narrow plunge of a canyon that can hardly be called a canyon — a chute, a slide, a five-hundred-foot-tall recess in a cliff face.

"You start with it today," he says.

I nod in acceptance.

A woman on the boat asks, "Is that it?"

"We can't carry any more," I say.

"All right, then. We're gone."

I pull the bowline from between the rocks and toss it back. The boat hesitates, then drifts from us, turning downstream with the metal-wood sounds of movement, two people settling into their places. We watch them for a moment, waving good-bye, studying our gear, watching again as the boat becomes smaller.

Our ledge goes nowhere. Either end dives into deep water. The only way from here is up. We both stand for a while, surveying our surroundings. On the other side of the gorge, spheres of sandstone rise above the walls, pressed together as if they might be giants wrestling each other to the ground. Beyond this commotion of stone are the lifted heads of faraway buttes. Behind us we see nothing but the wall, a cliff that swallows everything.

Customary languages do not suit a place like this. They are too simple, too general. Can I even call this thing above us a *cliff* or a *wall*? Such words do little to speak of the field guide of shapes in this country: twenty-foot benches, braided walls that wind in and out of each other, harrowing precipices, lone-standing strikes of rock, places that are gentle enough not to be called cliffs but where you die anyway if you fall, chalkboard faces seven hundred feet tall, and stubborn little pancake stacks of rock outcrops.

This unmarked route above us is a common man's cliff: perched ledges among gaping vaults, a variety of possibilities, plenty of vertigo interspersed with safe places where breath can be caught, rests taken. It is approachable enough to climb without ropes, just hands feeling for holds, eyes working the rock ahead.

I glance at the book of poetry lying like a fat brick on the ground, picture on the cover of some wire-muscled poet holding a Prince Albert tobacco tin in his hand. Our ride is gone, vanished around the bend, so we can't give it back.

Dirk moves into the gear, flipping through items as if picking at a trash heap for something useful. It looks as if we have been dropped into a safari camp with all of this equipment, but we've done this before. More times than we can remember. We will work it down until everything fits onto our backs, and we will again adjust to moving with weight through complex terrain. That part of the journey we know. What we don't know is this place ahead of us. We have only the maps, my memories from flying over, a book of poetry, and the words of an old man who hid out here as a child.

Fire Man

I remember a camping trip I took with my father when I was seven years old. I remember my eyes were drawn into the fire. Boot-splintered limbs of ironwood glowed furiously beneath the flames. My father moved slowly around the edges, like a potter tending his kiln, slipping in sticks, which the fire took with the hungriness of a dog. Neither of us could see past the shadows into the night around us. The entire world was made of fire and blackness.

Once my father's creation was perfectly balanced, he said, "There," and sat down beside me.

This campfire was not a badge-earning Boy Scout blaze with logs stacked neatly into a pyramid. The branches were crooked and gnarled, set into each other's crotches for support. The wood turned translucent in the center, breathing as the air shifted, white with heat.

"It's hottest in the coals," my father said. He was then a young, strongly thin man. "The flames just let the heat escape. The coals, though . . ."

He slipped a beer bottle into the fire, holding it by its neck, pushing a nest open into the coals. Then he quickly whipped his hand back from the heat. Slowly, the bottle bent into an amber glow. Its neck drooped into lenses of molten glass. My father did not smile at this. He only watched with fascination.

"Fire is a living substance," he said, not to me but to the fire itself. "It wants to spread. It calls out for wood, for anything. It is pure sensation searching for touch."

I traveled along his words, understanding only the trance of his tone.

"It is filled with desire. It is life. The way of things is written in it."

He stood and walked to the truck, bringing back an assemblage of items, cradling the ingredients of a bomb. One item was an empty bean can. He poured into it a small amount of gasoline, swirling the can around as if about to take a drink.

"If we really have been alive forever," he said, fingering three .357 Magnum bullets into his palm where I could see them, "then I was the fire keeper. Back before we had flint and bow drills, I was the caveman who carried embers and called up the fire each night. That was my job."

He dropped the three bullets into his bean can of gasoline, and again he swirled his concoction, rattling the lead points like

ice. He looked at me, judging my expression, seeing if I was prepared. He lifted the can to the sky, an offering. Then he nestled
it into the coals.

"Now, run. Get behind something."

I leaped to my feet and scrambled away from the fire, dodging into the darkness, where I dropped into the dirt-and-cobble
trench of an arroyo. I glanced up from the barricaded edge, seeing the form of my pyrotechnician-shaman father still crouched
in front of the fire. He rose, turned, walked swiftly toward me,
and slipped into my shelter.

"Don't watch the fire," he told me. "Stay out of its light."

I scooted to the bottom of the arroyo, a cheek against coarse
sand.

The first shot exploded, flashing the surrounding paloverde
trees as our campfire blew apart. Instinct jolted my body into
the ground. Before, there had been nothing in my night but fire
and its halo of darkness. Now there was only the bullet's discharge stretching through every spectrum of my hearing.

The second bullet followed instantly. There was no sound of
bursting windshield glass or the dead *pang* of metal struck with
a bullet. They must have both fired straight into space.

The third . . . we waited for it. Ten seconds. Twenty. How
long do we wait? Is it ever safe? Too curious to stay put, I inched
up to the edge. I saw burning coals all around the fire, as if a
building had just burned down and this was all that was left.
Small bunches of dry grass ignited, little conflagrations eeking
across the ground. Burning ironwood limbs lay scattered. What
an astounding mark.

The third. Any second.

I shrank behind the arroyo's bank, looking to my father for

instruction. I could not see his face in the dark. He lay on his back against the slope.

"Wait," he said.

Had the third bullet been blown free of the heat? Did it rest in a field of scattered coals, its gunpowder gradually warming? Was it on the cold ground as if dropped from a pocket?

I wrestled, waiting for it, thinking that I was about to pop, my heart ballooning in my chest.

My father heard the itchiness of my movement, clothes against the ground. Again, he said, "Wait."

Wait.

I sat in the secret dark beyond the fire listening through the snaps and whips of heat and flame for the sound. I held every sense in my imagination — the oily-sweet smell of creosote bushes, the burn of stars. They would be gone at any second, exploded from my grasp.

Wait.

POW! Sound bolted my body into itself, arms crunched against my rib cage. It was over that fast, replaced by the night's silence. How could it be? I wondered. Did it even happen? Did the third bullet really discharge, or was I eternally caught in this moment of anticipation my father had assembled, hovering like a bullet not yet fired?

My father stood and wiped his hands on his pants. He looked across the remains of our fire, and he called it good.

DAY FOUR

This stone is the color of blood stirred into buttermilk. It goes on for miles, nothing but solid rock and a single far-off juniper tree, a few flares of last season's ricegrass leaning wind-bent from the cracks.

Yesterday we left, climbing from the water up the gorge wall to this higher country of rolling stone domes, setting camp on a high mesa. Today, wind wraps this earth like muscles over a skeleton, some places bone-bare, others strapped by dense, streaming tissue.

Dirk stops, the weight of his life trussed to his back. He lifts his head into the cold winter bluster as if smelling for something. I stop, too, my head down to block the wind.

Suddenly, he starts shouting at me. Through the wind I don't get all the words. Something about high-impact urban police work, how this place reminds him of it. His hands are flying, so at least I know the nature of what he is telling me. I get bits and pieces, him saying that there are no sex crimes or daily murders here, but that just like on the streets, everything here happens on an elevated plain. I hear him shout that each brush of wind and chime of breaking glass was once filled with meaning for him.

If you want to survive you gotta understand tones of voices and how someone has parked a car, if it's parked hurriedly, if the engine's still hot. Same way here; there's a language of landscape. Rock ledges and thunderstorm floods and water holes. You gotta learn the subtleties.

At least that is what I think I hear. I would expect it. He has long believed that his work as a cop and his life in the wilderness are both driven by the same desire to navigate complex terrain. But he never says it calmly. Always, his explanations are thrilling. What brought it on this time? Probably this wind bearing down on us like a swarm of wasps. We've been walking for miles without conversation, and finally, his thoughts are breaking free. He comes right up to me, leaning on his argument, his face fearsome like a mad evangelist. Now he's poking me in the chest, and I can hear him clearly over the wind. I avoid his eyes.

With every poke, he tells me that he used to walk into bars and watch the eyes fall on his uniform, that he had to figure out his escape routes, who was going to shoot him, who was hiding a crime, who wasn't, and that here he doesn't see just a landscape but a web of possibilities, endless routes. He reads the land the same way he would read a person's face. Finger poking, he explains, "You walk into the landscape and you're wired tight, nailed to the fucking wall, every sense amplified."

The wind unaccountably dies, and we lean away from each other in the release. Wind does this out here, regulated by the tumescence of the land. We hear it elsewhere, hemming over far ridges, thrusting ferretlike into lower canyons.

The sudden void defuses him. His voice lowers. He takes a break. With the volume of a table conversation now, he tells me that this place is some kind of Tao, a way of living, something of religions and philosophies.

"It's not just some place," he says. "Not some piece of ground. It's a way of comprehension, one of the paths available to our minds. You can't help having an internal dialogue out here. You just can't help it. No wonder people keep away from places like this. This is the last thing they want, a completely undistracted internal dialogue."

I've got a sore spot from his poking, and I am wondering about his brain, how it must be just a mess of fallen boulders in there, busted tree limbs, dust devils whipping sand hither and thither. Still, none of his comments catch me by surprise, though I can never anticipate what he might start shouting in the wind.

We move again, drifting away from each other with the conversation unfinished, words replaced by boot scrapes and the *hunph!* of landing on the other side of a fissure. We travel across the stone like hunters, shoulders shifting to the terrain, ducking into parched flood draws and up their other sides. Miles of wind-eroded sandstone bells lift around us, many too sheer and steep to be climbed. This is the singer's territory. His childhood refuge lies some miles ahead, a region out of our view where the land descends into a cauldron of gorges. We only have theories about what it is like inside. The singer did not wag his finger telling us to beware; he never said anything about finding water or a thousand dead-end passages. He only explained that it was a place where no one could be found.

On the other side of all this we will eventually reach the water again, and a supply cache that we left hidden in sand. There, friends have agreed to meet us; they will float in and pick us up in the still of backwater. We have two weeks to get there.

The old man had told us that armies of the United States once rounded up whatever natives could be found in the Southwest and marched them hundreds of miles to winter encampments in the east, a walk that left a good number of them dead. A couple of dozen Diné broke away from this march, fleeing here to this lifeless quarter. Some came from near present-day Kayenta, Arizona, others from Black Mesa, forming a group of distantly related families, people who had found one another at the last moment. Troops were sent in pursuit, hunting these Diné families as they fled and scattered into the cliffs like birds.

I imagine the Diné's choices as they moved, keeping to this convoluted country, poking here and there, finding routes, inching themselves deeper into the terrain. I see them walking these high buttresses of sandstone, slipping out of the wind for a rest, two people sent ahead as scouts, pausing at the edges, one crouching, one standing. The land, it would seem, rose behind and around them, shielding them from the pursuers who found themselves lost in the outermost regions, where cliffs stand within cliffs. In the desert twenty miles behind where we are now, the confused and frustrated U.S. troops gave up the hunt.

Among the Diné who live in this part of the country there is still a palpable pride. They are descendants of families that never gave in, people who endured years in the wilderness. They were not captured and dragged away. When these few families emerged from the canyons seven years after their escape, they came like Moses off the mountain, carrying a new religion in their hands. They had found a ceremony in the far desert, an entire pantheon of rock formations and water holes that took on names and places in stories more ancient than tribal memory.

We begin working our way through house-sized boulders — not mansions, but modest homes, two stories tall at the most. The boulders end, and we start up a bald arc of sandstone. It is a cliff made round. Its grains feel like sandpaper. We slide our hands in front of us, taking holds, inching our bodies upward with our Sherpa loads of winter gear. Cursive patterns are raised from the bedrock, loops of rust offering texture, enough to hold the tips of our boots. I can hear the scratching of my clothes, and Dirk's breath below as he reaches up for a grip.

A cranny of a canyon opens through the side of this arc, and we file into it, finding a string of water holes along a narrow floor. They are ornaments of old rain and snowmelt set deeply into the bedrock. The sole kind of water source we expect to find out here. Like seals to a breathing hole in the ice, we both drop to one of them, head to head. Our lips graze the surface, and the water tastes grainy but clean. Our palms lay flat, shoulder blades up like wings. I feel Dirk's exhale. Water drips from his lips. His ripples pass across mine.

Done, we sit back, allowing the packs to take our weight on the ground. Dirk's expression is a sort-of smile, long-remembered satisfaction. It says, *We have been here before*. I lean my head back, same smile.

By evening we reach a high boneyard of boulders, setting our camp in a dry, wrinkled surface of weathering pits and crevices. In weary, automatic moves, my hands drape to unlace my boots.

The sun sets, and I glance up to watch it go. The air freezes. Night comes.

Gathered up into warm clothing, Dirk and I move to our chores. We have the same way of going about things, year to year, with no gap in conversation or in the sway of hands passing back and forth a black-beaten pan, a spoon, a small alcohol-fueled stove. Dirk lays out his dinner belongings as if arranging santos at an altar. He scrapes a comfortable clearing on the ground for himself, brushing away rocks, assembling his life.

I quickly find that my chosen spot, as usual, is not well planned. I am on a slope leading into a crack between boulders where a pen might roll, clattering beyond reach. I keep my belongings close to me like a worried juggler, aware at every moment of what might fall out of my grip. Looking at Dirk's spartan clearing, I realize how much crap I carry around, bits and baubles hauled into the wilderness. I never unpack after a trip, so my equipment is peppered with whatever I've collected over the years: a marble given to me by a boy in Mexico, a chestnut seed, a few shell beads, a magnifying glass that I hardly use but always carry, a broken pencil that I refuse to part with, figuring I can sharpen it with my knife if I ever need it.

Dirk relaxes in his sanctum while I balance a lighter on my knee, groping around for my spoon, catching my lamp before it slides away.

I do the cooking, making udon noodles and curry, handing the pot to Dirk when I am finished. He eyes it with his lamp, spooning his share into a bowl. When it looks as if he might be done with the division, he begins stirring the pot. In our travels I have watched him do this many times. I know exactly what comes next. He is unsure that this is an equitable split, worrying the noodles with his spoon, judging volume and weight. Finally, he takes a resolved spoonful from the pot, dumps it into his bowl, and now all is right with the world. He starts eating.

I take back the pot and look at him.

"What's up with that spoon ritual of yours?"

He chews, examining his spoon in his small cone of light. "I've never noticed," he says. He takes up a hot bite and mouths it to get it cool. Talking up over the bite, he says, "Gotta have order in the world. Gotta make things even."

"But you'll get more one night and I'll get more another," I reason. "You'll be hungrier sometimes and me other times. It all works out in the end."

Dirk stops chewing and looks straight at me through the faint cast of his lamp. "No," he corrects me, making a square with his spoon in the air. "Equal distribution. It's the only way." With stern strokes, he divides his square into even quarters.

I scowl at that. How can a man of intelligence believe in such rubbish? But I know this isn't about bowls of food. Dirk's talking about how the universe is supposed to work. He is a man of order. Still, it is rubbish.

"Oh, come on, Dirk," I rebut. "Even with your spoon equation you still don't know who has more food."

About to unearth another bite from his bowl, he stalls and wags his spoon at me. "You've got to have some kind of plan. Otherwise, you're talking chaos."

"Your plan is an illusion, Dirk."

"Doesn't matter," he says. "You find your order and you stick with it."

"That's living a lie, and you know it."

He's just eating, hardly listening to me. Grinning, in fact. Damn him. I launch a frustrated barrage at him: "Equality isn't a numerical thing. It doesn't matter how much ends up in your bowl; the line is randomly set. You're comparing irrelevant numbers to irrelevant numbers. We've got to let go of these petty illusions that the lines we draw are real."

Now he is listening, shaking his head. "Listen, Ope, on this planet we've got laws to live by. You start pulling that anarchy crap and no one'll know what to do. Then you have real inequity, lack of clarity, trouble, violence, combat, military intervention, sex crimes . . ."

I'm not eating. Just staring at him. "Bring it on, then."

He reaches in for the next bite, saying, "You don't know what you're talking about."

"I don't want to live a lie."

"We must have rules," he answers.

"I want an older kind of balance, something not restrained by the human mind. Something not poisoned with judgment or values. Where everything is just relationships; it's not that one side of the relationship is more important than the other. That's what this universe works on."

He takes his bite and talks through the food in his mouth, saying, "Your dinner's getting cold."

I put my spoon into the food. Enough said. I let go of my argument, feeling a bit foolish, but still in the right. The night settles in as we go through our meal, the quiet rippled by the last tinkering of spoons. For washing, we boil tea water in the same pot, adding bits of dinner's flotsam to our drink. The air is motionless under stars. I hear Dirk drink off the metal rim of his cup and take in a breath. Out of the dark, he speaks with a quiet visionary's voice,

Starlight travels into infinity
Yet we only see it when the night is black.

I say nothing, my cup warm in my gloved hands, pulled into my body. I look over stars and the dark earth below that conceals a thousand canyons, listening for him to go on. It's from a song, some music he's played to me in his living room before.

Dirk takes another sip and continues with his musical poetry,

This is the question the brothers and sisters fear;
What is the color of the soul?
Said Buddha, Jesus, Plato, and the poets of Old,
That evening is the color of the soul.

If evening is the color of the soul, Dirk, why are you so worried about your precious spoonfuls of imaginary order?

I finish my tea and set down the cup, the metal loud in the darkness. Straightening my wool serape across my back, I lie on the cold rock, arms pulled together on my chest, head on a piece of gear.

Dirk's voice stays with me, the theater of his words. I feel sometimes that I am a vine hooked into his woody branches, sweeping around his trunk with delicate feelers. I am holding on to him the way I hold on to this land. I need something firm, someone who believes in organization. It is not so much that Dirk might be a stable father figure to me, or even a watchful brother. He is a friend who has answers to my questions.

Before the age of sixteen I had moved sixteen times between Arizona and Colorado. Stepfathers came and went, treating my fleeting homes like doorways to someplace else. Everything, in fact, was a doorway. Every place led elsewhere. Maybe that's why I am so drawn to Dirk, why I set my camp near his sense of order.

After Dirk quit the force, he and his two brothers bought a Moab business that shuttles people and equipment to and from the wilderness rivers. They bought the outfit with its boats and fat-tired school bus and warehouse of gear from a man named Tex McClatchy. I used to work the rivers with Tex, so I came in to see who had taken over. Hands were shaken, small talk bantered around.

Immediately Dirk and I looked at each other like animals from different continents. We sniffed and paced around each other.

I was perplexed and enchanted by him: *You used to be a street cop? You've killed someone?*

And he had equal curiosity: *You just walk in the desert? That is what you do?*

Dirk invited me to his house. He sat me on a sofa in front of his full-power stereo, the Doors vibrating through the floor.

Dirk watched me as the music went on, his wife's zoo of cats wandering around us wide-eyed. I closed my eyes, nodding to the tune. After a few songs, he turned down the stereo and read Robinson Jeffers's poetry over a couple of beers at his kitchen table:

> As for me, I would rather
> Be a worm in a wild apple than a son of man.
> But we are what we are, and we might remember
> Not to hate any person, for all are vicious;
> And not be astonished at any evil, all are deserved;
> And not fear death; it is the only way to be cleansed.

I nodded to that, too.

For his final investigation he produced a piece of lined paper, revealing something in blue ballpoint that had come from his own hand. He read it with the pained conviction of a café poet:

> I face the fears that make you
> Piss the bedclothes.
> I find the truth that hides
> Beneath lies and chaos.
> I document the flowing wounds
> You inflict upon each other.
> I wear the equalizer
> The one to end your final fit.

Still, I nodded.

A short time later, I asked Dirk to join me in the wilderness. We went out together, hunkering in a snowstorm, eight days into the Utah canyons beyond the confluence of the Green and Colorado rivers. It was a place I knew, way out beyond public trails. That evening the air smelled of snow draping over stone. Dirk and I watched the great arms of a dead juniper collect thin white railings. Then the sound of water arrived, snowmelt coming down, a stream clattering like silverware on bare rock. We both turned at once.

He did not dumbly nod at this sound. He let go of his eyesight and became ruled by further senses. He was engulfed. That is when Dirk became a part of my mythology, the man who fell into the desert as if from out of the sky.

I had already spent much of my life walking the charred peaks and cactus basins of the Sonoran Desert. I had wormed my way through sandstone canyons in the high Blood Desert. My truck, in which I lived — having no address or phone number — was clogged half with hounded field equipment and half with papers and notes on the sediment loads of flash floods and rates of cliff erosion across the Colorado Plateau, things Dirk would have once dismissed as utter frivolity. After he began walking with me, he understood why I ask the questions that I do. He realized that asking questions was the only way to truly survive in this landscape.

No longer the man with a gun who flew high above all others, he needed an interpreter to read this new topography. I insisted to him that the world was not merely judicious, as he believed, black and white and sterile. There was room to move. There were ways of seeing beyond the confines that the city had branded onto him. My interests would have seemed laughable to his former companions on the streets. I had reasonable theories on hunting practices among the Anasazi culture. I developed methods of predicting eclipses without the use of modern astronomy or calendars. I identified a strain of corn eight hundred years old in an abandoned rock shelter. My obscure knowledge inspired my life in this shifting, convoluted realm through which I traveled. He wanted to know how it was done.

Of course, I was equally engrossed by him; spending time with Dirk was like drawing my finger along the cold metal of a knife's blade, admiring the craft of its handle, the cleanness of its edge. Like any hunter-gatherer, I wanted to keep this new tool close to me. I was amazed by its sharpness. His decisions were made without argument or vacillation. His convictions and oaths were carried around like papers to prove his identity. Dirk saw into the land in ways that I had not imagined, moving briskly through the terrain, his cop years having left his eyes unmistakably trained. He was alert to everything, like a hunting animal, a predator. I had seen this before in hawks sweeping into their kills. I had long envied them for their ferocity and sureness.

When we traveled it was as if we were tied together, flinging each other deeper and deeper into places we would have never discovered alone. Our treks eventually brought us to this night in the singer's country, to these stars, to my back cold against the ground, teacup empty. Ready for bed.

Dirk's light comes on, and I hear him opening the poetry book, his to carry for the day. Pages turn against the silence. He clears his throat:

> *The poet, who wishes not to play games with words,*
> *His affair being to awake dangerous images*

And call the hawks; — they all feed the future, they
    serve God,
Who is very beautiful, but hardly a friend of humanity.

The Projects

A call was sent from the most interior block of the city's government projects. It was a place Dirk knew the same way a novice
might know the innards of a car engine — it was made up of
numerous enigmatic parts and emitted strange smells, and little
about it was familiar. Still, the projects were a seductive taboo, a
place where he usually did all his talking out the rolled-down
window of his patrol car, rarely daring to get out and walk in the
open. Whenever he drove by the stale project buildings, he
imagined the unknowable and the unthinkable within, not sure
of what he might see if he was ever called inside. This morning
he intercepted the call and out of curiosity decided to turn his
car around. He was still a young cop. He intercepted calls
whenever he could.

It was midmorning in autumn. Gingerroot light fell on the
pavement between buildings. The engines of a jetliner strained
as the plane gained its first altitude over this gray clutter of
buildings. Dirk parked and walked along a row of hastily constructed cinder-block structures, no signs of immediate violence around him. Cars were abandoned in postapocalyptic
disrepair on the street. Scattered like windblown dust around

the buildings were broken bottles, wadded paper bags, and unaccountable pieces of oily fabric.

He came to a ground-level door, identical to every other door except for the number, and knocked on it. A girl answered, maybe six years old. She should have been shy or polite, but she was nothing. She pointed behind her, inside. There was a grimness about her that disturbed him. She was too young to have this expression. He could not muster even a smile, sensing it would have been naively wasted on her. He slipped around her small body into the dark of a room. She pointed down the hallway, to the bathroom.

The first information to come to him was the odor of a life utterly unlike his own. It arrived in layers: the dense smell of mildew; the acid of cat urine in the carpet from past tenants; blankets and towels overwhelmed by the territorial musk of a man.

He moved through the dark hallway and came upon a raw, metallic scent. It was the smell of fresh blood. Closer to the open bathroom door was a wash of meat-locker odors, as if a deer had had its belly split open. He walked around the door and looked in.

A woman sat on the toilet. She had swollen lips, one busted at the corner with a pastry of dry blood. One eyelid blossomed purple. She sat bowlegged on the toilet seat, mascara streaked in tears. In her hands she cradled the slick body of a fetus. Its umbilical cord raveled back into her own body.

He could see between her legs toilet water darkly feathered in blood. Rocking her dead child, as if sending it to sleep, the woman looked up at him. Her face was vacant, pleading like a voice too far down a well for rescue.

Panic rose through him. He tasted bile. His lungs jerked for breath. He swallowed to hold down his vomit.

He backed out of the bathroom like the swing of a robotic arm. He stepped from her view and pressed his back to the hallway wall, taking short gulps of air. His body trembled. His skin was cold. He felt an atrocious fear. He had stepped into hell. Even his gun could not save him here. He fought the hot taste on his tongue.

He was still against the wall when the paramedics arrived. They wore pale rubber gloves to protect themselves, their hands looking like the hands of ghosts. Even with their uniforms and paraphernalia-filled belts and handheld kits of official, precise equipment, they could not break the spell for him. They were only tools of the trade, men like him designed to plunge themselves in, grab what is needed, and plunge back out. He said nothing to them. He made quick, distracted eye contact and pointed, directing them to the open door beside him.

He went home at the end of his workday and sat on his couch. He turned up the stereo until the walls vibrated. His living room became a sheltering cave of music. He stared at nothing.

DAY FIVE

Dirk says, "No ravens. No sign anywhere."

He is dismayed. How can there be a land without ravens? There are no animal prints either. No bones. No knuckled fox vertebrae half buried in sand, no bighorn sheep ribs sprung over the rocks. No evening birdsong, not even the far-off, gravel-throated scratch of a wren. No sudden owls in back-alley canyons with wings that sound like breath. Neither of us has ever encountered such absence.

I would call it a dead land, but that would be an error. The place shifts in and out of itself. It is more organic than geologic, luscious foliage of sandstone grown beyond all reason, fed and sculpted by erosion, cliffs rising and collapsing. We move through this place in the morning with only enough gear for the day, our packs left behind so that we can walk freely, scouting routes. The morning is cold. Wind pushes small pebbles. The air smells of snow, a crystalline-wet scent. Stone-gray clouds buckle and turn over one another, ripping across the higher and farther rock formations. I scan the ground for a sign, for sun-bleached nut piles of bighorn sheep droppings, for a bone left in a dry basin where a water hole once sat. These are things we would usually see, the leavings of the desert. But the only organic life I notice here is the movement of our two shadows. They stretch with winter light, rippling, extending, and falling back in the changing terrain.

Dirk's shadow is crisp on the rock, kept tight, his day gear well packaged around his waist, climbing rope bound over his left shoulder with only the knuckles of the bight standing out. Beside him, my shadow is a billowing apparition. I wear a serape bartered from a Guatemalan textile merchant, its wool flanks turning in the wind, hood pulled to a monk's peak. My day gear is an assemblage of parts salvaged off my main pack, strapped together with extra webbing, water bottles hung like ballast.

Dirk moves to the edge of my vision. The drab color of his clothing barely shows. Still, I recognize his body, the cock of his arms, the spread of his hands. He moves toward the east, looking for easiness in the terrain. I know his shape, the loping pad of his boots on stone, his glance turning one way and the next in constant scrutiny. I am pulled in his direction by an invisible tether between us. This is the way we usually move together, aware of the other at each moment. In more familiar country, the line connecting us is allowed to go long, and we often separate for miles, ranging into entirely different canyons. Even then, I walk alongside Dirk's invisible pace and his unseen pauses across obstacles, trailing him with the crystal ball of my imagination. Always we are able to reel back in and find each other by nightfall.

Not here. This place is filled with uncertainty. We might not find each other again for days if we wander apart. We rarely even drop from sight, toting each other around like two young boys holding hands in a crowd. There are too many possibilities to vanish from each other. These dendrites and bifurcations, choices leading to choices, tumble-slope boulders and brief shimmies down to ledges, each promises to separate us. We stay close. I feel him lure me around the rim of a vacant water hole. A paint-peel layer of dry mud lies in the basin below me. I drop to the west of it, my motion lightly catching Dirk's attention, towing him back toward me.

Dirk follows the strands of lesser canyons while I loop in and out of higher domes. My mind is busy memorizing uplifts and crevices that might show themselves when we need them miles or days ahead. There is a constant internal chatter of navigation, like working a small, fragile boat across the sea.

Our paths meet again where a canyon cuts through the face of another dome. I am ahead, the slope steepening around me. I hear the hushing of my footsteps and the labor of my breath.

They sound as if they belong to someone else. Most of my attention lies in the slope and in the presence of Dirk not far behind. I let my vision spread outward, getting some idea of where we are going. Mushroom country ahead. It looks like the earth is overgrown, a field of enormous organic shapes making up for the complete lack of plant life on the ground. We could go in any direction, following a cascade to the west into what is likely a bed of canyons just out of view, or toward the southeast, where shoulders of rock rise to a towering, spindled crown, or into these sandstone chanterelles and amanitas just ahead.

My attention is drawn back to the steepness of the immediate terrain. Boot soles swear they will come out from under me. My heart gulps on a skid of sand, sending up a blood command. My hands flash out for balance. I pause, holding back my weight, judging the increasing angle, how close I might come to falling if I keep on going. A slip would roll me eighty feet down the slope, dropping me into a wind-rounded bowl at the bottom. I would lose much skin, break a few bones, but be alive.

Dirk comes. The ink of his shadow washes the face below me. Instead of pondering the next move, I watch his shadow. In it is skepticism, a scant lingering. In the presence of even his shadow I feel solid ground, a firmness in the bluster of my own life. I have questions. He has answers. The answer is clear in his shadow: This is too steep. I turn back. Find another way.

Lone waves of rock curl up from the earth's surface, lifting beside us, leftovers of long-evaporated groundwater, some aberration exposed from its domain once deep inside the planet. Caves scoop from the faces above us, where weaknesses are exploited by the wind. Bowsprit formations stand into the weather, and we walk by them, taking a moment to circle, then move on. We are heading toward a concentration of geological eccentricities, stretches of ground covered with hundreds of chocolate-brown marbles, hard as iron and up against each other in perfect symmetry. An octopus emerges from the rock, a vestige of some living thing that died in the dunes of a Jurassic desert.

If the sandstone here were much harder, it would stubbornly resist the elements, remaining stern as a granite face, its hunchbacks and disproportions unseen. If it were softer, it would be flung into dunes of blowing sand. As it is, strengths seem to be equal between ground and sky. It is an open conversation, erosion and resistance. Whales of sandstone begin surfacing around us, their backs curved, sleek as they slide through the wind. They dive by the hundreds, drawing the surface down with them into foaming boulders and beds of sand. We keep to their backs, following one to the next, rising hundreds of feet. In one of the spaces between whale bodies we come to an enclosure of plants, signs of life.

It is an interior garden where soil has been gathered from out of the wind. We circle it.

Dirk says, "Zen garden."

"Mmm." I nod my head.

This site is an assemblage of plants and small stones that is neither disorderly nor grossly formal. All of the plants are miniatures — weather-punished bonsai. There is a stub of a cactus, defensive as a scorpion fish; three turpentine bushes with winter-small leaves; sporadic bunches of snakeweed and ricegrass; and a centerpiece yucca, its flagpole still bearing a few emptied seedpods. Their potting soil is a black material, a single, slowly living organism, hundreds of years old.

Flakes of glassy rock gather like bits of beach shell across this dark surface. Each is a different color. These are what lure us down to a crouch at the edge of the soil, not stepping in where our footprints might remain for months or years. We have no wish to leave bold statements of our crossing.

Dirk and I lift these curious stones as if plucking spilled rubies off the ground, thumbing them between fingers, letting them go. Each translucent piece of rock is finely shaved. We know exactly what they are: human artifacts broken on the ground. Nine hundred years old, maybe older — five thousand, eight thousand? — hard to tell from this collection. There are no whole pieces, no notching styles that tell one cultural group from another, no finished spear tips or arrowheads that might argue a five-thousand-year difference in their design.

My weight rests on one heel at a time, shifting and reaching. My recollection of this posture is old. It is a cellular memory, habit, weight to the heels, drawing a finger over a sharp edge, turning an item to feel for its dimensions — the geography of body posture formed in order to read the geography of Earth. It feels good to stretch my muscles, to feel the ground with my fingers for a few minutes. This is what humans were left with when we began walking upright, our fingers no longer skimming the ground, our eyes suddenly and hungrily searching the sky. An entire horizon of questions and answers fell away from us when we turned vertical, so we had to learn this way of coming down on our haunches, hands turned into tools. Memories of planting; memories of hunting.

I lift a knife-curve of gray stone, something that had snapped off while a tool was being made. This kind of scatter is all over the canyon desert, bangles left across the land by hunters on the move. Another piece that I find is the remnant shard left from a hard blow. A third is flaked off thin as paper, peeled away by the palm-pressed tip of an antler, a square of leather across the thigh to soften the work against the maker's skin.

My fingers read these details, accumulating knowledge of whoever hunted here. I feel for the expression of a person cutting a tool, eyes turning up to the horizon in routine watchfulness, back down to the task at hand. I have done the same before, sharpening a knife or taking notes in my journal, my stare moving up now and then to keep track of the wind and the motionless boulders.

Dirk runs his berry-picking fingers across the ground, searching for the whole, ripe arrowhead. He does not do this to slip it into his pack, but only to lift the piece and feel its accuracy. There are no complete pieces, though. I pick up another sliver, a clear slice of red stone. I hold it to the light of the sky so that I can see the blood clots captured within.

"Check out this one." I lean my crouch toward Dirk, arm out, and pass it to him.

He tilts to me, takes it, and does the same, studying the universes suspended inside the rock. He looks up then, attentively rubbing it between his fingers, examining the terrain.

"You can scout game through this gap down here clear across this lower region," he says, using the piece to point in that direction. "Maybe for other unwanted hunters coming in from below or any sign of movement. And the wind is blocked from the south." He aims the piece south.

He is right. This is the place. It does not break the skyline, so a person can see without being seen. This is a hunting shelter, a place to sit and scratch out your tools. I think of hunters along my family line. They obeyed the same ritual that Dirk and I have fallen into, ducking into terrain that both protects and reveals.

From my father I inherited a box, a container of arrowheads that I now keep beneath my desk at home. The box is a 1940s Christmas greeting-card container originally secured by cotton string. Inside are items that my great-grandfather had gleaned from the land near his home in southern New Mexico: the elbow of a fired clay pipe; a piece of corrugated pottery around seven hundred years old; two carved stone pendants likely of Paleo-Indian origin; eight hand-chipped atlatl points, big-game variety, ten thousand years old, give or take; and thirty tiny arrowheads — pink, cream, banded black, and sugar-grained brown — as finely crafted as ivory figurines, some notched on their sides by desert nomads as far back as six thousand years ago.

When my great-grandfather died, my grandfather inherited this box of artifacts. When my grandfather died, the box passed to my father. When my father died two years ago, it moved to me.

Every now and then, I take out the box and examine a few of its pieces. I feel for subtle messages, codes inscribed across thousands of years. I slip my finger across the edges, thinking, You could not have known who would next interpret your communiqué. The pieces say *hunt* and *kill* and *watch*. Some say *rabbit,* others *deer, bighorn,* even *bison.* I know there is more written on them — age of the maker, male or female, hunter-made or done by a craftsperson who has never killed. But I have not become proficient enough to read the code that closely.

I sometimes imagine what would be read if someone studied my own knife blade or touched the edges of my journal. Would they know of my history, my entire family line, those who were eaters of rabbit, squirrel, quail, and white-tailed deer from the gale-beaten scrub of the Chihuahuan Desert? Most men in my family were hunters or fly fishermen patrolling the tiny boulder- and vegetation-infested creeks scattered across the highlands of New Mexico and Arizona. A great-great-uncle worked as a game warden in the West Texas desert, and my great-grandfather was a rancher who regularly shot and trapped predators. My father hunted coyotes. His methods were the most persuasive and evocative of anyone I have known, bloodless and far-reaching.

Dirk continues ferreting out the most colorful pieces and the ones with the finest edges. Suddenly, his hand snaps back with a bee-sting yowl. I am quick on him, looking for the culprit.

"What?"

He holds one hand in the other, thumb stuck up like a sprout. On it is a welling bead of blood. The bead blossoms, and a bright thread winds toward his palm.

"Damn," he says, truly surprised. "That one was really sharp."

A grin sweeps my face.

"I'm serious. Look at this. It's a deep cut." He sucks it clean, and before the blood returns, I see that the inside flesh is white beneath a superficial layer of pink. A deep cut indeed.

"Jesus, Dirk," I say, moving a hand across my face so I do not laugh. "Be careful with that stuff."

He considers the wound, pulling it apart to peer inside, just to see how well these tools actually work. He turns his hand to let the blood curve one way, then the next.

I draw the hood over my head to keep the wind out and continue scanning the surrounding land.

———

It is so rare to find soft ground out here. On the sheltered bays of a mesa top we come to more of these Zen gardens, fields of coral-reef soil: black, pointy, and layered by centuries of growth. We arrive at a large field, and immediately Dirk sweeps down to one knee, poking a finger into the ground.

"This stuff is in good shape."

I join him, hand grazing these tiny, friable soil heads as if passing over rime crystals.

"Nothing's been walking on this," he continues, glancing up, obviously searching for a way around so he won't have to crush it with his steps. "Old-growth crypto."

The soil is infinitely delicate. We walk, but there is suddenly very little bare stone to carry us, so we skirt every edge of soil we can, as if wandering the ins and outs of very small coastlines. This way of moving reminds me of childhood games — don't step off the rocks/the log/the sidewalk lest you plunge into boiling lava. It takes time, changing the pace of the day so that we do not leave footprints.

Anywhere that an animal touched this black molten earth, we can see a disturbance. We pause where a skullcap of soil has been kicked off, landing upside down a few inches away. The event happened months in the past. Rabbit, we conclude. Without the evidence of any other tracks, we account for the trajectory of the animal, the size (small enough to slip under a blackbrush broom just ahead), and the speed. Had to be a rabbit. Startled, perhaps. Moving fast, taking swift cover around these nearby dry bushes.

"Hawk," Dirk suggests.

"Yes," I agree. Hawk. Something that would not leave tracks but would send a rabbit quickly across the soil.

The concealment of this landscape makes subtleties such as this stand out far more than they would anywhere else. In sand or mud, a fresh track is bold, revealing species, genus, direction — the more available facets of an animal. Here, the animal shows up only in a stray step, a quick crossing, a suggestion of personality in the light paw scratch, the telling of age in this story trap of black soil.

I don't mean to say anything out loud, but a question slips past my lips. "Why are we so interested in tracking?"

Dirk's answer is quick, like a reflex. "Information," he says. "We want to know what's going on."

"Why?" I look at him. "Why do we want to know?"

He shrugs it off. "Curiosity."

I don't like his answer. I know it is more than curiosity. We track animals and hunt our way through the wilderness as if we would die if we didn't. That's not just trivial inquisitiveness.

I say, "But it's like we're trying to look through something. Like the world is camouflaged and we're trying to see through it. We spend all of our time at this. It's more of an obsession than it is curiosity."

"Whatever you want to call it."

I'm not done, though. Dirk is my sounding board. I feel as if I am a puppy springing at a wolf, and I trust that he won't suddenly tear my head off. I go ahead. "No. It's not whatever I want to call it. There's something about tracking, something about the way we move out here that is more than just nosiness."

Dirk responds by sitting on the naked sandstone. Now he's giving it some thought. I am suddenly not just a puppy. I have lured him in.

He looks at the print, the single tick of soil out of place, something that most people would never notice.

"There's an otherworld," he says.

He tells me that in order to amuse himself when he was a

cop he used to ask someone for his name, then, within less than a minute, determine that the person was lying and extract the real name. It was an exercise in vision, as routine as morning sit-ups, training to see through obfuscation.

He acts it out for me. "'Let's see your driver's license. How old are you? Where do you live? Hmm, that's a different address than what you just said. What's the address on your driver's license? Open your wallet. What's that? Yeah, that one with the picture. Yeah, that's you, but there's someone else's name on this. That's funny. What else do you have in there? Where did you say you live?' *Pow*. I got him. Then we start getting down to the real dirt, busting open the underworld, having a look inside. That's when you start seeing things."

I ask, "Why would you do something like that?"

"Just to fuck with them. To hone my skills. Who knows?"

I say, "You and I are hunter-gatherers, Dirk. We go around poking and prodding, picking things apart, figuring out how the world works. You have the ability to see through veils, see how things are put together. You look at some plain feature and know that written beneath its facade is an entire evolution of motives and actions that most people never witness. You're tireless."

"It's simple assessment," he says. "You look around and see what's going on. It's just business."

He is balanced at the edge of my trap. I want him to admit it. I want to hear him say that there is a sacred order to the world — not his goddamned illusion that we're eating the same amount of food every night, but a deeper order of animal tracks and canyons and water holes. I want to hear him say that he is pursuing this order, that his relationship with it is so intimate that it guides him from place to place.

"You told me a story once," I say. "You tracked a man through light city snow. Why is it that you had the skill to do that, while none of the other cops would have even thought of it?"

He smiles at the memory but comes back to me shrugging again. "It made sense. I was just patient. No magic mumbo jumbo. I just tracked a man."

It was a jewel thief, I remember, a botched robbery set against a fresh dusting of snow. The man had entered through a store's skylight. An alarm went off when the seal broke. He ran, taking nothing. Dirk was there fifteen minutes later doing the usual cleanup, compiling his notes on the crime scene. He walked into the alley behind the building, thinking, Is the guy at home watching TV right now? At the bar? Banging the baby-sitter? He looked below the fire escape ladder and saw fresh tracks in the snow. The thief was suddenly right there, falling helplessly into Dirk's circle of influence. Dirk stretched far beyond his physical body, carrying his senses all the way to the man, now at home. He started running to find him, closing the gap. The game had begun.

Dirk spent the next half hour dodging street to street, a patrol car following him as he swept in and out of intersections on the thief's trail. Tracks were lost at crossings, concealed under the prattle of more recent pedestrian tracks, regained along lesser sidewalks.

Perhaps the thief would have taken more care with his steps if there had been a good blanket of snow, a half foot of unshov-eled powder trailing him home, naming his every move. Instead, the dusting captured his overconfidence. It also revealed an inexpert fear, his crossing to unlit streets, turning slightly and too often to check his back. Not a professional, Dirk thought. He had noticed the same thing in the bungled break-in, the alarm ineptly tripped — of course there was going to be an alarm on a jewelry store's skylight! What kind of desperate fool was he?

The tracks were finally absorbed into the anonymity of a multistory apartment complex, but by then Dirk knew the man well enough. He knew how to scare him out of hiding. Two minutes of banging on doors and throwing a commanding voice drove the thief out of his bathroom window. He jumped three stories, hit the ground running, terrified. The chase went through a cemetery, out to a street-lit business district where a throng of waiting cops charged upon him and dragged him to the ground. When Dirk arrived minutes later, he counted coup on the struggling man: He walked up, turned his flashlight butt into his fist, and, with a single thrust, met the man's stomach and said, "You're it!"

I say, "Tracking isn't just a technical skill. There's something else about it, something more . . . preternatural. I think sometimes that the second you found his tracks in the snow, he knew you were there. Maybe he got up and turned off the light in his apartment and didn't really know why."

Dirk looks at me flatly. "Maybe, but who knows?"

"I know, Dirk."

"You do not."

"You track an animal until you know so much about it that it actually appears right in front of you. That's what you did with the thief. You gathered up so much knowledge about him that in a way you became him. There was no way he could escape you. He was inside you, so where else could he go to get away? It's the same out here. You move around until this place fills you. That's how you find your way through."

Dirk wipes his hands on his pants and stands. He laughs, shaking his head. "Fuck that Yoda shit of yours."

I have to grin in return. My trap just barely swiped him. He has to laugh me off because for a second there, he believed me. And for even longer, I believed myself.

———

Dirk doesn't want to step in this fragile soil because it is beautiful and ancient. He wants it kept clean. I don't want to step in it because tracks would expose me here. This is where the jewel thief made his mistake, feet touching ground, marking a place of vulnerability. You can be named and hunted by your tracks. I do not want to be judged among the healthy, rational citizens of my species. I am something other, a strange animal in hiding, prints found only in the momentary flick and scratch. My movements are those of a desert golem.

Finally, Dirk and I have to cross the soil and leave marks of ourselves. It is inevitable. We stop in front of a stretch that we cannot get around, its tiny castles standing by the hundreds of thousands ahead of us. Dirk goes first, his pace utterly changed. I follow, trying to become light, walking along whatever passage will leave the least mark.

The crust breaks through into powdery dust below, every foot sinking. I glance back, checking my progress. My prints look like bomb craters. Dirk checks his own tracks and stops, complaining, "I hate walking through this stuff with these damned clumsy monkey feet." I nod to that. We are giants here. Why have we not learned how to float through such places? In general, Dirk and I are difficult to track. We obscure ourselves across the soil in how we step and in the choice of our paths. Still, I see myself postholed into the ground, crashing through fragile universes.

This kind of soil is called *cryptobiotic,* literally meaning "hidden life" — ineffable and present at once. I know it by its hives of anchored organisms, the expansion rates of its cyanobacterial tendrils, the laminar patterns of its growth. Science is easy for me, with all of its neatly turning gears and ratios. I can put my weight against it in discussions with learners of obscure disciplines: fluvial geomorphology, osteology, microbiology. But I have also known that I should not put my weight there. With this limited human spectrum of sensations, our blithely unquestioned bias of self-superiority, how can I possibly confide in the imagined purity of science? Devastated beneath my boots are colonies of rare desert mosses and these brittle, creeping continents of blue lichen. Spore heads no larger than drops of mist bind and crush. Hard science barely allows for mystery, for true sacrifice and loss. It robs this soil of what I see right now.

I come to a crouch to relieve the pressure of my steps. I drop a hand. My finger searches the textures. I see a sanctuary in this ground, a Byzantine realm of shapes and misshapen, enigmatic creatures too small and too numerous to count. I imagine myself concealed here, an eel peering from subterranean holes, my mouth open to breathe. Here I will never be seen by those of clumsy feet, never even expected by those who thoughtlessly imagine all this to be dead. I am the hidden life in the desert. Cryptobiotic: a living man roving this delicate and barren wealth of earth.

My finger grazes the black scab of a yucca seed, and I press on it so that it breaks the surface crust and sinks below. There it might someday split open and drop a pale, vulnerable root. Hold on to the ground, I think. When you burst to the surface green and tipped like knife blades, this wind-struck environment is all that you will have.

The science tells me of symbiosis in the soil. Nutrients are stored. Vascular plants are at last given earth in which to root in this land of cold stone. Only the armored and the subterranean live here, grabbing on to one another. This is a garden of fugitives — dryland fungi, blue-green algae that were the first life to appear on the planet, and needle-proud cacti aside bayonets of yucca. The desperate lands, the deserts and the methane-spoiled atmosphere of early Earth are their sanctuaries. They have been alive for a long time. Their memories lie long before the comforts of cottonwood shade and soft grass.

I am one of these, an older creature. I have learned to seek secret traps and crannies, like a low-tide animal waiting for the water to return. But not only on this solid earth have I found my hold. I have rooted into my family line the same way these organisms fasten to this crisp and desiccated soil. I dwell in the genetic shadows of drunken redneck nobles from southern New Mexico, composers of obscene Chaves County bonfires and all-night gun shooting into the stars. In this family of oddities I am infinitely elusive. I am the hidden life. But I must be cautious. This soil is delicate. This bloodline is perilous.

Coyote Hunting

My father was once the fastest man alive. This was not long before I was born. Back then he ran 440 yards in a couple of tenths under forty-five seconds. Those who knew him at the time said *he burned*. He was not *on* fire, he *was* fire. Pure and swift. Not a stray thought in his head — a talent shared among particularly skilled hunters who can run down deer. As soon as word got out about this wire-muscled high school kid from the rural high desert of New Mexico, he became material for the Summer Olympics in Mexico City. Then, two things happened.

First, in time trials, he ripped a muscle down his left leg and came limping off the track as if clipped by a bullet. His coach hauled him to the locker room, fisting balm against the injury until the air smelled unbearably of eucalyptus and oil refineries. The man opened a kit, rattled out a bottle of prescription painkillers, fed them to my father, then put him back on the starting block.

Fifteen seconds into the next sprint, his muscle tore along the length of his calf like a cotton sheet. He was a plane touching ground without landing gear, legs, *wings,* cocking into the air as he rolled. He came to rest facedown, fingers scratching the black surface, sweat dripping uselessly onto the asphalt. Over the dizzy mask of drugs he felt severed muscles strangling around the empty space where there had been nothing but speed. Running was over for him.

Second, his consolation prize for not being awarded a gold medal in Mexico City was being told by his girlfriend that she was pregnant with me. I was the only child either of them would ever have. Their newborn marriage would last four years, punctuated by epic fighting and an affair with the woman he would marry next, whom he would later lose to another affair with yet another woman he would marry.

My blood mother became my bread and butter, my day and night. My father, meanwhile, was a distant and gleaming nebula who took me away to sleep in the out-of-doors. He was a man of excruciating cravings. When running had ended, he turned his attention to the universe at large, burying himself in philosophy and music, Nietzsche's mind-boggling void and the dark panic of eastern European composers from the late nineteenth century. His birthday gifts to me were Prokofiev's Fifth Symphony, Stravinsky's *Firebird Suite,* and Dvořák's *New World* Symphony, which I played endlessly on a tin-speaker toy record player.

I was a worshipful kickstand of a kid. I inhaled from my father what seemed to be a dense vocabulary, following him too closely, sometimes stepping on his heels, causing his summer sandals to snap against his feet. I hummed his words weeks and months after our visits together. Once, he took me coyote hunting, driving me out to the cactus-and-thorn-tree jungle of the Sonoran Desert. I was nine years old.

I loved riding in his rust-cratered truck with its cracked windshield, his hand batting against the window to get the flies out. There were strange smells in his cab — greased chains, the metallic scent of old bullet casings, and the gutted odor of cigarette smoke. I remember a small crescent wrench forever jammed into the track of his bench seat, causing the seat to jar whenever he moved it forward or back. The mass of objects behind the seat included a map of Arizona, a fishing map of Colorado, a U.S. Geographical Survey topographic map of the Chedeski quadrangle on the Apache Reservation, and a badly beaten road atlas.

As we banged over desert hill and dale, I foraged into his garage-sale floorboards, crammed headfirst in front of the seat like a cosmonaut. I found treasures down there — a stopwatch, a crop of ink pens, pieces of nondescript paper trailed with his illegible handwriting, a key chain from the insurance company where he worked.

I remember that he used words such as *cosmos* and *quintes-sential,* leaving me hanging on the syllables, no need for defini-tions. He venerated the sciences and littered my mind with *plate tectonics, supernovas,* and *velocity,* the last one particularly romantic, sliding off my tongue like light. I once announced, to the awe and disbelief of other children, that I had my very own *velocity* that I kept in my room and would show to no one.

I told lies to my friends at school, saying, *Well, my dad is a war hero, a five-star general,* when in fact I had no idea what my father actually was or how many stars a general might be able to earn. If I had discovered the truth, that he sold insurance out of a poorly lit office where he spent a good portion of his time thumbing through books on numerology and the Spanish con-quest of Mexico, he still would have been a warrior — all guns and heroism.

As I grew up, he kept telling me that I was to live in both worlds, never explaining what he meant. I was baffled whenever he said it and eventually stopped listening.

Gone coyote hunting, we parked the truck along a roadless desert arroyo and got out to watch the sunset, sharing cans of mealy pink Vienna sausages under the emerging stars. I regu-larly asked if it was time to hunt the coyote yet, and he kept say-ing that it would happen soon, and to keep my voice low.

My father was lithe and strong, still built like a runner. Even-tually, he would lose his shape entirely. He would become cor-pulent in his last couple decades of life, but for now, he was still a swift man. Leaning against a tire, he sat on the ground near me, an apparition in the fireless dark. Sausage cans rested on their side, their silver lids curled in the starlight. He talked qui-etly about quasars and neutron stars and the speed of light, gulping at a bottle of Yukon Jack, "a taste born of hoary nights." He was devoted to astronomy, to its suggestion of realms beyond realms. He explained to me the distances between stars, telling me how something small and faraway does not contradict its being unbelievably huge and close.

I was attracted to this word *contradict,* a clattering sound like a rock thrown down a well — hitting the side once, *con!* then again, *tra!* and finally dropping into the water, *dict!* I could tell that it was a tool, a mechanical divider between words, flipping like the small metal wing he had called a *governor* in the truck's carburetor, turning one way and the next to regulate the flow of fuel. I knew this would be a useful word in any sentence. *To contradict:* to separate. *To not contradict:* to bring together, to think of things as big and small at once.

He was drunk when he told me it was hunting time, his voice deep and slow in the dark but still intelligible. He was now calling me "my son," the tongue-bitten edge of his words leaving me more uneasy each time they were spoken.

"My life is for you, *my son,*" he said. "Your *Dad* would do anything for you. You understand me? I have died for you. You will live in both worlds, hear me?"

And then there was a long stare into the stars, the chime of air bubbles up through the glass bottle, and the steady coal of his cigarette.

He stood, snuffing out the cigarette with his boot heel and reaching down to pocket the butt. He rummaged through a box in the truck, orchestrating the sound of bullet shells and batteries, the cab light a strange beacon in the night. He brought to me a dying-rodent call, an oversized wooden whistle. He told me to blow into it with great force, opening and closing my hand around it to vary its sound, using all of my breath until it was time to stop — he said I would know when it was time. This is the sound, he said, of desperation. Coyotes can't resist their own curiosity. He rigged a handheld spotlight to a spare automotive battery.

Together we created a blaring circus. I threw my lungs into the horrible call, which sounded like an animal in a garbage compactor. The whistle was immensely pleasing to roar upon, fulfilling a childhood fantasy of shattering all known silences. As I did this he swept the desert with the white shaft of his light. It was utterly unnatural, the light casting surreal shadows, stealing the subtle steamy night colors from everything it touched, turning them barren and dry. The sound continued to screech behind him, a dying goat, a squirrel gutted but still alive.

The light panned until I was familiar with each detail — a particular paloverde tree, the firework arms of an ocotillo grove, the dusty gap of an animal path into a nearby arroyo. I hunted for any shift, a shadow in a different place.

I drained my lungs to the very bottom, filling them as fast as I could so that no pause would come to the coyote's ears. My mind glittered with colors and sensations, tiny worms of light across my eyes. I felt as if I might fall on the ground, knees buckling, but I could not, not in the presence of the great coyote hunter. So I blew even harder, spinning myself, demanding that the coyote come.

I had memorized the surrounding trellis of paloverde shadows so well that the moment the coyote appeared, its body stood out from those shadows as if burned onto paper. It ran from the thorn trees, head turned toward us over its shoulder. I dropped the call to my side.

The coyote froze across my vision. It was a strong, lean dog with heavyset fur. A tail like a bush on fire. I saw its hips rise and fall through its coat. A bone-struck face with a long, blunt snout. Brown-ringed eyes. The eyes seemed inquisitive and shocked. This was a creature of the wilds, something from *out there*, with a mind behind the eyes, a mind like my own.

I had heard coyotes so many times, howling in the faraway. I had seen their tracks and caught them spying on me from a half mile away. But never this.

Never even slowing its sprint, it made contact with us. I saw its recognition, a suspicion answered. In that instant it swerved and ran the other way, an amazing turn, never losing speed. The coyote was gone as fast as it had arrived. We had played some strange creature out of the ocean depths, and the line snapped just as it reached the surface. The coyote darted back into the darkness, and my father shut off the spotlight.

I had never been coyote hunting with him. I expected next the terrible blast of a handgun, the flash of white shooting into the dark. Instead, the desert became a deep and fathomless sea, a universe I could not touch, but one that I was carried into. I forgot about the gun. Paws struck silently across rocks and arroyo, fur brushing quickly through creosote branches. The coyote ducked invisibly onto an old path, recognizing scents along the ground, checking over its shoulder.

My father and I had summoned an animal who could run into the unreachable desert with us clinging to its back. I fled with it into the dark.

As long as I could hold my breath, the coyote carried me. But I needed to breathe. I resisted. When I gave in and inhaled, I let go of the animal and found myself standing exactly where I had started. Only then, when the mind glitter wore off, did I look at my father. I realized that he was unarmed. He had no intention of killing a coyote. This is what coyote hunting meant, a glimpse of a wild animal drawing us out of our skins.

He had not yet taken his breath. The light was off, and he was standing still, a dark form against the stars. His profile faced the coyote, motionless. The spotlight hung in his hand. His body seemed limp, shoulders dropped. He was being carried. I saw the thing that cannot be seen, the line that passes through: the union of father, coyote, and desert. In that moment he was far away from me, the fastest man alive.

DAY SIX

We pitch across a rock face under the weight of our packs. The earth is a sugar cube to my fingers, granules springing free, lifting into the wind. The angle is barely enough to hold us; we are ten grains of sand away from boot-skidding down. But we do not fall. We move deferentially, fingers on the rock ahead, body weight brought nearer to the core of the earth, thigh muscles hot as coals. Only the crescent edges of our boot soles do any good.

My world is the oilskin circle of my hat brim, the grade just ahead, and my tumbling heartbeat. I lift my head against my pack. Here: the cliff depressed barely enough. To my left: treacherously steep. Straight above: perhaps possible, but unlikely. The danger is not a deterrent. It governs our movement, buffeting our shoulders and hands. It leads us in the right direction. It leads us to safety.

Climbing straight up would require ropes and anchors,

multipitched ascents with racks of metal-alloy gear jangling like cowbells. But there is a way to go with bare hands. There is a course within the cliff. We follow the slope of the braid, crossing left to right to left only along its accessible exposures.

I glance at Dirk, fifty feet down from me. His hands are in front of him. He sweeps the face of the rock as he moves, lightly balancing himself, touching the surface as if clearing spiderwebs from his path. I see in the cleanness of his movements that he belongs here. He creates a path as he goes, closing it as he passes, a ribbon of awareness traced up this ascent.

We rise into spindles of rock left by the wind and climb through them, brushing their plump bases with the receptively soft undersides of our hands. With every step I touch something: the visage of a boulder soon to fall, a small crack, a salt-shaker knob of rock. This is a way of reading this landscape. I memorize the details because each will prove useful. I snap a loose pebble into my hand and roll it the way a starfish seeks weakness from a clamshell, discerning its shape, its friability. I hold it for two steps, three steps, then, once I've made its acquaintance, I drop it and it ticks hundreds of feet down the face, popping high over Dirk's head.

My sense of touch is volatile. The synapses between fingers and brain fire until they shiver. They tell of each meager change to grain or temperature or friction. In the past, weeks into treks, I have looked at my fingertips and found them bare. The prints had been sanded into inconspicuous pads by all the touching. But always, the prints regrow. I don't know where they come from, how such delicate and subtle circuitry is re-formed. I have watched the prints fan into place over the weeks until I am exactly who I was to begin with. I am inescapable.

In a saddle between rock formations I slide from my pack, letting it fall to the ground, banging it with my hand to make sure it is well planted. From there I climb free toward the top, the lack of weight sending me up, nearly flying. A minute ahead of Dirk, I come over the crest of an open, desolate park. My hands slide like whiskers around me.

Now I can see where I am. This is the top of the land, only the sky from here. I move immediately into the open space, crossing it to the other side, where it drops off.

Dirk arrives, no pack either, his arms outspread above this field of eroded, stellate boulders, over the whole of the earth.

I turn back to see him for just a moment, to make sure we are together, then keep moving. I walk straight across the basin and climb the low abutment of eroded rock on the other side, which leads me to the edge.

There, the world falls beneath me.

I find the place jutting farthest out and lower to a waiting and urgent crouch. One palm is flat on the rock, one knee on the ground, head pushed over the edge. Cloisters of canyons and haphazard stone fins gather in the depths below. This is the mad country I had seen from the airplane window on the way to my father's funeral. It is the place we will have to cross.

My hands are suddenly inessential, nothing but springboards.

Now my eyes serve me. Color, distance, depth, scheme. Everything is out of reach. As if searching for a thread's beginning in a terrible knot, I start my eyes in one place, then another, then another, unable to find a beginning or an end to this landscape. Schismatic shadows corkscrew into nowhere, vanishing into optical illusions of far and near. The place is a geographic rummage sale, pieces of canyons, buttes, spines, and ravines all over one another, no visible bottom. It does not even have an other side that I can see.

I recall a story that the Diné tell about coming through here. When they first arrived, unsure of the terrain around them, they sent a small dog ahead as a scout. The dog returned every day telling of routes and places to sleep. One day, as they neared this difficult heart of canyons, the dog vanished. They could hear it, but they never found it. As the story goes, the dog's voice is still calling out, forever lost in these cell walls of stone.

I am filled with a mix of anxious craving and atavistic fear. It is an alarming sensation. I want to be in this stronghold this instant, wrapped in shadows, stone forms launching around me. I also want to crouch at this vista and never move except to inch my way out, no sudden motions to draw attention.

Looking for a route just to get into this place, I cannot see any clear passage. Massive bulwarks of stone stand in the way. There is no repetition among landforms that I can see. Every item is fashioned by its own urges; an assault on civil, human principles; the result is the kind of reckless imbroglio that only the deranged might enjoy. *Seductive, though.*

Dirk walks to the edge beside me. He presses his hands against the heat of his thighs, still breathing hard. I remain in a feral crouch, waist high to him, my weight leaning forward, barely balanced, the dog on point, the gargoyle high in the gables of a cathedral.

"Bad rock wilderness," he says. "That is absolutely bitch country down there."

I say nothing. This must have been how Galileo saw the bespangled night sky, looking for consequence among the sweeping, self-propelled pinpoints of light, finding neither the sterility of divine order nor Satan's sex-craved bedlam. He saw meteorites fleeing the stars, planets minding mathematic rhythms, and the whirligig earth turning beneath so that nightly our universe changes, and changes back.

Dirk and I look from here into the garish mouths of canyons furrowing into unsolvable precipices, beams of stone as long as rivers. We have the jump on Galileo, I think. We can physically walk into it. There is no need for telescoping lenses of glass; we can travel through stars with our hands and feet.

Dirk's voice is soft at first, trancelike. "Look at these shapes," he says, his left hand tracing over the skyline. "Like clay all wormed out."

His voice becomes prophetically measured, a rising oration. I know by the tone that I do not have to respond or even look at him. His audience is the air, the land below.

"There are two landscapes," he announces from this pulpit of rock. "Two at once. The first one is this hard, tangible country, the one where you make decisions — *do this and you live, do that and you die*. The second one is what etches onto the silicon disks of our minds."

I think back to the trap I tried to catch him in at the single clip of a rabbit track in dark soil, how I had wanted to hear him say this.

He continues, "You can hear the needle scratching into us right now. Every little detail down there, shapes and colors we've never seen before. They all leave this mark, this second landscape inside of us. You can hear it. Like a pencil scribbling something on paper."

Both of his hands start moving, defining something in the air.

"A place like that land down there means countless numbers of contact points driven into the hard drives of our minds. This is where people won't go. They get their little bundle of record-ings and that's it for their lives. They turn off their eyes. The needle scratches too deeply out here, too much information, *No, thank you, I'll pass; just let me decline into my own intangible world, drooling into my bowl of corn pone."*

His voice lifts across the rims of canyons, growing louder. He is no longer speaking to the land. Now he's after someone else, someone far away. He is speaking, I think, to himself.

"The thunderstorm is just over the horizon," he warns. "The thunderstorm is just over the horizon every day, every place you go. Always right there, about to bear down on you. *Get it?"*

Then his hands cast out and he is shouting, every word barked to attention.

"Go back to your daytime TV and fucking sale prices at Wal-Mart and stay the fuck out of here!"

His shoulders drop, hands to his sides. He comes easily onto his rear beside me, knees up like gun sights, arms laid across them. He is done.

I sit quietly beside him.

Is he a madman? No. I've known him long enough. I listen to his outbursts as if they were poetry, strange mirrors of his mind. He is haunted. He has spent too much time in the secret hell of human civilization, which has twisted his language. I have seen people shrug unimpressed when they hear he worked not the streets of New York or Chicago, but lowly Denver. What they do not understand is that no one city is more tragic or violent than any other. Wherever people gather there are guns and lies and voracious predators. Beneath parking tickets and patrolling the schoolyards is always a cancerous layer of duplicity and habitual violence. It is not even an urban phenomenon. Park rangers are shot by drug traffickers. Rapists leave their victims dead in the desert. A rancid odor follows this species wherever it goes. Dirk carries very clear memories of this smell.

On the other hand, what judge am I over who is a madman and who is not?

Red Tricycle

Memories from childhood come mostly in bursts of color. This particular memory is the color red.

I was standing at the living-room window in a Phoenix duplex when a woman came screaming and beating against the glass. Her wrists were sliced open. Ferns of blood uncurled across the window. I stood in utter bewilderment.

The slashes across her wrists looked like two dark mouths, tight-lipped and violently sputtering. She howled for help, her hair wild with blood, the window in front of her slapped in fist prints. My red metal tricycle was the only object on the porch, and it was being lavished.

I thought that nightmares had been allowed into daytime. I did not scream or cry. Probably, no expression at all came across my face. I was helplessly thrown into another world. The home I knew was uprooted without warning, replaced with this bloody screaming and chaos. I could do nothing to bring it back into line. My life was now the panic of this woman spilling herself all over my tricycle. Where had she come from? Was this my new world? How long would it last? If my old world left me, would it come back again?

I turned only for an instant to look at my mother, who was standing at the far end of our duplex, on the other side of the couch. She was wearing only a bra, caught changing perhaps, and she was frozen with fear. I do not remember her ever moving from that position. She is still standing there, immobile in my mind.

Shouldn't something be done? Am I in danger? My mother's eyes said nothing to me. She was too young, too unfamiliar with the world. Perhaps, like me, she knew nothing of suicides. She would later explain this thing I saw as a fable; the moral: Never leave sharp objects lying about.

She told me that the woman had tripped and fallen on discarded razor blades.

I turned from my mother and looked through the window in time to see the woman streak into the street. She was a dancer followed by sheets of blood that my memory has turned into beautiful curves of red fabric tracking her every movement, filling the street, the sky.

At this theater of glass I watched people run into the street and grab her. A man with white hair, who had once been gentle and played with me, tied the woman to a dining-room chair, and suddenly she was a pageant queen. He wrapped towels around her arms, and when he could do nothing else, he stroked her face.

Then there were sirens and people in uniform all around. A white fire engine. The situation was cleaned up in a matter of minutes, leaving only the decorated window and my spattered tricycle as proof.

The memory diverges from there. It leads to a bathroom.

I picked up a razor blade off the sink and studied it. My

mother's boyfriend had left it there. The fable my mother had
given me to explain what I saw seemed so bizarrely out of place
that it broke the trust I had with myself. I could not imagine
how a woman might fall and slice both of her wrists on such a
slender piece of metal as this, such a small thing, harmless. My
eyes had expressed to me the truth of the matter, the violent
emotions of suicide, but my mother's explanation pointed in a
different direction entirely, to an accident, to formless happenstance. Razor blades had become dubious and powerful.

Here was a live one on the sink.

I needed to know for sure. There was only one way. With a
resolute slash, I split my palm open. For the first instant there
was no blood at all, and I stared in astonishment. Skin pouted
outward from a long white line. I knew immediately that the
woman's dilemma had not been a fumbling accident. She had
done this herself.

Then came the blood. With a burst of screaming I began to
flail, spackling the bathroom mirror with rubies.

It was in this way that I learned to ask questions, branding
quandaries into my skin in order to discern their reality. This
was my first time traversing the wilderness alone.

DAY SEVEN

There is a design to this landscape that is as refined and suf-
ficient as the cables and spans of a suspension bridge. I see it
as I move, cataloging in my journal and in my mind the subtle

variations in fracture patterns within the sandstone, how the weight of arches is supported by struts and cross beds in the rock, the way canyons are connected by stairwells of ledges. I feel beneath my steps great tidal surges of erosion and tectonics. The most primary elements are recorded here. Water, earth, and wind are only containers of still-older elements — motion, weakness, intention, resistance, desire. This desert speaks in ancient tongues.

I have heard that the beginning of the universe is often witnessed in places other than here. Echoes slap back and forth between the mysterious walls of nothing beyond the quasars. We have ears listening for them, radio telescopes dished toward the hinterlands of space. Our sky is streaked with aluminum-foil satellites tracking the tail of the big bang as it floats off to nowhere . . . as if we had not walked this viscera of earthly geology and found ourselves surrounded by the original pops and hisses of the embryonic universe. I hear old-universe echoes booming among blowholes in the rock where wind pours through. I see in the ellipses of floods left in dry tarns of sand the primeval patterns that we still live by. I find all of this here in a water hole drilled like an Einstein scribble into the rock, twisting downward, its ceramic walls shrewdly incised.

The water hole is seated in a canyon floor, something we have come upon during a day's exploration. We have been walking without our heavy packs, moving freely, recording what we find, moving on. A map is being made, one that defines this land for us before we dive in with our packs and start moving camp into the abyss of chasms.

As part of this map, we chart the water holes by taste. Yesterday we took water from a shallow saucer of a hole flavored as strongly as an Earl Grey tea bag squeezed into the mouth. The morning before, we relied on two owl-eye holes, huge circles of water, one mealy with dead insects and a faint slime of winter algae, the other clean and snowmelt sweet.

Today's water hole is deeply inset. Dirk waits above as I climb down toward its storage. My boots and back brace into the turn of its wall. At the bottom is a smooth, indigo mirror that shivers as grains of sand fall in one at a time.

Below the water is a gathering of smallish rocks, edges rounded smooth. When a flood comes, these rocks will leap into action, spinning, wearing the hole deeper. When the flood stops, they will fall silent to the bottom. They have no hope of escape. The way they rest, the shapes they gouge from the walls, these things tell me of history, the kinds of floods that are generated, the grain size of local geological currency.

As I inch down, feeling the cool of the wall behind and ahead with both hands, I imagine floods pounding over this hole, boulders obliterated with dark-sounding smacks. The rocks down here become like worry stones played in the water's hand. In the floods, these rocks are as powerless as I am, thrown and ridden by the currents, hopelessly driven by incomprehensible forces.

Coming low, I reach a hand down, scoop up a palm of water, and put it to my lips. Diamonds of cold droplets land on my pants and soak to my skin. The water is lightly spiced with blackbrush leaves and the taste of rust from the rock. We will not treat this water with chemicals or force it through a filter. It is good water.

Dirk hands down canvas bladders and plastic bottles. Anchoring my weight, I fill one after the next. The coldness cuts my skin as I sink an arm, serape pulled and draped on my shoulders, shirtsleeve rolled to my elbow. I am surprised there is no ice. It must be the insulation of this wraparound enclosure that keeps the ice from forming. I stretch the containers up to Dirk. His arm hangs from the edge to grab them. Water traces down my arm, streaming past my rolled-up sleeve, marking the warm skin of my chest like a razor.

I climb out, coming to the open country above. Dirk is leaning over his gear, securing his water. The canyon below us is jeweled with water holes, most easier to fill from than this — I had wanted to climb in only to feel its throaty shape of erosion. The ground surrounding us has been drilled into so many cavities that it is more of an absence than a presence. In other parts of the desert, we are used to water holes made of smooth eggshells or shallow stone dishes deep enough only to kiss. Occasionally in our travels we have come across wildly constructed wormholes, but nothing like these here. This place is a sculpture garden. Each water hole is flood-burrowed, like a fist twisted into fresh bread dough. The holes stream in and out of each other, as smooth and worked over as hand-thrown pottery. This elaboration must have to do with a consistency to the rock formation, perhaps a function of runoff patterns across so much bare stone.

Where to now? This is the still point. We stand for a bit, drinking from the bags, wiping water from our beards and gaping at the scenery. I buckle water containers into my gear and strap everything over my shoulder, around my waist.

"*Down,*" I shout, and I start running into the canyon below, skimming the edges of holes, the weight of water beating at me.

I hear Dirk complain, "*Jesus,*" behind me, and I turn, not slowing.

I call to him, "Let's get down there, see what this place is made of."

Making his voice into a caricature of a Southern accent, he

shouts, "You a damn foo runnin' around lack some craized monkeh! Get yosef keeowed!"

I am getting out of reach. He jogs behind me to catch up. Then his body snaps into action. We are in flight. Hollow black water holes are cleared in jumps, bodies pressed centrifugally across their sidewalls.

I feel like a marble coming down a track, swerving around one object, rounding into a dead end, and, without losing speed, spinning out of it and rolling on to the next ramp. The land draws down, stretching away from us. Our hands reach back to push ourselves off, or to hold ourselves in place for a half second before leaping ahead. There is no bottom to this place. The closer we come to it, the faster it falls away. I like the running, though. I do not have time to stop and consider. The land builds and collapses quickly, and still no sudden edge stops me. We speed in and out of massive sandstone formations, cold arcs as steeply sided as shark fins, their summits so high that they are out of our view. By the time we stop running, gulping our breath, it looks as if our canyon will end. It is quickly tapering. I pull off my serape and roll it up. I hang it around my back. Dirk unbuttons his outer shirt and strips the bandanna from his head, pulling off his sunglasses to let out the fog.

Water holes pass around us as we continue, slowly now, stopping to look into the olive water. We are still skirting the outer edges of this lower chasm realm, not yet able to find a way into it. New topography is revealed every ten, fifteen feet. Dirk is out in front, and I can see his head drifting above the quirks and jumps of his body like a gyroscope, the way a small bird steadies itself as its grass stalk dips toward the ground.

We stop where a thin hallway of the canyon falls ahead of us. Our eyes hunt in and out of it.

Dirk turns to me and says, "If anyone else was here right now, they'd be sure we were completely lost. They'd be thinking, *Where are we going? How are we gonna get out of here?* They wouldn't know that we're piecing together our knowledge, that it's the only way to make it."

I lean my back against the wall, watching him, listening to the instruction of his voice. He has to stop every once in a while and set a benchmark, speaking out loud as if the moment must be understood in English before we can move on. It is a way, I imagine, to keep from getting lost, to verify that we are indeed here, as if otherwise we are dreaming. I imagine he did the same when he was a cop, turning to his partner and riddling him with observations and explanations.

"Lost?" he asks, and then answers himself. "No. Nervous? Yeah, maybe. A little nervous. Kind of like a blind date. It's a willingness to suspend intention. Let the place talk to you. Let it direct you. You've got to examine things, see what qualities make this place what it is."

His finger lifts to trace the canyon around him. "This sudden narrow here," he says. "It's something different. Something to remember. Why? The drainage is cutting through rock a little harder, more resistant. We should know about this. It'll show up again, and maybe it will be even tighter, maybe impassable. Everything has something to say here. We need to be fluent."

As we walk ahead, the narrow stretch tightens further. It shoves us down into a smaller and smaller hole. The grace of isolation is overwhelming down here. Sand gathers around the canyon's inside turns, remnants of lost winds. The outsides are scraped raw by floods. The bedrock carves into snaking hallways of stagnant water, the overlapping walls no farther apart in some places than our shoulders. Our voices dampen whenever we find something to say. We walk bend by bend, the sky swerving drunkenly overhead. In the rubric of geomorphology, this is called *sinuosity*: a canyon's urge to twist, a straight line made into a ray of curls as the laws of stone and fluid dynamics rub against each other; the desire to live.

We palm the bare rock as the canyon closes. A dark wind moans over its depths. I see Dirk ahead of me, his arms spread as if in flight, and I know what it means.

"Ends here," he says.

I come and look over his shoulder. The canyon falls away. There is no route. We have marked another doorway to nowhere. I can see a few ledges inside. We could shimmy down if we wanted, jump from one ledge to the next.

"We could try it," I say, but I'm not serious. This is one of those places we would tumble into and our bodies would never be found.

"Fuck off," he tells me.

We both retreat to a higher platform of rock, up in the sun, unloading small bags of food, nuts, dried fruits, sharing back and forth. As he is passing across the nut bag, his hand meets mine. It is rough, skin chipped and scabbed from the dryness and the rocks. Sometimes I can't help imagining his hands in combat. I see him wailing his fists into someone. These thoughts are so out of place that I try to put them away, but then I remember that this is why I am with him. He teaches me of a world I can scarcely imagine. He is a foreign animal. I am alert in his presence.

I've asked it before, but out of the blue, I have to ask again.

"Did you ever cross that line?"

He looks at me once. He knows immediately what I am asking. Did he ever become the beast, the cop who kept hitting someone out of sadistic, uncontrollable pleasure? Did he ever slip through an open door, warrant in hand, hoping to fire his weapon into someone's chest? I have asked him before, and his answer is always the same.

"Never," he says.

"I don't believe you," I say. And I don't. With his methods of structuring the world, he could put the line wherever he wants.

"I never did," he insists. "Sure, I danced the edge. I mean, there is some madness you've got to work with. Going to some woman who had her geraniums stolen when ten minutes ago you were fighting fucking tooth and nail for your very life, some goddamned shoot-out, bar scene . . . whatever it was. And you have to put on this face that says, *Oh yeah, I'm perfectly sane and rational now. How many geraniums were stolen?*"

He eats his apple, thinking about it, shaking his head. "I've been there enough times. That cop shit was too intense. Scares me to think about it." Then he laughs, almost as if he shouldn't. "It was a fucking gas. I'll give you that. It's like walking out here. You're just on fire. Everything has a story. But you cross the line and you're on the other side. You never come back."

He feared he would someday cross the line and find his logic, his cleanly organized world, vanquished like a house of cards. Someone would die at his hands, and he would not be able to turn around and step back to solid ground. He could never trust his own mind again.

"You really think you didn't cross the line?"

He stops chewing for a moment. "I've been in the emergency room," he says. "The doctor pulls up the pant legs on this guy I just hounded with a nightstick, and I'm looking at these lacerations where I've split his shin meat wide open, thinking, Damn, that's got to hurt. I did that. *I did that.* Could I have found another way besides beating the crap out of his legs? Did I go too far? It would have been so much easier to just write this sort of thing off, go home, listen to some music, never think about it again. But I'm in bed wondering, Did I enjoy that? Who am I?"

I watch him carefully. He holds his face still. Did he just admit it? I wonder. Does he even know whether he crossed the line or not?

Ten Minutes of Thrill

The air around him smelled of electricity, oil, and water. Somehow it was a fresh scent, a restorative city night after a freezing rain. At midnight the wet pavement had just a touch of ice. Snow had been shoved off the freeway by weeks-ago snowplows, turned black with exhaust.

Dirk stood outside his car finishing a report on the arrest of a drunk driver. The driver was gone, hauled away in another patrol car. Now the only actors left on the side of the freeway were Dirk and a tow-truck driver grappling his chains around the car's frame, yellow warning lights turning lazily. The chains sounded barbaric, industrial.

Dirk's own red and blue lights tracked across the asphalt. He leaned against his car, clipboard in hand, pen checking boxes, recording the event. He was proud of his reports. Unlike most police reports, they were written like stories, colorful details added. He let his pen hover, planning the next words.

The arrestee refused to perform any roadside sobriety maneuvers and referred to this officer as "you cocksucker" numerous times.

He could hear a car chase coming through the radio. A stolen Camaro was darting through urban streets with a wolf pack of sirens behind it. The Camaro had just left the scene of a house robbery. Its backseat was piled with stereo equipment and pillowcases stuffed with whatever household baubles attracted the driver's raccoonlike fascination. A low-grade amateur burglar. The night was alive somewhere far from Dirk, city streets turned into a barrel race.

The tow-truck driver went through his routine of tugs and pulls to make sure everything was secure. The two of them did not make eye contact. They were both tools of the city, the mundane clicking and turning of mechanical parts.

Dirk brought the pen to paper.

This officer observed an empty bottle of Wild Turkey liquor on the passenger-side floorboard in what appeared to be a pool of vomit.

The radio voices sounded calm in their chase. He knew the blunder they were avoiding: appear excited or fearful across the airwaves in such a moment and you have confessed to every patrol car. The voices ran steadily, as dull as if they were reading a grocery list.

"Near collision at State and Main. Still going . . ."

"He just busted a red light . . ."

Dirk listened beneath their tones. The cool-cop voices in the lead spoke secretly of radical danger, incredible speeds, insurmountable concentration, critical judgment, barely contained rage. It was like fast, nasty sex out there: a grainy, subterranean atmosphere of speed and viscera that had everyone's back arched, eyes dashing like bullets, feet drumming impossibly hasty rhythms against floor pedals. Cross streets ticked off like the spin of a roulette wheel.

Dirk listened to the progress, his pen winding down the page to capture further details of the arrest.

Elsewhere, the Camaro struck the same interstate he was on, hauling a net of swirling red and blue lights behind it. It ripped into the median to shake them, fishtailing, then jumped to the other side into oncoming traffic.

Dirk peered along the freeway's sulfur-yellow globes. Embers of taillights faded at melancholy, law-abiding speeds. He flipped back through to check his work.

The Camaro was sailing in and out of the median, pouring through oncoming traffic, headlights splitting around it.

Dirk signed his report and stood away from his car. He could now see the fire glow of patrol cars coming toward him from the opposite lanes. Clusters of headlights appeared far off in their own lanes — Blameless bystanders, he thought, if there is such a thing. The clipboard hung from his hand as he judged distances, calculated speeds. People were going to get killed here. Someone needed to end this game.

He opened the door, swung into his seat, slammed the door, seat belt sliding from hand to lock. The clipboard landed in the empty passenger seat as the siren yowled to life. He banked across two lanes and pointed straight at the headlights, driving the wrong way down the freeway. Engine pistons bunched like gathered muscles. Ahead, the Camaro appeared from the opposite direction, hitting bottom over the median, carving a U-turn.

Canals of shadow and light flashed inside Dirk's car. The engine raged through his body. The thoughtfulness of his report was gone. He was now part of the violation, a predator in the night's horror, his life poised. He glimpsed the Camaro running up from the median, tires about to catch pavement on his side.

He played his accelerator, calculating exactly when they would meet. Lines of equations stabbed across the asphalt into his eyes from the oncoming headlights, from the Camaro, from the other patrol cars, from the glistening surface of the road. The driver had not checked his sideview mirror. Dirk lay undetected.

The Camaro's tires grabbed wet asphalt on the shoulder, shrieking. It lurched forward, gaining sudden speed. Dirk dropped back on his accelerator, then pressed it to the floor. He jerked the steering wheel to the right and was instantly pummeled into his seat belt.

The Camaro took most of the force, folding at the impact, its back axle firing out of the body like a spear.

Dirk's driver's-side door remained uncrumpled, the hinges intact so that he could be on the ground as soon as he stopped. The two cars grazed across the slick surface, spinning, welded together. They careened into the median. As the spin wound down, Dirk snapped out of his seat belt. He opened his door, watching the grainy, cold earth slide by. The moment it stopped, he was out and moving.

He pulled his flashlight and torched the inside of the car. The driver's head hung unresponsive. Dirk tried the door. It was locked. With the back of his black-gloved hand, he knocked on the window.

A young man lifted his head from a far-off place. His eyes

barely found the side window. He moved from Dirk's holstered gun to the pen in his breast pocket to his face. He understood nothing. A moment ago he was on fire, terrified and frantic, the world writhing behind him, everyone's eyes on his taillights. Inexplicably, he was now hovering in space.

Dirk irritably pointed at the lock. The driver followed this pointing and came back to Dirk's face utterly baffled.

Dirk turned his flashlight butt-first. He drew back and smashed through. Kernels of blue glass showered inward. The man lifted his hands to cover his head, feeling a rush of cold air, the door unlocked from the outside and thrown open. He felt hands. Then he was on the ground, wrists instantly locked together by cuffs.

Dirk pinned the man's body into a sharp pile of old snow. This was the game. Dirk was the victor. He grabbed a handful of snow, crushing it in his fist, then ground it into the man's face. The man squirmed and screeched.

"You like that?" Dirk barked, bringing his face down close, a terrifying vision. The man was in an unbearably hypnotic stupor. Dirk was the animal, the guide hauling him to the other side.

"You like running from the cops? You like causing mayhem? You like trying to get people killed so your sorry ass can get away? Yeah? So you can steal your little shit? What is it you got that's worth anyone's life, huh?"

Dirk grabbed more snow, jammed it into the man's clothes, packed it down his arms, milled it cruelly into his chest. The man screamed and flopped, but Dirk held him.

"How about this? You like this, too?"

Dirk saw the other patrol cars sweeping in. He knew that

these officers were probably raging. The dynamics of a chase. Heat would be in their blood for hours. They were shivering with wrath, and if things got out of control, they might shatter this man's ribs, sinking fists into kidneys until they bled. This snow rubbing was like a good, hard spanking among cops, not the torment that might be demanded. The man got off easy in Dirk's hands — Dirk, who showed up to this chase at the last minute, not yet burned on adrenaline.

Dirk fisted him up by the collar and said, "I'm your guardian now, you stupid fuck. Just keep still from here on out. I'll keep them off you."

The man's eyes found nothing, stopped searching, in fact. No more screaming, just moaning and drool spurting across his shiny, wet lips. Dirk examined him for a moment, thinking, I am the end of your road. He could see the man's future. Ten minutes of thrill and now he would go to prison. He would be let out on parole but would never be accepted by most of civilization. No hopeful jobs. Little meaningful sex. He would commit another crime, go to prison again, and again after that. He would kill someone finally. He would never escape.

Dirk flipped the body over, grabbed the back of the man's head, and scrubbed his face into the snow so that he could be seen by all, the horrible pleasure streaking up his arm as he ground harder. He claimed his kill right there, his and no one else's, while the other cops arrived growling and panting, their words snapping at the air. The man did not move. He did not have the ability or wish. He was an unresponsive sack of garbage tossed into the median. Dirk stood and wiped snow off his gloves. Ice grains drizzled onto the man's back.

He kept his feet planted around the man, making eye contact with each approaching cop. *This one is mine.*

DAY EIGHT

Camp is in the wreckage of eroded boulders. A sand-salted wind comes strong. It is the new moon night, clean and dark. There are no clouds. Dirk sits against his pack not far from me; it is too early for sleep. The sky is sown with bright seeds of stars already dead for tens of thousands of years. Twinkle, twinkle . . . are you even there?

Dirk and I spent the day poking through the land, finding routes in the shifting light of morning and then afternoon, in the constantly low angles of winter sun. Now we make fists against our chests, protecting our gloved fingers from the wind's sting, faces occasionally nettled with blowing sand. I set down my journal and plant a rock on it so that it will not be blown out of reach. A buckle snaps wildly at the end of a strap. I grab it and pull it back, running it through my pack to keep it secure.

I know that Dirk's belongings are neatly arranged right now, packaged in the lee of a boulder. He will wake in the morning and know where each item of his has been placed. He knows the location of his bandanna, where he has stored his sunglasses, his lamp, his lighter. He lives to this day with a tactile knowledge of order like the timed collision of vehicles.

What do I know myself? I know that wind comes through, that it pulls me apart, that it threads this landscape and carries me off. All night I will wonder what part of me has blown away. Will I wake to find even my soul gone? I have too many loose ends, I think. All of me could be snatched by the wind overnight, every small part whisked into the sky until I have been scattered like a dead man's ashes.

Tonight I am ruled at once by a thousand hissing voices. Messages bay from far off, tunneling through air alien to this desert, never staying long enough to sit native with its land-forms. There is nothing worth talking about in this kind of wind. Just hold on.

I pull my day gear close to me, open a zipper, and rummage for my lamp. In the dark my fingers find small objects. First there is a wad of twine, then binoculars, then a red Swiss Army knife. I dig into an unintended cache of black-cinder grit from a desert far south of here.

Each object I find is a distinct and capricious memory. I think of what it is like in Dirk's pack. His belongings are placed like salt-and-pepper shakers on a suburban family table, always the same. After this trip, he will clean his pack out, wash every-thing, and put things back in perfect order. I could fault him if he were a grossly tidy person, but he is not. Instead, he is quick and efficient.

Feeling around my gear, I believe that I am an animal. Not a fluid killer like him, but a wood rat surrounded by midden, sticks and rocks and inappreciable items that are there year after year. My pack constantly grows heavier.

Like this thing that I find with my fingers, a limp bag of nuts crushed into powder, emergency food from how long ago? Ran-cid, probably. Better to keep it, I think. Times will be desperate again.

I find a small knife sharpener in its hand-worn leather sheath. Without bringing it out, I turn it, feeling through my gloves into its memories, drawing open the leather flap and slid-ing the stone into my hand. It is too worn and pitted to be of use anymore. I cannot remember when I last got a good knife-sharpening off it, yet still I carry it around. My father gave it to me. He owned it for decades before passing it to me the morn-

ing after we'd had a fight. We were camped in a canyon far
north of here during an ad hoc family reunion. The details of
the confrontation are difficult to recall and probably do not matter. The outcome was that he charged me at the campfire. I was
old enough to be charged, somewhere in my early twenties. I
grabbed a bone of driftwood to wave around, bluffing him, but
he called my bluff. He rushed me, landing in the center of the
fire, standing there like a violent flame-lit god trying to wrench
the wood from my hand. I remember how he did not burn even
as the flames stroked his legs. Sometimes I think it was the alcohol that protected him. Sometimes I think he was an apparition. In the struggle, he was struck with the wood in the center
of his forehead. A line of blood began to flow. There were others
at the fire when this happened, some of our family, some of his
wife's. They all jumped in, shouldering us away from each other.
He kept touching the blood and looking at it on his fingers, muttering, "That son of a bitch."

That night, cousins slept in a defensive circle around me.

The next morning, facing each other in the yeasty smell of
the Colorado River, campfire burned down to floury ash, my
father pulled out this stone in its leather wrapping and handed
it to me. It was the one true item of order that he carried in his
life, the stone that sharpened his blades. By the way he gave it
over and said, "Here," I knew it was mine to keep.

Humans in this world are fragile. My father had made me
certain of this. We are thin as a spider's strands, snapped at
almost any misstep. Tonight in the wind I think of what we have
done, of the web that my father and I left hanging with debris
and limp filaments. I hear beneath tonight's roar of wind the
piercing, wasted sound of glass clinking in a cut-rate bar. I hear

the night my father lit the couch on fire with a cigarette and stormed the room where I slept, threw open the door, and roared, *"What the fuck is going on in here?"* then slammed it closed. The odious smell of burning plastic followed right behind him.

My father needed to have the volume turned up at every moment. The spin of alcohol, the surge of the fight, the throwing of words. He needed life to be sharp, the same way I crave tonight's unrelenting new-moon gale. I hear the whips of wind at boulder tips, and the memories flow.

As soon as my father gave me his sharpening stone, he laughed that he was still going to kick my ass, that he wasn't through with me yet, pointing at the cut on his head. I took the stone, utterly baffled. How could I tell my father that I did not strike him in the head, that in his drunkenness, in the fire, he had clubbed himself? I needed to get out of his madness, but how could I escape when I understood too well his demand for an accelerated heart, when I disappeared for months into the desert so that my every breath would be amplified? The stone that he passed to me was calming. It was his talisman. It told me, *Please, my son, I love you, don't let us die this way.*

In the wind, I think, My father is dead.

I let go of the stone and draw my hands up to my face. I begin to cry into the wind. Dirk cannot hear me over the roar, so I wail, head falling into my arms. This swell of heat rising through my chest is uncontrollable, as if dissolving my organs. A horrible groan bursts from my mouth. It is long and drawn, and I think it could not be coming from my own throat. I bury myself in the wool of my serape, biting down to hold my voice.

It must be much later when I open my eyes. I am startled awake by quiet as the eighth day barely lets go and the ninth almost begins. The night sounds now like a train that has just departed, the tracks barely humming behind it. A light diffuses through the atmosphere, so faint and dry that the sky is green. I am curled among boulders with my bag pulled up around me. The air feels cold. The wind is gone.

This green light turns a lunar blue, a single color that spans the sky. The blue gives way in the east to pages of violet. I crawl out into the dawn. Dirk is not in his bag. I dance around in the cold, finding extra layers, and see Dirk in the distance. He is perched like a stone Buddha, breathing the silence of the morning. A cliff descends below him, and he balances on its last point of purchase. I walk to him, swirl my serape around me, and settle onto my heels.

Every morning in cold like this, a translucent drip forms at the tip of Dirk's nose like a sacred little gem. He reaches up with his gloved hand and wipes it away.

The landscape below, this is where my attention must lie. We will need to move our camp into it, the first true steps of our crossing. Portals appear below us, doorways dropping through canyons into inescapable holes and lengthy, unseen passageways. I know what Dirk is doing. He is playing chess, arranging the possibilities in his head, working out every step.

This is not a mountain for me, not a north face of an unclimbed alp. It is my own mind, my life laid out in stone. I do not play concerted games with it. I will walk in and find the way.

If I know nothing else of the world, if I am only a frightened animal hoarding objects and memories, I know at least that I can walk through this. I have gained the eye that tells me how to track fracture lines. I monitor water holes. I'm able to read places I cannot see long before I reach them, places that maps do not even suggest. I turn back through history, through a conversation held with the old singer in his hogan. The Diné families who came here, escaping the U.S. armies, knew nothing about this place other than the old stories that told them it was the end of the world. Still, they came to this forbidden land and found the way, just as Dirk has made it from the street to here, just as we will somehow walk through this maddening place below us.

Where to begin? I think. Which one of these open doors far below our camp? I wonder where my father made his first wrong turn. How deeply did he get himself lost before he gave up, his blood turning to poison out of fear or neglect, his heart finally ceasing? I imagine that no one in my family had this opportunity that I now have. This is how I will survive. I will walk into the maze. Rather than sort unaided through the cold box of my mind, I will step into the real, tangible landscape, a country of tangle and perplexity.

Without looking at me, in a low cadence Dirk says,

According to what one of the elders said, taking an enemy on the battlefield is like a hawk taking a bird. Even though it enters into the midst of a thousand of them, it gives no attention to any bird other than the one that it has first marked.

Dirk stands, gestures *Go* with his chin, and walks back toward camp.

PART TWO
CROSSING

In Flashes of Lightning, with these he ran.
In the Body of Black Wind, with these he ran.
In the midst of Thunders, with these he ran.

— *night song of the Coyoteway*

DAY NINE

As sunlight first slides over us, we heat licorice tea, drinking the residue of wind sand from the bottoms of our cups. Movements are free without last night's drumbeating gale. The ninth day has begun. We strike camp easily, loading our packs, and travel into the country below.

Sandstone lifts into steep-sided rock slopes as we move. Small routes unfold around us. Possibilities feed us through fissures and unpredictable slopes, lines connecting dots that from a distance seem impossible. Each way is delicate and revealed only when we come to it. We must put our hands on the rock to see. From far away, these routes appear too daunting, untouchable.

In front of me, Dirk lifts his hands as if commanding the landscape, outlining geological, geographic matters. He uses terms of geology — *imbrication, sinuosity, cross bedding*. I pause behind him like a servant, begging into my journal, writing quick details about rock fractures and wind patterns.

Dirk turns to me without warning and says, "If you smile just before you punch someone, it's much more effective."

I write that down, too.

No observation is invalid at this point. Everything is evidence for the way through. As we come down I note a huge fissured X in the wall beside us. It is a phenomenon of pressure in massive, homogeneous sandstones, an effect we have seen throughout this landscape. The same kind of fracture always appears, the same angles — 60 degrees and 120 degrees to each intersection of lines. It is as if a voice once reverberated through the earth, a single word shuddering the stone. The cracks formed around the word.

Both hundreds of feet tall and as small as clusters of jacks underfoot, these Xs erode out of the surrounding rock, changing the landforms, influencing how canyons and cliffs interact. It is good to know how the rock breaks. The top-heavy X carves away and collapses, its fulcrum left behind as a ridge that we can follow. Farther down the line, it acts like crosshairs gunning into the rock face, revealing weaknesses, opening passages in otherwise impassable stone.

We come down through slopes scored with Xs, moving in and out of their rows. We take a canyon that falls open beneath us like the bottom of a kettledrum. It drops farther into baritone tiers of alcoves, none that we can reach, and we climb out of it on a ledge that follows the contour around to another canyon. From there we are sent along a high rib of stone. One moment our walk is not far aboveground. A minute later canyons have fallen to either side. Dirk stops and looks into one of the canyons, suddenly aware of our height.

"Where the hell did that come from?" He looks back along the course. "How did it get so deep so fast?"

I look down in confounded agreement. It feels as if the land is beginning to move beneath us. The Xs are hinges, and their great doors swing open and closed. I walk to the edge of this rib, seeing if there is a way down. There has to be a way. Otherwise it is hours back to the last option on the other side of last night's camp. We might retrace steps only to find another dead end.

I need to think precisely here, but the shapes around me leave my mind grabbing at nothing. I am in a crowd. Conversations pass in and out of each other, and I cannot stay with one for long before another steals my attention. I want to grab Dirk's hand and hold on.

I quiet my mind with even breathing. There will be a way. It will show itself. Keep moving. It will be there. Just over this edge.

The edge of the rib bends downward. I shuffle my boots to its terminal steepness. This is far enough. I am looking over a waterfall of a landscape, a monstrous Niagara of stone. Streamers of canyons fall around me, dissolving before touching bottom. I snap open my arms for balance, a raven holding against the wind. My body tilts forward and back. How much traction do I have here? How good is this surface? I slowly back up on my heels.

"No way down here," I report to Dirk. "This is death."

The next possibility is a slender wormhole of a canyon tunneling into the rock. Dirk is ahead of me, scraping down its edges. He wedges himself, head craned to see below.

"This thing just pours off into oblivion," he calls. He crawls back and passes me, pointing behind him, masking his emotion with a quick Southern accent. "This ain't goin' nowhere."

His voice triggers me. He is afraid.

As he goes, I climb down to see for myself. I trust him, but I need to feel it with my own hands, see it with my own eyes. I shuffle along this brief spool of canyon to where it drops under me, a hatchway into space, and there settle myself into a groove staring straight down. Pinheads of sand slip from under my boot.

Our previous days of easy walking among domes and the backs of whales have ended. This closure tells me that everything is now narrowing. A new and critical decision must be formulated every few steps.

I let one hand dangle into this dead end, feeling the draw of gravity. This is why mazes are so frightening. The passages lead nowhere, and eventually the notion of a way out becomes as meaningless as all these false options.

Where are my eyes that see order in chaos? I had them this morning, it seemed. They have left me. I cannot see the way. I remember once standing in an art museum, studying a heap of vertical and horizontal sticks composed by Sol Lewitt. When I moved my head one way, the sticks leaped to attention, revealing grids of passageways and stairsteps coursing faultlessly through the sculpture, the way molecules ring into chains. Then I moved my head the other way and the sculpture fell apart. The causeways collapsed into an insensible mass. I spent a good part of my visit standing there shifting my head back and forth, thinking, This is sanity; this is insanity.

I remember the museum, the quietness of footsteps. I was safe there. I could look at the art and walk away.

How do I shift my head here? This hatchway leads to nothing. It is an empty passage. I wedge a boot and push myself up.

Dirk and I leave our packs up top and scout along enormous horns of rock, slots below filled with sharply cut boulders. He slides down into one of these thin slots, climbing along as I cross over his head by leaping here to there. I can see him under my feet, his body inventing itself, bending, bracing, and throwing. I know which of his muscles are sore, how he favors his right leg. I see the compensation. So much of what is done here is devotion, a gymnastic conversation between body and terrain. It is the finding of our minutiae, the same thing that children get from playground equipment and stream banks, the innovation of perception. Into adulthood, some of us still crave this learning. We want to feel the articulation of our skeletons as we reach and pull.

Descending this exploratory chute of boulders, Dirk and I both reach the end at the same instant. Dirk braces and looks over the edge. I stand on the boulder above his head and see exactly what he sees, the gape of a cliff falling below. Dirk looks up as if checking the rafters of a ceiling, testing whether there is a way to go up. My glance follows his. Not there either.

"We're getting too deep in here," he says as he turns around. Too deep and he will no longer be in control. The land will swallow us both.

Dirk says, speaking mostly to himself, "We get too deep in the wrong direction and we'll never get out. We need to think about this. We need to do some map-looking."

The map. What good will it do? It occurs to me that there may be no way through. We are walking the Rubicon, about to slip to the other side, forever barred from return by the layers of routes we will be unable to recall. Back to our packs. I grab the map, walk it to a good vantage. It hangs from my hand, folding along its creases in the breeze. I pull the map tight. We both review it, Dirk moving in, supporting a corner with his hand.

The map tells of inclinations, of potentials, but not of what is actually here. True topography falls between all these printed lines. The real landscape is made of replies and commands. It is made of our hands touching rock, our eyes discerning shadows, our minds sent ahead to find the way. The aimless movements we make during our days are painstakingly intentional. The color of stone is as much an informant as the shape of a cliff. The shape is as instructional as how much water is left in our packs, as the free fall of an exposure, as the sharpness of a kernel of sandstone caught in my boot and digging at my ankle. The route binds all of these variables. Where is it?

"There's a trend here," I say, running my finger along a southwest-to-northeast axis obeyed by several canyons on the map. "Looks like a fault system along here. Enough to carry us across."

Dirk looks from the here I indicate on the map to the one out there. Our view is blocked by overlapping barriers of sandstone, unknown canyons in between. "That doesn't tell me how we get off this piece of rock."

"Rope," I say.

His face crunches as if I had told him that we could sprout wings. "Forget it."

"Then we have to jump." I grin at him.

"You go ahead and jump, Mr. Wizard. I'm getting through here alive."

Dirk takes the map for himself, studying it more closely. "Now wait a minute. This canyon here" — he points to it on the page. "This doesn't match up at all. Doesn't seem like the map could be right."

While he wrestles with this, looking around him and then back to the map, I continue scanning in front of us.

"No, not right at all," he mumbles. "Look at this. It shows a canyon coming around over here and that one . . ." He points, but loses himself, the chess game taking on too many levels and dimensions at once.

I gesture down a descending curve of sandstone, smooth in the sun. "What about over here?"

"The hell you say," he blurts. "There's no way I'm going down that with my pack. No way in hell. I know where my heart would be the whole time, throttled up into my goddamned throat."

"What if it goes, though?"

His voice starts drifting. "Moving every second with someone zeroing a gun right between my shoulder blades? No fucking way out of it but death. I know my limits."

"But what if it's our only way?"

"Only way to where?"

I just look at Dirk. He knows what I am talking about. This route may be what we are stuck with, climbing down an insanely steep passage to start our way in.

Dirk reads my face, my mouth, my eyes. He sees me as a reckless person, someone willing to risk death just so I can validate my being alive.

"I know your dark side," he accuses. "You want to haul our packs into the abyss and rope them up the other side with loops of intestine extruding from our rectums."

I shake my head at that. But he is right. I want strain and fear. I want to tease the edge of death so that I am forced to clean the clutter out of my head. I want to be whittled down, get rid of this sloppy flesh of mine and get down to my bones, the only things that are finally true.

I used to walk the bombing ranges along the border of Arizona and Mexico, the Sonoran Desert, the Desert of the Fist. I walked for weeks and months in this endless terrain. My cadence of footsteps turned into the sound of a relentless chore. My head swayed in the heat, and at times I feared that I was stumbling in endless loops, days of gratuitous circles. Then, invariably, I would come upon an unexploded missile planted in the earth, a remnant of military exercises. It was like finding a white sand lily. I would kneel beside these exiled weapons and lay my hands on them as if palpating a shark. Then, to see if the warheads would wake, I would heave back on them with all of my weight.

A flash of light. A plume of dry smoke that no one ever sees. My remains evaporated in the solace of endless country. Each time I did this the warheads remained asleep, of course, and I opened my eyes to find myself still alive. The desert would lie around me in divine silence. In those moments the stillness of the air seemed purposeful, intentional even.

Dirk sees my breathing, the hunger in my eyes as I look down. He studies the route in front of me, and then my posture. My body tells him that I am ready to plunge down these slight ledges below us and vanish into the dark. He is not interested.

"Listen, I've seen this beast already," he tells me with a tired voice, dropping the map to his waist. "You remember what I did for a living?"

I just stare along the slope, remembering what Dirk did for a living. Is he going to flaunt this at me? He once taught himself to believe only in right and wrong, and he falls proudly, easily back on his former beliefs. But now he is hounded by the desert like a stone reworked by the wind, the sharp corners of his oaths dissolving every day. I want to remind him that he was a cop for the sheer acuity of the experience. This is also why he came to the desert. He came to feel uncertainty, and the certainty that is found within. He came for the wish that if we climb down this sloping cliff we will be carried by the land. He came for this risk of not only finding himself, but reaching beyond himself.

I say, "Don't start flashing your badge at me."

"No, listen. I was the guy who came in and cleaned up after people had their powerful and terrifying experiences," he says, his voice going off somewhere. "It was all just blood and broken glass. That's it. You think it brings you some kind of quick-thrust enlightenment, that if you delve into some dark horror you will receive promised salvation."

Dirk gestures his chin at me, saying, "You think if you cross over the edge, you'll go right through death, and there you'll see the Giant Carp opening its mouth to vomit out the true meaning of the universe for you?"

I do not look at him, even as his eyes shoot into me. There is no venom in his words. I know he is not lying. He wants to make sure he does not die here. He trusts his old ways.

"Self-knowledge is not commensurate with self-destruction," he continues. "I saw where people had their revolutionary moments. Whether it was something criminal or drug related or just out-and-out stupid. All I saw was destruction. I have no doubt that there is this incredible emotional momentum behind each situation, but there is this other thing called *the here and now*. The here and now was my job." A finger stabs straight down. "Come in and stop the momentum. Grab somebody by the shoulders and wake them to the immediate consequences around them."

Dirk returns to his examination of the map, his voice calming. "I don't want to go on some mad venture down that dome just so we can talk to the Giant Carp. I think we can find another Giant Carp somewhere over this way." He waves with the map and starts walking back to his gear.

He stops and looks back at me, concealing himself in one of his accents. "We ain't here for no walk in Central fuckin' Park," he calls. "Let's go."

———

"Hand!" I shout.

Dirk's hand shoots out like a dart, meeting mine as my foothold gives below him. My body and the weight of my full pack falls into him, my second hand knotted into a crevice.

The foothold is a small chip of cliff that slides away, grumbling against its parent rock as it tumbles and shatters down the Dome of the Giant Carp. We did not take my original route off the dome, but maybe this is just as bad. I kick and wedge, dragging myself back up to Dirk, flopping onto his ledge.

Rarely do I lose a good foothold like that. Once a year, maybe. I can't get the rhythm of my breath back. The solid earth has collapsed beneath me. What can I trust now? I look at Dirk. He is laughing. I have to laugh with him to defuse the adrenaline. We are always this close to each other. We are children growing up together, and like me he wants to learn the reach of his body, the design of this world that he has been born into. He wants to get off these cliff bands into the canyons below, where he can walk freely. I am breathing evenly now. I scoot back from the edge and stand.

Skirting down elsewhere, Dirk finds a stairstep of giant ledges, one leading to the next, and chains of boulders heading toward an open, barren park.

"Gentle as a mother's love," he gloats as he rides down the rocks in front of me, arms spread for balance.

We need this, finally, a gentle route that cleanly ends our day. The smooth stone field beyond us opens into a number of farther canyons heading off like highways to unknown points beyond. We come to the base of a rock eminence, a giant obelisk left by the wind. Along its warm south face of apricot-colored sandstone we lay our packs. Immediately we see color-ful flakings of rock left on the ground. Toolmaking. I doubt that they are of Diné origin. More likely, they come from before the Diné, hunters on their way through this landscape a thousand years ago. Lifting one of these hunting stones to my eye, I imag-ine that cultural affiliation is of no matter here. Maybe these fluted, chipped stones are like the ropes of DNA that we carry from one generation to the next, the same hunting stories con-stantly written across this desert. Dirk's and my movements become instantly fluid, relaxed once we know that people have been here before, even if a millennium or two ago.

We grab empty water containers and head off, following the angle of the closest canyon in search of water. Our route will be proved here, I think. We will walk and see that this route leads straight across. Walls will open because this is how the land has broken itself, the direction cleaved into the earth. This canyon will be the needle that sews us through the country.

The canyon steepens as we follow it. Its walls lift and curve overhead. Cold air washes up from below, and I am struck by apprehension. Why is this cold air here? It feels as if I am descending into a root cellar.

The floor becomes narrower and more complex, funneling us into pour-offs and lodged boulders. Obeying our different ages, our preferences in stride and handholds, Dirk and I sepa-rate. Soon I am in front of him, out of view. The canyon falls with such drama that I move by impulse alone. I do not think I can stop.

In front of me a black seam lies in the earth. It is slender, an unimaginably deep gash bisecting my path.

Wait. There was nothing like this on the map.

As I come closer I find myself within the gouge of a landmark deeper than anything Dirk and I have seen. I cannot call this a canyon. It is a different species altogether. The closest name I can possibly conjure is *chasm*. I inch closer to it, peering over its edge. There are slight ledges, barely enough to hold me. I am far below the nearest sunlight and far above the floor with its shadows piled one on top of the next. I am nowhere, tucked within the wings of an impassable slash.

I lick my wind-brittle lips and lean out my head as far as it will go without pitching me over. Motionless gulfs of dark water lie below, and there is no way to reach them.

I would be relieved for at least a choice — turn left or turn right, upstream or downstream. But there is no choice here. How did they do it, I wonder, the Diné refugees who came through here, who lived here a hundred and twenty or so years ago? I know that they found a way. Maybe that is enough.

The stories that have survived from those refugees tell of mythical expatriates wandering ragtag in the wilderness. One of their stories that I remember, a tale reduced to religious figures and symbols, is about two sisters who became lost in the desert. After some time of walking, hungry, thirsty, and forlorn, the siblings arrived at a country of holy people. What now might be mistaken for towers of rock, for the spans of sandstone arches, for deep pools of water holes, were then and still are the bodies of these holy people. The sisters were taken in, comforted, fed, and given water to drink, but it was made clear by their hosts that the two sisters did not belong here. The girls asked repeatedly if they could stay, but the holy people were People of the Water, *Táyi'jí dine'é,* and they said that this was not a good place for their kind. In the same breath, they said that they would provide a miraculous means of returning the girls safely to their origin.

The two sisters were sent home. They told others of their survival, and their account was absorbed into the oral history of their children and grandchildren and great-grandchildren, passed on even now into my own memory.

My eyes fall into this chasm in front of me. It is overburdened, its wings monstrously heavy. Its eyes are dark alcoves recessing into the walls. Above this drop, my water bottle and day pack hanging off me, I feel as if I'm balancing cups and saucers in my hands. The Diné families must have felt this same precarious balance as they moved into this landscape.

I hear Dirk from behind, and I slowly turn my head to look at him. He is glancing around as he comes, nodding *Yes, yes. Here is something beyond us. Here is something that does not bend to our will no matter what we do.*

"It cuts us off," I say, the low tone of my voice echoing as if I have called into a drum.

Dirk scratches down to my ledge, stands beside me, sticks out his head to peer over the balcony.

"It's not what we thought," he says.

"Was this on the map?"

We scramble back up to safer ground. Dirk reaches back, unzips one of his pouches, and pulls out the map. He unfolds it, and we each take a corner and review our location. There it is — a thin meeting of contour lines that suggests a long crack in the planet. The tightness of this chasm hides itself on the paper. There are three of them, now that we are looking. Three chasms in a row lined up like a gauntlet. This is the first. The second and third lie even deeper, farther than we can see.

Dirk and I unclip our gear and leave it on a shelf. We slip off one ledge to another, dropping in and out of cracks, scouting for a possible route. Alone again, I see below me a tower of cliff that has broken away. A fissure runs down its side. If I could get myself to the platform atop this tower, I would be able to see clearly if the fissure turns into a chimney, and if the chimney leads to the floor, and if the floor goes somewhere. Never would I consider such a maneuver with a full pack, maybe not even with my day gear, but now I am curious and moving lightly. I might learn something.

With my face pressed to the cliff's curve, I lower myself. As a rule, going down is more difficult than climbing up. Gravity will help with the return trip, giving me better traction. But going down . . . About to lose my grip, I push off, skidding down a short distance. I land on the platform below.

I remain crouched at the center of this leaning rock slab, a place as wide and flat as a writing desk, a hundred feet or so tall. My heartbeat is quick. Coming down here might be an unnecessary risk, but now I can see along the chasm's gullet, how it bends out of sight upstream and downstream. From here, at least, I can clearly see the cold lagoons of water at the bottom. This chasm has no give. It is pure erosion. I can see no way of crossing it, making this pillar of rock feel like a spike rising through the rings of hell. I am enchanted and horrified at once.

I stand and step to the edge. Lines of rock cracks fall away from me, light-headed fractures gathering below until this tower melts back into the cliff wall. I walk around the perimeter. The fissure I had hoped would work vanishes over the side. It is useless to me.

I return to the center, feeling for the gravity of this tower, testing it with my presence. I come down, balling my weight again into a crouch. I remember when I was young, seven maybe, I used to sleepwalk. I would wake up in strange places around the house, on top of cabinets and furniture, in closets, not knowing where I was or how I got there. One night I came suddenly alert while crouched on a flat surface. I was in my underwear, the baggy white cotton briefs that boys are often condemned to. I began feeling around, discovering that I was perched on a platform in complete darkness. There was no way down. Even by slowly working my hands I could not find an exit. I made myself small, imagining that I was balanced on top of a slender pillar that stood in infinite space. Dread washed into me.

Eventually, a faint light became visible. I recognized a window blinded by drapes. The surrounding room slowly surfaced. In my sleep I had climbed onto a desk in the house of my mother's boyfriend, got myself up there using a chair. Even knowing where I was now, it took me some time to shake off my fear. I crawled tentatively to the edge, foot down onto the chair for safety.

At the tower I bunch my hindquarters and leap like a spider throwing itself to the wind. I hit the wall, every part of me grabbing, using my momentum to bound upward. I snatch a good handhold, swing up to a ledge, and stop there to breathe.

This chasm below is untouchable.

———

Dirk and I retreat into the night, setting up camp in the security of the sharp-edged hunting stones we had found earlier. The night is comfortable. No wind. All is frozen. Not Arctic frozen, but merely stiff, a temperature best not touched to the lips. Dirk has arrayed his life around him, a snug spot for sitting and sleeping cleared of stones. My pack remains strapped and full from the day. Dirk says that if I get the pot out he'll cook dinner. I'm huddled away in the dark, buried in a Genghis Khan assortment of warm clothes, using a small lamp to chase my pen across journal pages. I look up at the cold and intimidating form of my pack. It will be a commitment to dig into it.

"Yeah, dinner," I say.

My pack is lying on its side. A few items are scattered around, nothing that can blow away: a knife, a water bottle, my day pack. I walk over to it, kick it to loosen the straps, and start pulling things out, hauling the cooking equipment over to Dirk. Within half an hour we are eating steaming, mashed beans with hot sauce and rice cooked in water found in a nearby canyon.

"You know what it is?" Dirk says, tapping the air with his spoon. "I'm feeling constantly on guard down here. We don't have any of our usual bail-out points. Not like up north. I don't mind if our routes fail there. We know the rocks and the canyons well enough to get back out. But here . . . failed routes add up pretty damn quick. I feel like a cat. I'm not hissing yet. I don't have my back up. But my tail is fuzzed out, on alert."

I finish chewing, one hand absentmindedly fondling the stone ornament hanging from my neck. I say, "Mmm." Agreement.

After dinner we lay out our bags, Dirk close to the wind shelter of the wall in case weather comes, and me out with the broken stone artifacts. I hear Dirk throw a sudden obscenity. He calls me over. His light casts onto the shiny globe-shaped body of a black widow spider.

I crouch to her level and watch her move. She is methodical

and observant, tentatively exploring the hood of Dirk's bag. He had set his camp too close to the wall and snapped her web. She is just down to repair her anchors. Her fine legs study the terrain. She is uncertain. Something is not right in her world. She knows we are here but is not sure who we are or what we might do.

I slide my journal under her and carry her away. As if saving the drips off an ice-cream cone, I turn the book this way and that as she tries to leap off or skitter up my arm. I find a place and let her go.

I come back as Dirk is moving his gear away from the wall, meticulously clearing a new spot. As he finishes he says, "Good thing you showed up. I might have killed it."

"Never kill spiders," I warn. "Bad juju. Especially down here."

We take our lights along the wall to tally the local widow population. Their webs are numerous and catastrophically sloppy with matted and windblown detritus. Unlike the perfect, geometric nets found beneath house eaves, black widow webs seem voracious, their strong wires laced back and forth in every direction so that nothing escapes. Unconsumed insects hang dead on the peripheries, too far out on the web's suburbs to make eating them worth the while.

At even intervals there are two, four, seven black widows down the cliff, their spherical shadows lingering on the rock surface. With needles for legs, they hang from their blizzard-strewn webs, their black abdomens suspended as round and glossy as fresh drops of blood. The hugeness of their abdomens is alarming compared to their tricky little thoraxes and even smaller star points of eyes. What kind of animals are these? They live among their rice-paper balls of abandoned egg sacks and husks of the dead. Their fresh egg sacks are incessantly caressed by the tips of their legs, cradled like something precious. They float, listening with unmatched stillness for any quiver along any strand.

We focus our lights on one of the black widows. I am tempted to touch her web and watch her posture change, see her snap like an animal hearing a sound, but I cannot break the tranquillity of her concentration.

My question: Is she conscious?

Dirk's question: Will it crawl into his bag and weld poison into his blood?

We move close to her. In the expansive darkness of this landscape, we hover around this single spider, our eyes inches from the perfect blood mark on her underside. Dirk turns his light toward a much smaller, frailer spider clinging to the farthest corner of the same web.

"Bedmate," he says.

I turn my light. It is the male. He is also listening. The female has enough poison to lash him into death before he can lift his legs against her. For now, she is his god. He feels for her weight, for the bow she makes in her own web. He knows where she is. He senses her every concern, listening down the line.

She slips a single leg forward, one measured movement, a question: *Is someone there?*

The male keeps silent, hearing her in the distance, hearing guns, thunder. He thinks, *The female moves.*

Should we be watching such an intimate dance? Dirk and I pull back our lights and return to our world of down sleeping bags and our stainless-steel cook pot. We sit beside each other in the quiet.

The image of the widow hangs in my mind. I have long held beliefs about creatures such as spiders, that they do not move dumbly about the world, that they do not suspend motionlessly from their webs out of brainlessness. Even (or especially) in childhood I saw a consciousness within the dark, shiny, hairy arachnid souls. I imagine what it might be like to wait in a web with all senses ultimately alert.

Finally I say, "I want to learn to be that observant."

"As the black widows?" Dirk asks.

"The way they were hanging there listening to everything."

"You're anthropomorphizing again, Opie."

"I don't want to hear about anthropomorphizing," I complain. "What other eyes am I supposed to be looking through?"

He shrugs.

I say, "When I was little my dad took me into his garage. A black widow was climbing on the wall, and he told me to get up close to her, watch her movements, get a feel for her. I remember him telling me that she was alive right then, just like me. Breathing. Heart beating. Aware of the world. Then he took his boot and flattened her against the wall. Just like that. Bang. Dead. A black streak on the wall."

"Mmm . . . ," Dirk says, waiting in the cold. Then he asks, "Did I ever tell you my red boy story?"

I say no. He has, but the night is cold, and I've given him my story of sudden death. Now it's his turn. He makes himself comfortable.

"I was in second grade, walking home from school with a bunch of other kids down a suburban street. Standard city sidewalk over a creek crossing, iron railing alongside. A lot of times kids would stop there, you know, throw rocks in the creek. There were crawdads, so kids would go down there, try to catch something. There was one boy in the first grade and two girls walking behind me. The girls were playing a game with the little boy. He was trying to steal their purses — they had these little-girl purses, shiny plastic things. I remember it so well because we'd all paused at the bridge. One of the girls reared back and said, 'You won't get my purse, I'll hit you with it!' In mock terror the little boy turned to run away and darted straight into the street, no warning whatsoever. A car was coming at thirty, forty miles an hour, not speeding. The kid ran out and *WHAM,* it just center punched him. Very little braking, it happened so fast. You know, he was short, so it knocked him down on the pavement. Front tires skidded past him. The back tires of the car — because now it was starting to swerve — caught him and skidded him along. Eventually one wheel bounced up over his head. The kid was lying there in the middle of the street, all broke up, blood gushing everywhere.

"The car came to a halt. This woman got out. Early twenties. She was wearing light-colored clothing. She started shrieking. Got the kid, pulled him into her lap; she was covered in blood. I mean, the kid was lifeless. He was dead. And I'm thinking, How can there possibly be so much blood coming out of one little kid? She was rocking him back and forth, crying inconsolably. Then this guy came running out of a house with a blanket and wrapped up the kid. That's all I can remember. I kept thinking about it after that. I was only eight years old. That's when I began noticing stuff around me.

"Within days I found a dead baby bird that had fallen out of its nest, a little hatchling on the ground. I stood there equating things. Dead baby bird. Dead kid in the street. Death. Mother-fucking capricious thing.

"The thing about it was that after I saw him die, I was terrified of crossing the street. I mean it was bad. I was embarrassed to go out with my friends because I just couldn't do it. So I went out by myself and hid between two parked cars. When I heard someone driving up, I darted out and ran to the other side. Then I counted how many seconds passed before I would have been hit. Seven seconds that first time. I got away clean. So I started cutting it closer, hiding and jumping out in front of cars like some mad little dervish. Five seconds, four, three. Pretty soon I was the king of cars. I'd have them skidding sideways, brakes screaming, and I'd keep running street to street, clipping right between them."

He throws his hand, a chop through the dark. "They never got me once. I was in command."

After Dirk gives the story time to soak into the air, he laughs to himself, shaking his head. "The shit we do to figure out the world."

I stand up for bed. "The shit we do," I agree. I walk away into the dark to sleep.

The Graveyard Shift

Graveyard shift members moved like cat burglars through the city. They were the ones who loaded their own bullets at home, illegally adding more firepower than was allowed. In the checkerboard patterns of streetlight and darkness, they would work unseen, bending and stretching their own laws to match the heightened crimes of night. The graveyard shift grew into a union of secrecy. Day cops would wake in their midnight beds, hearing hurt-hawk screams of sirens racing through the distance. They would listen with envy and disdain.

On this night, a crack addict was roving the city with a gun. He robbed convenience stores one after the next: forty dollars at 11:15 PM, a bag full of singles and fives at 12:30 AM. He was the most unstable, perilous brand of criminal available. A description of the man and his orange Dodge pickup with a camper shell had been circulated. Each member of the night team carried a photograph of him from a surveillance camera.

The events that this man initiated on this particular night would ripple through the graveyard shift for years. One officer would be murdered. Another would end up committing suicide with his duty weapon. One would become a desert nomad, and another would turn to Christ. Others would be dismissed over matters of conduct and ethics.

Shouting furiously down the barrel of his .38 caliber handgun, the crack addict had just robbed a 7-Eleven of eighty dollars. Immediately, Dirk and the second in command, a man named Ed, searched through a nearby parking lot, moving slowly in a crouch, flashlights shifting beneath cars, through windows, guns out. They watched each other, listening to shoe soles touch asphalt, judging the speed of shadows cast by their flashlights.

This was the same night that higher powers at headquarters decided to lessen the visceral prestige of the graveyard shift. Night cops had been teasing the daytime crews with bad habits. Fearing that this nightly brotherhood had become too tightly bound and dangerous, those in command assigned each man to an unfamiliar location. The delicate choreography — hands reaching for hands, bodies sailing outward to meet a perfectly timed grasp — was upended. It was the same night that manpower shortages left numerous positions on the graveyard shift vacant.

While the addict came out of the dark, grabbed money at gunpoint, and slid back into hiding, each cop was awkwardly handling his new placement. The angles of the city, the curious shadows and escapeways, were offset and alien. Nerves twitched at every unexpected sound. They had a name for this kind of tension: One Call Away from a Cop Getting Killed.

Going on about nightly business, Dirk left Ed in the parking lot — standard procedure — and cruised the neighborhoods. Thirty minutes later, he heard the call. Everyone heard it. Ed was alone. He had found the orange truck parked in a mobile-home court. It was exactly on the east-west boundary of two police beats, hazy territory for everyone.

Ed called for backup. They all knew the voice. Ed was a man who usually sounded bored, even in the most tense situations. Now he seemed nervous. Nothing was right. He said he was going in to have a look.

The brotherhood scrambled. If everyone had been in place, an unbroken perimeter would have been created like trenching around a wildfire. Each member had a position and knew his own streets: streets that could be taken at ninety miles per hour without dips or holes, ones with views, ones without blind corners, ones linking to alleys to other streets to other alleys. But tonight the city was a newly made web, strands upon strands that would paralyze.

No one got there fast enough. The gun battle between Ed and the addict was quick. Both men fired shots from no more than three feet apart.

A stranger's voice came on the radio. A citizen. He was frantic. "One of your officers is in the street," he said. "He's been shot in the head."

The hive roared. Sirens exploded across the entire city. The orange Dodge peeled from the neighborhood as patrol cars fired in behind it. The freeway was right there. Speeds were instantly well over one hundred miles per hour.

Dirk jumped to the freeway. He sped the wrong way up an off-ramp — not enough time to get to the other side. Aiming for an interception, he raced opposite the chase lane, lights spinning wildly. Oncoming traffic appeared through a tunnel.

Dirk glared straight into the speeding headlights, muttering, "Get the fuck out of my way." The cars spilled around him.

Out the other side of the tunnel, Dirk watched one of the patrol cars swerve in front of the orange truck. Brakes hit. Smoke blasted from under the car's tires. The truck barged into the rear of the patrol car, clear into its backseat. The fused mass of truck and patrol car skidded into the median. Dirk snapped his steering wheel to the right and went down after them.

Another officer made it there first. He fired his shotgun into the driver's door, pitching sieve holes into the metal. A second officer pulled to the other side as the man tumbled out unhurt and threw his gun to the ground. His hands flashed straight into the air.

The second officer steadied his gun on the man's heart. He had a clean shot. The man begged, baring his hands to show that he was done; he had killed a man, and now he was finished — *Please don't kill me!* The officer held his gun, his weight on the trigger, knowing what would happen if he fired, the sudden solution, the unstoppable darkness that would come over him. Muscles tightened in his face.

Dirk arrived with the entire wave of uniforms. They poured around the officer standing with his gun, passing him frozen in the current, still struggling with the shot his training and his personal codes would not allow him to make.

This would be their justice. The man's bones were going to be crushed. They would take him right to the edge. Ten, fifteen cops from across the entire city descended onto this man. The scene was immediately overrun with shouting, with unfamiliar faces, people from other precincts, voices lifting: *You're dead, motherfucker! You're dead!*

Dirk saw down this path. He felt the aimless agony that would flood their lives if they mishandled this moment. They would have crossed too far. They would never be allowed to return to their lives. They would stumble home and never sleep again.

"No! Be fucking cool!" Dirk bellowed, dizzy with confusion, his head blaring with hatred and fear. Another officer shoved into the crowd with him, both of them yelling for calm, grabbing shoulders and arms of other officers, making eye contact, shouting, shouting.

"We'll lose this!" Dirk yelled. *"We'll fucking lose this! Don't let it happen! We've got witnesses here! Pull it back! Calm it down!"*

The wolves circled and bit at the air. Muscles hammered at themselves. Men fell away, necks straining. No one hit the man. No one drove the man's face into a knee, into the ground. The horrible sea wailed back into itself.

The man was trussed like a pig, handcuffed at his back, cuffs around his ankles pulled up to the handcuffs so that his body lay bound and useless. He was tossed into the backseat of a patrol car. The crowd of uniforms wandered, wailed, and eventually dispersed.

At Ed's funeral, Dirk felt his organs collapse inside of his body. As he sat in the pew, he began lurching with sobs. His wife covered him with her arms, but Dirk was gone. He reached out a hand to bury the sounds, but they broadcast from space, burning through his palm. He coughed up tears and fell into himself.

Three days after the funeral, Dirk found his way to the desert. He negotiated a canoe and entered the Green River in Utah, its gorge as barren as bones. He had been there before, vacations in the wilderness, few-day outings to the canyon desert.

Dirk floated for days. Cliffs lifted around him, each shifting slowly behind the next. Not far from the Green's confluence with the Colorado River, he pulled to the right shore. The canoe scratched and banged against boulders and rocks. Dirk dragged it from the current, tying off its bow with a length of dusty rope. He climbed silently from there into the jumbled boulders of a side canyon. The climbing infected his mind. Dirk felt the familiar span of his body, the quickness of his hands. The land was made of fire, every touch a scar, a flood of information. He felt his balance, his step, as if his gun were drawn, as if he had opened fire, each bullet racing to its mark.

Dirk climbed into the fern grottoes and the shadows of dripping springs. Cloisters of cottonwood trees appeared between enormous boulders, their trunks knotted and turned by floods. His hands dragged across their beaten bark, and Dirk thought that the trees looked like true living creatures, ones like himself, that he was just catching a glimpse of them frozen in time as they threw their roots into the ground, bracing themselves. Some were dead, snapped at the knees by floods. Dirk touched these, too, thinking that living and dying were always this close to each other.

Finally, he came to a pool of water, its edges sheltered in blades of cattail leaves, the tan seed heads ready to explode and madden the world with life. The water was like museum glass, absolutely clear. Dirk had never seen a thing like this. He had once imagined this desert as most people think of deserts: nothing at all, forever, drought and rock with no place comfortable to sit. He crouched at the edge of the water, touching it with his fingertips, watching the spread of ripples. Shadows ribbed the floor.

Dirk stripped naked and slipped in. The water rose cold to his chin. He drifted across. From the gravelly floor he clutched a stone with his toes and lifted it to his hand. It was black and small, one stone in a countless world. Dirk kept it. He thought that the desert could sacrifice this one object for him, an offering for his survival.

DAY TEN

In the cold before dawn I wake. I crawl out and swing the serape around my naked body, the wool like wire on my skin. I prance barefoot over broken sandstone and come to the last black widow web along the skirt of cliff at our camp. There I bring out my light. The black widow still waits in her web. The male to her left has not moved all night. He listens for her without rest.

I am met with a sense of inextinguishable patience. I bring my light to the red violin printed on the black widow's belly. She is poised at the tip of my light, every change registered by legs more slender and precise than any tool humans have ever made. She is infinity, I think. She sees all. She contains in her stillness every disenchantment and sudden ecstasy. I turn the light toward the male. He is still waiting for his move. Go, I think. Gather yourself and go. It is the only way you will find what you are looking for. And she will kill you.

I return to my sleeping bag and pull on my clothes, take a slug of water, and from there walk alone toward the roadblock chasm that had stopped Dirk and me yesterday. I just want to have a second look, a pause before daylight, before we set off to scout the next route. The sky rises prismatically, with violet, sienna, and a cool, thoughtful pink. I leave these colors for the dim below. This canyon I am entering is the one that I had believed would be our salvation. I stop at one of its inset water holes, pull back the hood of my serape, and kneel to drink. The water tastes of rock and algae, a good taste, different from other holes, robust to my tongue. I slip the warm hood back over my head and continue.

Dirk is conspicuously gone. I had not realized until now how closely we have traveled these past several days, leaving company only long enough to dig a hole or shit on the drying south slope of a boulder. Urination has been candid, done in front of each other like scratching the back of the head, forgotten as soon as it is done. The terrain is so unfamiliar that without much thought, we have not stepped away from each other.

Even this morning, apart feels barely affordable, though I am pleased to walk alone.

The final passage drops into a thickening center. The chasm surrounds me, walls of shadow far over my head and far below. The air is cold; it's as if I'm standing in a room of ice. A hollow sound rises from every move.

The map tells us that we must make three crossings. Three crosscutting chasms like this lie in our path. I can feel them now, like three new moons in my sky. I feel as if we have begun to sink beneath the surface, digging ourselves in as we struggle. This first chasm is darker in the morning, less forgiving than yesterday. I reach up and toy with the carved greenstone hanging around my neck.

I brought the map, and it seems no more useful down here than sheets of paper towel. It is stuck into my belt, and I had planned to stand here with it open to see where I am. I do not slide it out. Opening it would be loud and showy. Instead, I pull back my hood, my head free in the cold air. I listen unencumbered to nothing. I come to my haunches, a crouch for staring down the barrel of a canyon, a skeptical, curious posture, poised to lean as easily forward as back. I am a mound of wool laundry balanced within the abyss. My gloved hands gather beneath the serape.

Eight days in, I think. The orderly atlas we are trying to make out of this place is not coming together. We need to internalize the rhythms of this geography so that we are not continually reinventing our steps. Instinct is required; we must travel as if we belong here. Instead, there is an awkward discord thrumming in our heads. We search for patterns, but we are thrown. We follow fracture lines, and they shift as soon as we make their acquaintance, abandoning us on piers and ledges. What other language is there besides geology to follow? I wonder. What am I missing?

I remember a game that my father used to play. It might have been nothing more than a parlor trick, a sleight of hand that I never caught. I watched him carefully when he did it because I knew if it was not a trick, then my father was indeed immortal.

He would write a number on a piece of paper and give it to me, a long and random number like 12,876. Then he would ask me a series of maybe twenty questions with numerical answers, answers he could not have known — the age at which something transformative happened to me, an estimation of miles I travel in a year, and so on. In the end, when he had not looked at my numbers, I would add them, and without fail they equaled the one he had given me.

From then on I believed that invisible cords ran through the world, connecting impossibilities to each other. Otherwise, how could my father have reached the number on the piece of paper? There was no random luck to it. He had found the secret order to the universe.

My father performed this trick on three occasions that I remember, and I asked him each time how it was done. I pestered him for weeks, but he only smiled, said, "It's in the numbers," and no more. He once played it with three people at the dining-room table, a grand master of ceremonies asking his wife historical dates (her being a history buff), asking me questions about stars and geology, and asking my girlfriend at the time, who was a rural cowgirl, questions about horses and livestock. The numbers came out exactly as he had written them on three different pieces of paper.

If his game was nothing but a rabbit in a hat, I still could not find the trickery in it. Eventually, my father stopped playing the game. If I ever asked him about it, he became quiet, inward, then angry, so I stopped asking.

Looking down through this chasm, I think of my father's number on a piece of paper. I think of it as a destination.

With a quiet voice, I ask, "Where is it? Where is the way?"

I look up and around, my hushed request reverberating unexpectedly like a chant.

When I return to camp, I find Dirk coming up from his own dawn journey in a nearby canyon. He says he saw a way, a ledge leading to a nose of rock, leading off somewhere else. A possibility.

We start gathering our gear. This will be Dirk's day with the giant book of poetry. Before packing it into his gear, he flops it open. Half a book of pages drapes either side of his forearm as he reads,

As to the mind's pilot, intuition, —
Catch him clean and stark naked he is first of truth-tellers;
    dream-clothed, or dirty
With fears and wishes, he is prince of liars.
The first fear is of death: trust no immortalist. The first desire
Is to be loved: trust no mother's son. . . .
Walk on gaunt shores and avoid the people; rock and wave are
    good prophets.

We load camp and carry our full packs a short distance, stash them in the side of a canyon, and continue with only enough for the day, scouting the next leg.

In this landscape of remembering, the light is bent and pressed like steel glowing beneath a hammer. Folded and refolded, it is a light of subtle strength carried into back canyons, shifted to cobalt and the wine red of worked leather. This land is a governor of light, a prism, a divider. The ground is made of shapes and mirrors, great lenses of sandstone gathering shadows that play off each other. Even in the still cold of morning, the colors are exaggerated, the way they are during a forest rainstorm.

As we move along Dirk's imagined route, in and out of shadows, I am concentrating on the number my father used to pull out of his hat, the number that will show us the way through. A simple wave of a conductor's hand might bring the three chasms together in an hour or two, putting us on the other side. The walking should be delicate, a run of catwalks and meager paths. Everything is vertical here, a warren of cliffs. The miles are a fractal between them, the span of the entire earth held in a cluster of crystals in the palm of a hand. We are treated the same as the light, split into our constituent parts, sent this way and that.

As we come down a bony canyon, our motions are articulated like those of a cat on patrol. Weight softly shifts from foot to hand to foot. We are walking slowly now, admiring the titanic scenery, as if we have enough time for leisure, as if we have found the way already.

When we reach the floor of a nearby canyon, I stop and hold up my hands where I can see them.

"The light is different down here," I say.

Dirk does not hold up his own hands. He looks at mine for a

second. Then, in a menacing gang member's voice, he chants, "The streets look safe but they narrow."

His voice lingers. A warning.

We are in the ribbon of a flood path. The walls have the consistency of flame, flickering in and out of each other, dancing and pulling, one becoming the next. Not far down from here, we arrive at an untouchable slope of stagnant water holes. The holes are black. As we look over their edges, a pebble comes loose from one of our hands and drops. It strums the water of a pool twenty feet below.

Suddenly, there comes the sound of a bird, the downplaying, chromatic scale of a canyon wren. The call builds on itself note after note, as if the damper pedal of a piano has been floored, rising through the canyon in clouds of tone. One bird fills the entire space. Our heads turn every which way trying to find its source. I hear the flit of small wings. Dirk lets out a long breath.

We head upstream, and this puts us onto a shelf on the other side, tweaking down to a thin line, not enough to hold even our boots. I try some unlikely option above it, climbing while Dirk watches, a spectator with hands on his hips, calling to me from below. "Even if you find a way up there, I am not following you."

"Just let me check it out."

"You hear me? I'm not with you on this."

I get up high into this route, overextended, full of fear. No handholds. I climb down jittery, flashing a sheepish glance at him.

"Not the way," I say.

We backtrack to a break we had seen in the canyon wall. It takes us up a cliff-cut ravine full of boulders. They are enormous, entire pieces of planet fallen inward. Climbing not on them but among them, I throw a hand down for Dirk, who is struggling. We lock arms. We do not make the weak link of a handshake. We grab each other's wrists so that we will not slip apart, making a knot of ourselves. With a shoulder blade and a boot, I anchor into the earth. His weight comes onto me for an instant as he lets go of the rock. His free hand snaps up, jams into a crack, and then he lets go of me.

I scramble back out of his way.

Climbing this chute of loose boulders is an act of pure meditation. Every rock has a center of balance. Information bypasses the fat of our brains, straight to the spinal cord, absorbed by our skin, carried into the bloodstream. I land on a tractor-sized boulder. It groans to life and begins to tilt. Before it can lean into a fall, I negotiate it back into place with a quick jerk of my shoulders, listening for the dark-throated clack of resettling. I jump off to the next one.

The boulder field strings us up through a crevice. There we reach a notch that drapes over the top and down the back side of a cliff. Dirk and I both begin nosing around the broken rock and flat spaces of the notch. Some sign of animals should be here. We have seen hardly a scrap in these days, but a pass-through like this is nearly a guarantee, a place where animals must leave some remnant of themselves — a dropping, a track, a scraping away of small stones for sleep. If we find any of these prizes, then we are given a clue.

"Come on," Dirk says impatiently, hands braced on knees as he scrutinizes a wind bowl of sand. "Give me a track."

I come to my haunches and lift a powdery white plug of animal scat from pale dust. It is seasons old. Dirk steps over and crouches beside me.

By its shape, this dropping is certainly from a predator. I imagine the animal's movements here. I think of its eyes situated toward the front of its skull and of the way its head turns, scanning the territory. It is a coyote or a fox or a mountain lion: an animal that lives like a sheathed knife waiting for the flash, hungry. I follow its daily habits, finding in my mind how it travels through here, where its routes are, how far it goes to find prey, its sleeping places, its pathways. It rests in quiet oblivion, sometimes in the open on a sun-warmed rock, where a rabbit or a songbird would never pause. Each of these images tells me what the land ahead will be.

The weather has been at this scat for a while. The original shape and size are difficult to read. No seeds or threads of grass: It is all digested meat. No wings of grasshoppers or little mouse bones: an eater of big things. No fur: a fresh kill, meat taken first. Cat, I imagine. Cats are exclusive about their eating habits. I hand it to Dirk.

He is immediately focused. I see him spreading his map open in his mind. Bobcat, he ponders. Mountain lion, even.

Mountain lion. The idea brings up certain images, an entirely different way of travel than the open lope of coyotes or the quick darts of foxes. A mountain lion's terrain is made of holes and cover and shadow, an intricate place of hiding and watching. This animal has to have room to move, plenty of routes and back routes, an onionskin landscape peeled open.

Dirk leaves the scat and looks across the ground for more data: If there is a predator, then there is prey. If there is dark meat in the dropping, then there are others. Nearby he finds a few cracked seeds of bighorn droppings. He holds one in the air as if inspecting a diamond.

I move over, picking up a second of these dark, round nuts, a nipple pinched from its end. Bighorn sheep. I crush it between my fingers. It is sawdust. The animal is long gone.

Dirk turns the dropping between his fingers. Speaking to it, he asks, "Sure . . . but where did you come from? Where did you go from here?"

"This is the clue we get," I say, standing, clapping the dust off my hands. I am already sure that this is the way. We might as well head back, grab our packs, and haul them through this pass, adding ourselves to the parade of creatures. "There has to be a way through here."

He glances up at me. He is not certain that this is the way, but he sees in my eyes reassurance, validation of these clues we have found. He thinks that he never would have come to this place alone. This maneuvering that goes on between us, hands reaching to hands, possibilities verified in glances and words, has magnified his abilities. Alone, he is an ordinary man. He lives in his fears and his own hoarded memories. When he comes to me, he feels the broken and jutted pieces of his life fit into mine, forming something whole. We become the light and the dark, carrying inside each of us a part of the other. Together, we are no longer ordinary men. We will find the way.

———

Leaving the animal droppings in their places, we cross through the notch, coming around on interior ledges to the edge of another canyon. I had not imagined that there would be something deeper, something less passable than the one we just crossed. But it is here, a parting of stone as fathomless as a glacial crevasse. We would need a bridge, a rope across, something other than what we have.

I had just begun to fill in spaces on the map at the pass, but now I have to reconsider. Where did these animals go?

Trying to enter this new canyon, Dirk and I climb into palaces of newly shattered boulders, haphazard explosions that lie along a steep cleft. All the boulders are sharp-edged. Sharp means freshly fallen, homeless, no time to erode. It means that everything is delicately loose. The chaff of boulders clatters down between our steps. I glance at Dirk's posture to see what he thinks. He is glancing at mine.

Soon Dirk is below me. I leap off a boulder above him and it falls. I shout. It starts a slide, picking up everything it touches. Dirk flies out of the way, jumping from the electric smell of impact. We each take to bedrock ledges, where we watch the mobilizing mess I have created. A hundred centers of balance fall away as rocks explode into each other. White flashes of powder shoot into the air.

From the canyon floor that we cannot see come distant detonations. Echoes rise into a sound storm. The high pitches of rocks striking water pools are covered by deep cleaves, boulders cracking in half. Thick plumes of dust burst upward.

This is too much noise. I feel like the male black widow, small and so thin that I am almost invisible. I have tapped the web. She knows that I am here.

This is not the way.

Dirk and I retreat up the cleft and traverse a high sidewall, hands slapping for holds. Friction-climbing. Heading up, we first have to go down. Left takes us right. Out leads back in. This landscape, I think, is a riddle, as truly contorted as a Zen koan.

The cliff steepens. I feel something cold, the subconscious shiver of a nightmare. The depths are increasing around me. We work across the rock face, following whichever step is most secure, constructing an improbable stairway.

Dirk throws himself up the wall above me. The point above him narrows to a single edge blending into a higher cliff, which blends into a still-higher cliff. If we can climb up and over this point, it will lay us into a canyon just to the east. Still, we will have to backtrack the entire distance at the end of the day to retrieve our packs. We're getting too deep.

When Dirk reaches the very top of this point, his body suddenly shrinks. His head faints into his shoulders as he turns and crawls down toward me like a crab. A half-made word spits from his mouth, and he sits immediately on the nearest foothold. He does not look at me.

I have never seen him cower like this. I cannot alter my momentum without losing my grip, so I pass around him, not asking what he has seen. I will see for myself.

I clear the top. Where there should be a short climb off the back, I freeze at an open fall. This piece of cliff we are on is separated from its mother rock. It stands completely alone, soon to topple.

Instantly my muscles seize, and a cord of breath untangles from my lungs. My body dwindles back. We have reached the tip of a needle. This was supposed to be the point of delivery, the line of travel we follow to cross chasm after chasm. But it is nothing. It is an end. I feel suddenly unmoored, set loose. I am no longer on solid ground.

I recoil from the tip and crawl down to Dirk.

"Shit," I say.

He mutters, "Tortuous fucking place."

I settle onto a ledge, fondling the stone at my neck as if it were a rosary, scanning the utter lack of routes around us. I reach down and unclip my day pack. Carefully, I pull it around front. I open the zipper slowly, every motion weighed out. If a pen were to escape my hand, a bag of nuts, my water bottle, it would float free. It would ride down the face, disappearing into this land of giants.

I look over at Dirk. His eyes are staked down by something far away, something that is not there. He had not been expecting this. He is no longer scanning for possibilities. This is not where he should be.

With a distracted drone, he says, "There are parts of myself that remain inside. We aren't meant to be entirely open books like this."

I pull out a bag of nuts, open it, and offer some to him. His eyes come down. He regards the bag as if I am holding a snake.

"Eat," I urge.

———

We return to our packs defeated, no routes found, knees weak from fear and strain. Under this weight we move slowly into the end of the day in search of a place to camp. Dirk stops, head suddenly turned to the side. He hears something. His alertness calls me to stop behind him. I am tired, my pack heavy, but my senses sharpen, mirroring his.

A flock of small birds, juncos, slips around a canyon bend and into the floor with us. They are winter nomads, flown down from the higher snowbound mesas, finding seeds wherever they can. They rain onto a nearby sandbar of sparse vegetation. Some of them land to survey the surroundings from a dead juniper's branches, while others drop to the ground and begin snapping up ricegrass seeds. Their ensemble of faint twitters sounds like the chirps of children in a field, each secretly aware of the others. Dirk does not stir. His breathing seems to have stopped. If either of us moves, a thread will be plucked. They will all fly away, messages sent between them faster than sound. We have seen hardly any other living creatures. We watch, amazed.

I sense the vigilance of these small birds, thinking that this is how it needs to be done. The juncos have an old way of going about things, the protection of fellowship in a place ripe with hazard. Their unanimity seems like a bright point in a country as friendless and dryly cold as space.

At once, by command of a mutual mind, they dash to the air and flit down canyon from us. The hungry are fed, the watchers relieved. Not enough seeds here to stay.

Dirk stares where they vanished, and once their sounds are gone, says, "You can't help feeling allegiance with anything else alive out here."

We start walking again. I come around front and listen to Dirk behind me, hearing exactly how he negotiates a loose rock that had barely tipped under my step. Without looking, I know that he steps over it differently, warned by my body that it might give way and trip his gait. Every signal between us is like this, minuscule details alerting us by the half second. I listen to the rasp of his clothes, to the scrape of rocks beneath his weight.

Our minds are emptied by fatigue, so we walk with less and less cogitation, like water now, flowing and turning into eddies. The land opens and closes as we slide through, still behind the first chasm, hardly farther along than when we awoke this morning.

We find a good camp. Down in the compound of canyons: an alcove carved into a wall by a tiny, eroding seep. We climb into it, inspecting the line-dried laundry of black widow webs. Widows have not lived here for some years. We drop our packs and sit beside each other, our bodies hanging loosely from our shoulders like work coats put away in the closet, still warm and sweaty from the day.

This is the first night that we will not leave ourselves out in the open. We have a roof of hollowed stone. It leans over our heads, protecting us from the sky, from the eyes of stars beaming through gaps in evening clouds.

"Fire," I say.

Dirk smiles. "Yeah, a fire. That sounds good."

A fire will be a reprieve in this immense land. A thing made by our own hands. We will be able to rest at the flames far into the night.

I do the cooking. Dried flakes of potatoes and hard cheese crumbled with salt. While I stir the pot over our fist-sized stove, Dirk gathers the dry wood of last year's yucca stalks. He breaks the wood in his hands, placing it into neat, small piles: a stack of dry grass to get the fire going, slender twigs for kindling, and thumb-thick stalks to last into the dark. He tinkers with his piles, arranging wood, laying out the kindling so that pieces can be selected according to quick need.

The alcove feels like home. Even Dirk's belongings are scattered idly on the ground, as if he had tossed himself down on a couch, feet up on the furniture. The sounds of our movements are comfortably boxed in, muffled by the ceiling and the floor. Dust and rocks.

This alcove fulfills a very old longing, I think, probably from back when animals first learned about mutual interest, when protozoa began fluttering around each other for protection. Some of these same protozoa gathered in dark nooks behind rocks, like this alcove, when the bigger predators were about. With our modern human houses and our fenced yards and our sleeping-caves, how do we *Homo sapiens* imagine that we are brilliant above all others? We have had the same desires since we turned away from chlorophyll and started bustling about, eating other animals. We have wanted our caves, our shelters made of hide, the door flaps constructed to seal closed behind us like garage doors at the end of the workday.

Dirk starts our night's fire in a lock of grass, burning it in an aluminum dish so that the ashes will be contained. He selects his kindling and begins setting pieces into the flames. I enjoy watching his command, how he gazes over his cauldron. He chooses how high to make the flames. He arranges the sticks so that they catch but do not burn and die too quickly. Then he sits back as the fire burns on its own, a music box wound to play in front of us.

There is a faint light beyond us, in the surrounding canyon, a slim blue of the newly waxing moon. The fire soon takes this other light from our eyes. We are quiet with our small flames. Wood snaps and hisses.

Still stirring the pot, looking at the fire instead of my work, I say, "This is why television was invented."

Sparks sizzle out of a splinter of juniper wood. Dirk stares into it. He says, "Everybody's got to have their home fires. A little candy to come home to."

I blow out the clean blue flame of our stove and hand the pot of food over for Dirk to divide. He does the usual, weighing the food in his spoon, debating over the final amount. Later, as I eat, I study the lit ceiling, the black streaks where runoff storm water pours in — not all the way back to our camp, but close. I cannot clearly think of this place as a sanctuary. Even in this shelter and this warming light, the air is taut with apprehension. I am well aware of the darkness, the three chasms left to cross.

Dirk finishes his meal and turns to govern the fire's wood. He pushes small pieces into just the right space so that there is no smoke, only flame. He lets the coals burn down. There is wood left, but we do not burn it. The fire has had its time. I reach out with my stick, mending the coals, brightening them. The glow subsides, turned and turned so that it is nothing but fine ash. Now it will easily blow away. Our remains will be erased. We will pass through undetected. I plant my stick in sand to keep it from smoldering.

I do not know where we are. On the map, yes, I could find our camp. But what use is this map? It tells of a land that is not here, a place that can be rolled out flat. The land that Dirk and I know about is a series of interconnecting passageways. Regions are defined by our personal movements, by the second landscape Dirk had talked about days ago, the place that etches into our memory. Now, it feels as if we are not even on the land. We are moving through the shapes of our own minds. We have found the space in between passageways. The Diné reached into this same space. Somewhere in here, they found the Protectionway. They found a sacred safety, a wilderness ritual of discovery in which the oldest of stories are revealed, the ones that tell how we survive. Dirk and I will pass through this place undetected because, like the Diné who came before, our presence is sheathed here. This is not a place of humans.

But we are not lost, I remind myself. We are still learning how to move, that's all.

Then I think of my father. He knew about paths in the land and talked sometimes of the places between, the balancing points that perch at the peripheries of worlds. I think of the times we sat in the night desert together, the fires we tended side by side. I grew up with him and his fires. I remember the long talks as he described the universe to me, how there is a preciousness to the dark, to the stars, to the wilderness. He would never have walked this far into the desert, but he would have understood why Dirk and I have come. He wanted this sensation of the eternal in his life. He wanted to sleep with this infinity. He would have enjoyed the strange quiet here.

I mention this to Dirk.

Dirk looks up from the last hot bellies of coal that I turned over.

He says, "Your father was a pathetic drunk."

I look at Dirk's coal-lit form, not sure of what to say. I shouldn't have brought this up. Dirk never met my father, but somehow the man has become a bane in Dirk's mind, an agent of vicious chaos. Maybe I didn't explain things well enough to Dirk. Maybe I only told him that my father was a vile man. I never adequately described the nights we spent together around campfires.

"I don't think you can define him so easily," I tell Dirk. "Even his madness was something of value. I learned about this unexpected element to the world. I think I learned to crave it."

Dirk is not in the mood. He begins fiddling with his own stick, tapping at the coals. All he can add is, "Your father was a stuporific, alcoholic potato head."

I say, "But sometimes I think he died because he understood this kind of place so well. At least he understood it in his mind. I think there was a wilderness inside his head. His heart exploded, maybe out of desire, or unmet desire, or I don't know . . ."

"He died of a heart attack." Dirk points with his stick. "It isn't some mystery. You gotta be careful about worshipping this corruption that surrounded your dad. If he was really hungry for something in his life the way you are, why didn't he take it by the horns?"

"I don't know. I mean, I just can't tell if he was some sort of pure animal or if he was a destructive waste."

Dirk plants his stick in the sand so it will not burn and says, "Destructive waste."

I think, How I love you Dirk, how I trust you. But there are illusions of certainty I cannot sleep with tonight.

Brawl

My father and I went to a Phoenix bar to play pool. I was twenty-seven years old. The place was flooded with music, street punks with their metal piercings, and urban drunkards in black T-shirts, tattoos flowing up their arms. My father strutted around the pool table like Aristotle. He ordered shots of whiskey for both of us and hailed me with a toast, calling me a master of an ancient art, the commander of stories. I had just published my first book.

"Stories," he announced, "are the tools of transformation."

He slapped an empty shot glass on the nearest table and bent over to send his eye down his pool cue.

"But transformation is a hoax, my son," he said, measuring the smooth wood of the cue in his hands. "You must know this. Four in the corner."

The balls clacked against each other. The four ball shot into the corner pocket, choking into the table's underside. He launched his stick over his shoulder, never once risking his back to me.

My father said, "Transformation is the bullshit we use on ourselves as a distraction in between birth and death. It's a lie, a pacifier we pop into our mouths and suck on."

He walked to the other side and leaned again, sawing the cue back and forth. He fired. The ball sank. "You, my son, are the master of bullshit. My young Marcos de Niza, coming out of the desert crying, *Cities of gold!* Cities of fucking gold."

I polished his voice in my head, every word bathed and examined. What was he telling me? By now I was used to thinking of him as a gate swinging back and forth, a man of endless contradiction. I could not tell his lies from his truths, and whether he was sober or drunk, he always said that there were no such things as truths or lies. "There is only what is," he would always say. I turned his words over and over the way I might a small stone in my hand, feeling for subtle messages.

The master of bullshit, I thought. *Transformation is a hoax.*

My father's pool playing was brutally graceful. He set himself up superbly with every shot, twisting me around backward, leaving me with nothing. I hated his ruthlessness. I slopped the balls around after him, inaccurate and clumsy.

"Both worlds," he said, commanding me to balance my game, to find my grace as I steadied my cue. His words made me crazy with rage, and I slipped my shot. The cue ball stretched straight into a pocket and sank into the table's clattering bowels.

"Fuck you," I said to him, moving away so that he could make his next shot, never showing my back.

Three games lost out of five; it was after midnight when I

drove us both home in my father's treasure-trove truck, drunk on the backstreets, dangerous. Should have walked, should have tossed the keys on the pavement at his feet, but I didn't. My father's wife was awake and reading in the kitchen when we got there.

I should have thrown down my gear in his backyard to sleep. I should have fled for the desert. But I stayed. My father and I fell into a set of kitty-corner couches, dredging into a conversation mostly about the rate of universal expansion and whether we will all die in cold nothingness or collapse into a lively fireball. We had philosophical differences on the matter. My father stared at me with repugnance. I told him to screw himself.

The conversation roughened, rising from astronomy to feminism. Dreaded feminism. One of my primary studies in college had been feminist theory and historic women's literature. When I graduated, I stood with the women's studies department. This had been an indisputable insult to my father, a man of great womanizing reputation, an admitted misogynist.

No way out of it. Now that feminism was on the table, there would be blood.

A coffee table sat between us.

I had a drink in my hand.

He called me a bitch.

I pounded my drink against the wood rim of the table, knowing that the glass would shatter. It did.

The air exploded. My father's cigarette hit the floor. He leaped over the table, breaking whatever was in his path. Surprisingly agile for a fat man.

I threw myself straight into him, a blocking move. I buried my right fist into his gut, a shoulder up to shove him away, my mind dancing with the thrill. I could feel my father's body, a tightness, cables of muscles leaping beneath his fat. The rest was just movement, our bodies thrown into each other, hair grabbed, the blunt drive of a fist once, twice. I felt his grip. I had not seen it coming. It closed around my throat. My breath left me. I snapped backward just out of his range.

It was as if I were watching my father dance, observing his steps, while I floated barely beyond him. I recorded his movements, seeing weakness in his swing, strength in his forwardness, momentum to his mass.

The only word going through his mind: *kill*.

I heard screaming. His wife. There was blood. I didn't know whose or from where. The broken glass? My hand? His face?

I felt my father's fingers on my throat again. *How did he get here so fast?* His fingers worked for a hold, not yet revealing their full strength. They searched the way a mountain lion tracks the spine of a deer, feeling for the space to open with its teeth.

His wife dived between us. She screamed, raging her arms in the air. His grip was hurled from my throat. She plastered him with her open hands. With her back she shoved me out the nearest open door. It was just behind me, leading to the porch outside.

As I stumbled away, I saw my father's eyes. He was calculating over his wife's shoulders, dodging the obstacle of her head. He tracked me perfectly, in search of weakness. I was still dancing, amazed, enthralled.

His wife reached behind her and slammed the door shut. Suddenly it was quiet. Moths stooped and stalled around the porch light. I stood alone, my heart thumping into my throat, my body shaking with formless electricity.

An hour later I was still standing in the faint porch light out in the yard's hinterlands. The back door opened, and my father stepped out, the sound of the hinges and the closing so familiar, like a potent smell from childhood. I turned my head skyward, looking for any impression of stars over the city. My father walked up beside me and stopped. He must have stood there for ten minutes, searching the lemon-lit sky for stars, saying nothing.

"I was going to kill you," he finally said. "I didn't know who you were. I just knew that you were younger and probably stronger. I knew I had to kill you quickly. I had no idea who you were."

He's lying, I thought. He's grabbing the nearest answer.

I could not say anything.

"I don't want to kill you," he said.

"That was your last chance," I told him.

He lowered his head, cupped a hand. My father's face flared as he flashed a lighter to a cigarette. Leaning his head back, he blew smoke into the city sky.

DAY ELEVEN

At night I dream of movement. Nothing is still. I slide through canyons, floating, touching ground only with the tip of my foot, a finger, a palm. The dimensions and the atmosphere of these dream canyons are identical to the ones we travel by day, equally as quixotic and gripping.

Dirk is with me in my dreams now. Every night he is an

observer beside me, not a subject, but another dreamer himself. In this dream it begins to rain, and he watches along with me. Then it snows. The rock turns to ice. I panic. I am in a windowless box of canyons, trapped. Where has Dirk gone? *Where is he?*

I wake at the very edge of dawn, and the air reeks of moisture. I have not tasted this in a while, not even in the last swirling of low, dark clouds that days ago gave us nothing but wind. This smells wet at the back of the tongue.

I open the hood of my bag. It is past dawn. Whatever morning light gets through is stricken to a faint blue by the canyon, hardly reaching all the way down to this red alcove. I listen for rain. Nothing.

Actually, the air smells of snow. Snow is a poisonous dart in this part of the desert. It hits the nervous system, unravels motor reflexes so that a person is left helpless, every rock face as slick as oil.

As I lie here I go through the routes behind us: the one that led to here, the one coming down behind that, the one to there; tiny steps and holds, indecisions, gateways, balancing points. The impressions are too many and too vivid for my recollection. If we packed at this very moment and retreated, how long would it take for us to retrace our steps? And then where?

Dirk and I talked briefly last night about the last-ditch effort it would take to tuck our tails and back out. We agreed that this kind of failure would be too daunting — not because of the failed accomplishment, but because of the inability to come to terms with this landscape and, worse, to transform our knowledge into a pathway.

I slide naked out of my bag to feel the damp, breezeless air. Warmer than usual, but still sharp with ice. I pull sweaters and a work shirt over my head, the smell of my body scrubbing across my face. It is a sour smell, a strange, personal pleasure.

Dirk looks over. He has a pot of water heating already. He nods good morning. Steam spurts from under the lid.

Into my pants, I am completely out of my bag, stepping into boots, their leather much more flexible than when I took them off last night. Everything feels moist. I head out the front of the alcove and urinate across a span of stone twenty feet below. I can see a little bit of sky between the canyon walls overhead. Aqueous clouds are moving low and fast.

"Out of the south," Dirk says to me as I come back in. "Smells like gulf weather. You want tea?"

"Yeah, thanks."

I throw the serape across the ground and sit on it, scooting small rocks out of the way with my butt. Dirk reaches for my metal cup, drags it through the dust to his side, and drops a paper tea bag into it. He pours boiling water out of the pan, grabs the cup around its cool rim, then passes it across. His motions are a performance. I have seen them over and over, as if he has found these small paths of least resistance and memorized them, perfected them. These are the tasks of sanity.

The tea is too hot. I set it down to cool. Every morning, the same.

"Smells like snow," I say.

Dirk looks at me. Snow, he thinks. He pours his own cup.

"I scoped a route this morning," he says. "Up out of the canyon behind us. It'll take rope for the packs." He sips off the top of his tea, then clutches it, warm between his hands. When he finishes drinking, he stands and says, "Let's pack up and cross this route. Have breakfast up higher."

I cinch my lips, looking around. "Smells like snow," I say again.

"Well, let's make this one push. Get ahead of it."

"I mean, it smells sooner than that."

He shrugs and goes ahead with his packing.

When my tea reaches the right temperature, a hissing rain falls into the canyon. Dirk and I both breathe heavily upon hearing it, sighing out of both anguish and appreciation. The cliffs around us darken. The rock turns slick. Water begins to move. It is time to reform our ritual.

For now, it is only rain. The sky rolls into a steady shower. A minute later its wind-brushed sounds are interrupted by sheets of water pouring off the cliff above us, pulsing into waterfalls. The water machine of the desert has been set into motion. Holes are filling, pouring over. Water has nowhere to go but down, always down, barely kept by this bare stone. Individual tones evolve into a single roar. At once, rivulets ride across the underside of our ceiling and pour onto the ground, led by drips and streamers. Water moves on every open surface. This is a country of floods.

Is there never true quiet in this place? I wonder. Never a calm space? Every element shifts beneath us, new sounds and smells, sudden detours. We push our gear farther back, collecting it away from the splashes and inletting trickles.

Then, snow. It blows in fat, driving away the rain. Slow, dense flakes twirl over the mouth of our shelter. Dreaded, but fantastic. The canyons fall away from our reach in that moment. I feel the depth of the desert, the immeasurable weight of it brought down like a stage curtain. We have found our way in, and the door has closed behind us.

We cannot traverse this kind of terrain in snow. There is nothing we can do.

I pull on my serape and walk with Dirk to one corner of the alcove so that we can inspect one of the louder waterfalls. It is deafening, more boisterous than any wind. We have to shout in order to hear each other. We stand behind its streaming wall as it smacks the stone surface far below us, the sound of cymbals clanging against rock, the thud of driven stones. We reach out our hands, letting the tips of our fingers feel the water. It is cold. A stream forms in the lower canyon, galaxies of spinning foam.

Thick, dizzy flurries of snow. The flakes are like feathers. They touch rock and melt instantly into running water. I pull my hood into place and slip outside through the gaps between waterfalls. The sky is dirty with snow, gray piles of fabric collapsing upon me.

Might as well take a walk in this new world. Turning back, I see Dirk still standing in the shelter, looking at me as if I've dumbly walked into a sandstorm.

"Why not?" I ask. "The door's open. Let's have a look around."

Dirk thinks about it, then follows. Together, we work slowly down toward the floor of the canyon, every step slick. Where yesterday we had been skittering lizards, now we are infants learning to crawl, hands molesting the wet rock just to hang on. Old ways of moving are useless. Heavy-grained sandstone like this is marvelous on dry days, clinging to boot soles as fervently as we cling back to it. Wet, snow-slicked, every surface is a negotiation, a careful planting of the body. Our arms hover through flying snow as if grabbing ropes to balance ourselves.

At the bottom, water holes are filling, reaching their rims, draining to the next topped with a frothy head. The clockwork of these water holes becomes clear, why some have been full in these past days while others are empty. There is a pecking order. Some holes are merely dampened, waiting, while others fill their deep, gluttonous bellies before overflowing. As they fill and pour down their pitcher spouts, speed picks up, holes filling faster, toppling over into each other. I am enchanted by the motions.

We move along the canyon floor, quietly calculating the potential for a flood, watching for sudden exits and impending bottlenecks. It is not the right kind of storm for a big flood, but we walk alert anyway. My serape smells like a wet dog, like a just-watered garden.

I stop at the siphoning drawl of a stream sluicing down to a pool. Ahead of that comes the bell chimes of a small rivulet jangling across rock. To have water out here, running water, is a blessing. But this snow, this clogging storm, will slow us down markedly. Already we are low on food and will soon have to make a dash south to cross our three chasms. We have discussed what needs to be done after the failure of our route yesterday. We have trained our fingers over the map, postulating future routes, marking them with a pen so that we can look at the map, look up at the real world, and look back at the map without having to find our place again. We found only two options, neither certain. We will lift our packs and move headlong into one of them as soon as we can. If it fails? Then option two.

If the second fails?

And now, snow.

Snowmelt running across rock sounds like a madman whispering in my ear, clucking and laughing. There are so many adjustments to volume and tone that my senses are filled. I pause at each change to the sound, the increase of a waterfall, a sudden flush coming over a rock. My awareness is momentarily heightened, even above these past few days of travel. The easy ritual of making tea and drinking is gone for the morning. I look ahead for Dirk, who is nearly lost in the blizzard. Everything is in motion. The landscape throbs and recedes.

Dirk stops at a water hole that is almost full and waits for me. Stars of air bubbles rise to the water hole's surface below him. The water turns slowly clockwise. It is dark, heavy with dust and sand. Snowflakes dimple its surface. As we stop to watch, the water rises and pours over the lip, and the motion carries it to the next hole, where a raft of cream-colored foam begins to spin counterclockwise. This hole is much smaller and fills almost immediately, then spills into the hollow of a much larger hole below it, giving the water a clockwise whirl.

I recognize the pattern. In the nomenclature of fluid mechanics, it is called a "vortex street." The same kind of alternating swirls can be seen in smoke rising from a flushed candle as the filaments of vapor start to turn on themselves. This form is the delicate balance point between stillness and motion. It appears in the vibrating hum of wind across a tightwire. A car on a dirt road kicks up precise rooster-tail patterns in the floating dust. Cyclones and anticyclones spin from the earth's equator, brushing storms clockwise and counterclockwise across the two hemispheres. There is a law to these things.

Watching the water run, I am grateful for this order that I see. It defines for me how the world functions, that my being pushed one direction and the next in my life is not a matter of chance. Opposite forces drive each other. Dirk and I could not help meeting, coiling around each other, day and night, the known and the unknown, shifting and bending together into a circle. It was commanded by nature itself.

Dirk watches the turning of the water holes. He sees a cause-and-effect maze, a pinball dropped into a trough, knocking over a line of dominoes, snapping a mousetrap, lighting a match, popping a balloon . . .

"You know what it is about this place?" he asks.

I know not to answer.

"It doesn't lie," he replies to himself.

Coming around to me, he skirts the courses of holes, water spilling beneath him, snow applauding his shoulders.

"It doesn't have the stench of human duplicity. Everything's right on the surface. Here and now. You might misperceive a place like this. You might not have the proper intimacy to find your way through. The light might trick you, and you might get yourself killed. But that's the whole thing — you get *yourself* killed. You make a misjudgment in a place that has hard and fast rules. There's no deceit or artifice about it. That's what this place is. One hundred percent. Intact."

I don't believe him, of course. Humans, wilderness, desert — it's all the same. How can we possibly imagine ourselves as unnatural? Nature is inescapable. Indestructible. We're playing along just like everything else.

Dirk comes right up to me, his blue, snow-dazed eyes brightly lit. Only a thin corridor of wind and snow separates our faces.

"Fuck the map!" he shouts. "We got snow. Look at this shit. The world is over for us. We ain't goin' nowhere. We're goddamned born again!"

I look up through the snow, hoping to see cliffs, to get some idea of how much of this is sticking. If I could see that, then I could know what chance we have of getting out of here. But how long will this storm go on? I cannot see the cliffs. I only hear their shedding of meltwater, all spatters and growls. Yes, we are born again.

We cannot push through this snow with any force of will. We must rely on the vagaries of weather and stone. Admiring his own sense of freedom, this peculiar feeling of helplessness, Dirk spreads his arms in abandonment, capturing snow across the stem of his torso.

"You have to obey," he says.

———

Bulwarks of clouds fall away, tripping over cliff heads in their retreat. The sun emerges in long bolts of raw light. We stand suddenly caught in this changed world, the ground blinding with snow and light.

"Just like that," Dirk says from the canyon floor. I am up above him on a shelf.

"You ever seen it clear out so fast?" he asks.

I have, but I say no, because it is always this shocking, as if I had never seen such an abrupt change before.

"Sun like this should melt off some of these south faces," he says. "If it lasts, we've got ourselves a thin little escape here."

For the next couple of hours, this gap in the storm holds. Slabs of snow fall from slopes of rock. Some of the straight-south sides melt, but every shaded cranny still holds its snow. We take turns testing the next route, one at a time balancing through shelves and ice-strewn faces. In the afternoon my hands slide across rock. I am high above the floor trying to quiet my heartbeat, fingers dancing for something to hang on to, everything so cold and stiff and slick up here, even in the sunlight. I retreat, lowering slowly hand by foot by hand. When I touch flat ground again, Dirk is watching. I shake out my hands.

I have done this very thing before, tested snow slopes in the desert through a gap in a storm. Moments like these always come, when it feels like a domestic journey and my senses are tools of repetition; it's like kneading bread dough for the hundredth time.

"Another half hour, maybe," I say.

Dirk looks southwest, toward the birthplace of this storm. Not much can be seen over these parading cliffs, but he can see the edges of bluish black, the next wave of clouds coming. Dirk thinks that if we can at least get out of this canyon, we will be in a better position to try crossing the three chasms from a different approach. I think we've got to wait until the very last moment.

"Half hour," he agrees.

Half an hour passes. We load our packs. Garlands of snow remain along the northern and southeastern rocks. Time to move. The ascent is like balancing small rocks atop each other, the stack growing precariously taller. Soon we are edging around nibbled handholds, the canyon floor small below us. We climb slowly, but with quick intentions. The coming storm is dark with moisture. It obscures and swallows the high rock formations to the southwest. Like an advancing column, it takes one place after the next, rolling and splashing forward. A wet wind dives in front of it, flashing across our faces and hands. The smell of water, snow. We cannot be caught on this rock face when it arrives.

Our route is not a sheer cliff. It bulges inward and out. Shoulders of rock lean overhead. We test areas with boot scrapes, backing off where it is too slick. Very little of what is possible to climb is left for us.

The route becomes steeper than we can take with our packs. We slide out of our shoulder straps at once. Dirk pulls his rope, and I reach to take it from him. With the coil over my shoulder, I climb the nearest crack. My movements are swift, back and forth between the angles of an eroded wall. When I reach the top, I look southwest at once. The storm bucks its full weight out of the next canyon behind us. I send the rope down, and Dirk ties off the first pack. Pulling it up is a strain, my back given to the work. I drag the pack to my feet and plant it beside me.

Taking apart Dirk's bowline knot to release the pack, I feel the knot's succinctness, a message sent up from below: calmness, accuracy, certainty. This will without fail hold the weight. It can be undone quickly. I let the rope back down, reading it as it goes, feeling Dirk's hand clasp the other end, sensing his work in its tugs. Without looking down, I feel every turn to his hands: a swift tuck, an end of the rope sent through, the two-handed tug to lock the knot. He yanks the rope to let me know the knot is set. I pull it tight and haul up the second pack.

Dirk comes. He is groaning with the climb. Veins stretch at his neck. "I don't like this shit," he sputters.

I send a hand down to him, jamming my boots into a hold.

"I'm good," I say.

We lock arms into a single bind, and I hold him as he climbs to me.

Up through the cliff levels, we can no longer see the floor. We move through the canyon's middle world, blind from both the top and the bottom, and gather in the shallow grotto of a ledge where we quickly strip gear off our backs to hand up the next crux.

I grab Dirk's shoulder straps, cold from sweat, and hoist his pack up to him, on and on, ledge by ledge. The rope comes out again. Dirk does the scramble this time, rope over his shoulder, as I stand waiting.

Suddenly, I have nothing to do. Dirk is performing the work. I am helpless as the storm winds up the canyon, the wind hard now. I wait. I wait.

I can appreciate this place in such a moment. We two are strangely small, squeezed between the force of the storm and the invincibility of the landscape. So small, I think. Are all living things like this? Do we all bend to fit, forming into the wind and shaping around the rock?

Dirk shouts, "Rope!"

The coil wings into the air. It slaps the ground to my left, and I tie one pack through its straps, snapping closed the waist buckle so its tines will not break. I send it up, and it floats over my head, grabbed up foot after foot. A minute later, the next goes up. I climb behind, handholds gripped, pulled. I throw my weight, shoulder into a niche, next hand up. My body wants to fall, wants to tumble off this point, shredding all the way to the canyon floor. I resist, clamping my fingers into the smallest cracks, suspending myself. The wall becomes a misshapen ladder under my touch.

I cannot find the last hold. My right hand pats frantically for it and finds nothing. Dirk's hand is there that instant. I feel his skin, his fingers grasping my wrist as I do the same to his. He does not lift me. He just hangs on as I put my weight into him.

On the top I do not take the time to retrieve my breath. I lurch my pack into place, and we are moving. The climb is over. We have reached a higher level, a new landscape of farther canyons. Obstacles spill around us, massive drops and exposures, and in this we see a sliver, a low, approachable canyon. Without agreeing on it out loud, we jog east along the easiest spine of rock from which to drop into it as the storm moves over us.

We both see our destination at once. A span of ivory-red cliff has fallen and rests against its parent wall, a giant lean-to. We scramble up a flank of pale, cascading sand and drop into the mouth of the shelter.

Dirk and I enter a stone-slab hallway, something the ancient Egyptians might have constructed, unnecessarily tall and elegant. The walls are enormous, each sheared absolutely smooth by some cataclysmic act of geology. The passage is long, the sound of wind muted behind us.

Our movements change once we are inside. The sprint is over. The air is still. Time is different. It is not faster or slower than it was moments ago, but it is of a different quality, smooth instead of grainy, spiced with cinnamon instead of pepper.

Female landscape, I think.

We both let our packs drop onto earth made of drifted and settled sand. As dark comes on, we build a small fire of wood-rat twigs. A delicate cast of firelight leans up the walls, and the storm stays outside.

Dinner is dehydrated potatoes and bits of hard, sand-pelted cheese with salt and dried, leathery kale. After the pan is set aside, the meal finished, we sit in this sweet light, eyes stolen by the flames.

Again, I remember my father. I must tell Dirk that I used to sit with my father like this. Dirk will have to listen.

"My father would never camp in campgrounds," I venture. "He always took these horrible roads. And he used to make these great fires. He always started them with gasoline and a lighter. I don't even know if he could have started a fire with just kindling. He used to create this magician's spectacle, lighting off giant explosions, standing there with his face lit up as if he were calling the ancient powers."

I lift a stick, mending the fire by turning coals.

"Then he'd sit up all night poking at it, talking about fire being alive, and how if there are past lives, he used to be the fire starter."

I look over at Dirk, his eyes also consumed by the back-and-forth skipping of light.

"I always have memories of my father from things that happened at night. Why is that?"

"Night is for the observant," Dirk answers.

Fitting, I think, for the man of the graveyard shift.

Dirk breaks from the fire to look at me. He seems suddenly irritated. "You talk about me being nothing but black and white. Look at yourself. Only black and only white. One minute your father's a violent lunatic and the next he's a wise and ancient mystic. You live on extremes, Opie."

The fire. I look at the fire instead of Dirk. The beautiful fire, shifting, pulling, alive.

Dirk continues, "You see a continuum and process to everything around you, but you insist on living only at the farthest edges. It's like you live in two completely different worlds sometimes, like you can't bring them together."

The fire. I keep watching it. I think, I could say the same to you, Dirk. The two sides of your coin, my crooked genes . . . maybe this is why we ended up together. We both stand between worlds, between cop and wilderness, between madness and sanity, and we have not yet learned to sustain the graceful balance.

Dirk keeps on. "You think you're a madman, some kind of van Gogh hacking off your ear as a prize. God, sometimes I need one of those Taser guns to use on you, just zap you so you fall down and stop and realize that you are absolutely sane."

I stand and wipe my hands free of dust, pulling all of my warm layers of clothing straight.

"Gotta pee," I say, looking for a way to get out from under Dirk's scrutiny. But I cannot escape it. I move through the fire-light passage knowing how he sees me in this world, my shadow flashing against his walls. In his pantheon of criminals, of people capable of horrible and disturbing acts, I fall into the category of the good. I am an innocent. A good and innocent man cannot at the same moment be a madman.

But Dirk, I think, I am not one of the good. I am one of the many. I am confounded. I cannot see my way through. We are all mad.

I walk to the mouth of our shelter, unzip my pants, and uri-nate into the boulders below. The storm has broken into wan-dering pieces, leaving me with the false light of a clouded moon, the stiff cold of unmelted snow. I can just begin to see the night terrain around me. I see the birthing rooms of canyons and their haunted moon-colored boulders.

I glance back into the shelter.

Dirk is showering sparks out of the fire, bright birds startled from the brush. I see hundreds of millions of years in the fire-light, calligraphic layers of this wind-driven rock formation. Boulders lie crashed at the far end of the shelter, a collapse from not long ago, a deafening explosion, the ozone smell of impact and dust.

Migrations fill this room. Meanwhile, I bang around myself like a stone in an empty box. I wish to be one of these objects fallen into this land and not a human. My insides should be exposed, broken open, my life told by my passage, by the way I have scattered my gear once again in the dust, and by my attrac-tion to the exacting hand that Dirk uses at the fire. I want to be an alien here no longer. Release this notion that I am a man subject only to the laws of men. Come, wind, wear down my edges and build new ones of me. Make me more than black or white. Abrade me into a world without end. Turn me to sand and spin me through the air. Bring me to the ground again and I will build the next civilization of stones.

I walk back into the shelter and sit. We say nothing to each other. I watch Dirk's face as the fire softens and finally dies, and all that is left of him is the coal glow of his eyes.

Small-Town Cop

Dirk thought it would be good enough just to leave the city, get out of the heat of his job. He decided to move with his wife, Linda, a police dispatcher, to a Colorado ski town two passes away from Denver, up where the snow starts early and buries the place in winter.

Prior to this, Dirk had been working in a part of Denver that had no extraneous vegetation or geology. He was moving through a landscape of rooftops and alleys, a secret world that everyday citizens never visited. The places that seemed even remotely organic were only the slick dark undersides of overpasses, the popcorn-vomit smells of small midnight bars. It was maybe this barrenness that had been wearing most on his mind, and not so much the gunfire and the photographs thrown into morbid investigation files. Too many junked televisions and

weather-crisped fliers pasted to the buildings, not enough blowing leaves along the streets.

Dirk was afraid that he would die in this place. He imagined
himself sprawled on the ground, feet oddly askew the way they
always are among the dead before clean-up crews arrive. He
envisioned pulling over a car for some meaningless traffic violation. As he requested to see a driver's license, Dirk would barely
feel a bullet punching into his skull from out of the backseat.
This would be his end. The mountains, he figured, would be his
salvation.

So Dirk moved away, but instead of taking a job at a café or
with the snowplow crew or shelving books at the library, he
found work as a local cop. It was reliable, something he knew
how to do.

All the cops there had nicknames, as did most of the resi-
dents. Blue and Rooster and Red and Smiley . . . that sort of
thing. Dirk considered this, then said that he would take the
name Puss-Eyed Pete. They called him Dirk.

Not long into this new life, Dirk shot someone at a gas station. It was a late-night robbery, after closing hours. The burglar
walked straight toward him even as Dirk held a gun in his left
hand, flashlight in his right, announcing that if the man came
any closer he would shoot. The burglar kept on, reached into his
coat, behind his belt. There was a glint of metal. From a crouch,
Dirk fired once. The bullet traveled ten feet in five one thou-
sandths of a second. Bone shrapnel from the man's left shoulder
sprayed across the ground. It was a nervous shot — could have
just as easily hit the head or chest — but all the same it ended
with the man crumpled on the ground.

Dirk's friends in the city called him a shit magnet. He

couldn't go anywhere without having it fall down on him. It turned out that the burglar, mad with a heavy dosage of quaaludes, had been unarmed. The glint of metal had been a pair of channel locks pulled from his back pocket.

It began to dawn on Dirk that no matter where he went, cop work was always the same. Far quieter in a small town, it was still a job dealing in deception and violence. His days were still marked with domestic abuse, thieves, dead bodies, car chases . . .

The last high-speed chase of Dirk's rural career came from a whale of a white Buick blazing from county to county, dodging through back roads, jumping on and off the nearest interstate. Dirk intercepted the Buick on a mountain pass, overtaking the other patrol cars, sliding in close on the turns, overpowering the runaway driver by boxing him against the guardrail.

The Buick touched ice, spun off the road, and impaled a snowbank. Dirk, the first on the scene, dragged the driver out and immediately got to work, shouting into the man's face, rolling him handcuffed against the car, driving his fists into the man's kidneys. Suddenly, Dirk stopped as if yanked from a dream. He turned to look behind him and saw a row of faces. They looked like children on the first day of school, none of them sure how to behave, a couple of sheriff's deputies and a highway patrolman in his crisp park ranger–style hat. Their faces floated in the night silence, all staring directly at Dirk.

Dirk glanced at the driver's crumpled form, then turned again toward the hanging faces.

"This is how we do it in the big city," he explained.

"This ain't the big city," one of them accused.

Dirk studied their eyes. He grabbed the driver by his collar and tossed him into the snow at their feet.

"Then he's yours," Dirk said.

Cop work is cop work. The small town gave him nothing but low pay and poor benefits. A job opened up in Denver. Dirk took it. He moved back to the prostitute-laden beat along one of the main avenues, eventually dropping into the underworld of the graveyard shift, like an addict once more.

DAY TWELVE

Today Dirk and I will make the crossing. Snow has melted from any south-facing rock. There is only a scattering of white pockets in the north. We have scouted and been turned back enough times. Food is running low. We are only five days from our pickup on the backwater bend where we left our supply cache. Last night we agreed in the firelight shelter that today we would slip on packs and find our way through. There would be no more questions, no more scouting. The land would spread open. It would have to.

The first chasm that we have been unable to cross hangs below us in a suspension of crevices and minor gorges. We stop under the weight of our gear and scan the cables of sandstone holding this place together. Dirk reaches to the ground and picks up a single gray arrowhead. It is perfect, hand-cut from glassy stone, no damage at all to its fine, napped edges.

Dirk grins, holding it up, announcing, "I am the goddamned Yo-Yo Ma of finding shit."

He hands the arrowhead over, and I pass it like a faceted gem between my fingers. There have been so few artifacts out here that I have mistakenly imagined we are the first to step in one canyon or another. This is more pleasing, though — evidence of another person's passage. Human populations have been sudden and brief in this place: the archaic nomads hunting bighorns and rabbits five, eight thousand years ago; the Anasazi in the eleventh, twelfth centuries AD; Paiutes driven out by Diné warriors some few hundred years ago; the Diné fleeing the United States in 1883; the singer in his childhood; Dirk and me today, seeking refuge against the gravity of these histories and our own. We are next in the lineage, even if we are too short-lived to be named. We are only passing shadows, as were all the others before us. Even the names that the Diné gave to some of these landmarks — Head of Mother Earth, Talking Rock — will eventually wear away while these great stones will still lean against one another. I pass the arrowhead back to Dirk. He sets it on the ground and looks up, continuing his study of canyons spreading down from us.

"Choose your door," he says.

This will not be a coin toss. There is a pattern. Somewhere in this is the scheme, and we should know it by now. Some canyons fall into strings of traps. Others lead the way through. We need a route that goes down, crosses the chasm that has so far stymied us, and then takes us up and out the other side. From there we will need another, and then another. One crossing, two, and three. Today.

There is one thin, fissured canyon. It is heaped with boulders. The canyons surrounding it, seductive hollows winding out of sight, are clean of boulders. This messy, boulder-racked canyon before us looks purposeful.

"This is the place," I say.

Dirk agrees.

We start into it. Taking ledge by ledge down toward the dark, we sling off packs and lower them to each other. The formations lift and cover us. We are quickly down inside. This must be what it feels like to stalk a great animal, I think. We check over our shoulders, aware of the smallest details: sandstone polishing, a battered shrub of mountain mahogany leaving windblown claw marks in the wall. I think of the Arctic Inuit hunting whales or polar bears: laying a hand into a fresh track of a massive creature, or from a kayak, seeing bubbles rising from unknown depths. This is what it must feel like to expect a sudden appearance, a confrontation. Dirk and I have little mechanical advantage here. The rope is useless on most of these clean faces. We have our bare hands.

The canyon becomes a tiny gap within the earth. We lean palms against one wall; our packs grate against the other. What if this closes? What if this swallows and leaves us here? My face is against the rock, my chin, my lips touching sandstone, elbows cocked back. Boulders are jammed in here like skulls. It takes time to slip out of our packs and run them to each other. My hat catches and hangs above me, the brim wider than the canyon itself. I stretch back and swipe it down. Stagnant water waits in the lowest reaches, black with the rot of floods backed up from the main chasm. I wrestle off my boots, my pants, quickly tying laces together to contain the bundle, strapping it behind my neck. Every sound is muffled.

Ice water bites at my legs as I enter. My cold-fog breath curls and vanishes. The floor is sand. No mud, I notice. An almost complete absence of fine organic matter. With this information, I move up the chasm in my mind, the only way to travel the length of this place. I try to imagine a spring, a nest of horsetails or cottonwoods, and I find nothing but a barren expanse, a few desert plants grabbing at the cracks. Old flood foam clings to my legs. With my toes crisply aware in the cold, I feel the belfry of a buried boulder and the flood depression just behind it. The water leads me into the chasm floor. Walls sway in and out of each other in the faint blue light of day, and I feel as if I am walking into sex, two bodies of chasm walls wrapping around and obeying each other. Above my head: wall over wall over curving wall.

We have reached the floor of the first chasm. Finally. Our incoming fissure of a canyon bisects it like the arms of a crucifix. I hear Dirk behind me. Water gulps and echoes as he wades across. His head is ducked, as if he's walking through a cave of ice.

He murmurs, "This is one deep, tangled bitch."

I say nothing, staring up through the walls.

Dirk and I dry ourselves on the back of a boulder. My feet know every shape they touch, the textures acute. As we wipe off with bandannas, we keep an eye on the dark vanishing points up and down the chasm. Dirk and I both leave to investigate these causeways, our pants drying our reddened legs as we move. The chasm buries itself in either direction. Downstream is a flight of water holes intricately constructed among pilastraded walls, a church of Gaudí. Upstream is a bed of ice protecting an inlet where waterfalls sometimes plunge.

The way out is neither. The way out is in the mirror image of the overhead fissure we came down. This second fissure looks as if a city has fallen into it, an entire skyline of boulders swallowed by an X-shaped crack. We load packs and begin climbing hand over hand. There are dark places behind boulder heads, and cleanly exposed tips of rock that we clutch, our boots scraping off small pieces that glide unheard back down to the chasm we just left. I glance over my shoulder. Pebbles shower through the air, and they appear for that moment to be birds taking to the air, signs of life. Then they pop open, become quick, white dust against whatever they hit.

Each part of my body comes into play: hand planted to the left, boot choked into a crack, pack thrown from my back into the wall as an anchor, other foot as high as I can reach, and then the burn of my thighs. I taste bile in my nostrils midway to the top, coughed up by the hardness of my breath, a deep reach into my body for strength. At every stretch my face muscles involuntarily pluck at their cords, as if I were hoisting a backbreaking weight into my arms. My face comes near a crevice filled with meltwater. I move toward it, lips touching water, groaning to draw it in for a drink.

Dirk and I reach the top at an arc of rock in the sun. The land falls away from us on all sides. Enormous dishes of sandstone lift from the fray, wedges of earth crossing each other's shadows. The land has been stirred, churned, folded into itself again and again. Dirk's pack slides off and lands hard at his heels. His face is slick with sweat.

Hurling his voice down the crack we just ascended, he spews, *"Fuck me runnin' with a chain saw!"*

He whirls to me like a drunken man, swiping the bandanna off his head. I am sitting, tilting so that my hat brim lifts just high enough to let Dirk into my world.

"Pull all the fuses," he sputters. *"Pay no attention to the man behind the curtain. We are inside the beast. Come on, you pussy! Is this all you got?"*

Oh, Dirk, please don't.

I lower my head again. The sweat falls. Each drop dabs a dark circle onto the stone.

Now where? The second chasm is just ahead, close enough that a loosened rock would clatter all the way to its floor. If we could become small stones, we would bound. But we have these arms and legs. We are vulnerable, fragile creatures. Together, Dirk and I study the map for a moment. The second chasm lies to the south. Our only option from here, though, is to head west. Our world is tightening. The surface to the west reclines down a shield of rock. We begin to creep along its falling crest, our palms and cheeks resting on its walls, ankles cranked sideways to hold ourselves.

I hear Dirk, his breath huffed out, a nervous sound.

"This ain't the way," he mutters, and scrambles back, crawling up to vaguely level ground.

The quickness of his retreat freezes my blood. I am getting myself trapped. I cannot even see the bottom I might tumble into with my breakable bones. What are we thinking? I inch back to join him.

Dirk and I pace the ledges. We spy into amphitheaters beaming over our heads. The rope is useless here, nothing to tie off to, no anchors. Every surface has been worn smooth, polished into the ice of clean sandstone. We move quickly, no time to scout for the day. There is only one way. It is the one that Dirk did not like. We return to it and I begin.

My shoulders drop. Boots drag at the slope, barely lifting for each downward step. I turn my head in order to stretch my neck, breath filling my lungs, released. One choice. How fast can I strip out of my pack if I lose purchase? Not fast enough. There is no recovery from a mistake.

"No blunders here," I warn. "Clean out your mind."

Once I am on the open face there are no ledges, no knobs of rock exposed, not even enough to grasp with the tip of a finger.

We are crossing the face of an enormous globe. I creep with hot breath. My boot soles test by the half inch. I let my eyes turn down once, only for a moment, and I see the last visible surface curving away below me, sliding over this palisade of smooth stone. I would plunge into shadow, I think. I would disappear.

From above, to my right, comes a sickening rasp of fabric. I hear Dirk. An inhuman language jets from between his teeth. I know the sound. He is falling.

No.

I cannot turn my head quickly without throwing my balance. My forehead plants against the rock, and I turn only my eyes.

Sharp hisses and consonants scratch from Dirk's mouth as he starts to glide by my side. His fingers drag down the rock. Anything to anchor himself. Any sound. Any muscle. His left leg extends below him, boot catching at aberrations. Missing them.

I whisper, "No."

Dirk's leg bones will spring up through his chest, I realize. His ribs will decorate the remains of floods. He will be gone.

I cannot reach for him. I can hardly watch him. His pack carries him. Too much weight. He fights uselessly against it. Every muscle leads to the points of his fingers. I can see the white of his bones, knots of knuckles hard as coal.

I knew this could happen. I always knew we could die. My friend. This will be all I know of Dirk. My beloved. He will die quickly, and I will waste in this hall of mirrors. In the lifetime of hunting for his body, I will perish.

My eyes drop as far as they will go. I cannot move my head. I feel Dirk's weight, an invisible rope from the center of his chest to mine. I have never felt it like this, tangled into my organs, pulling me. I press my body even closer into the rock so I am not pulled off, so that we do not both plummet, tied to each other with this unseen accord.

Remember who you are! You are not the man who is falling! Keep your hold! He is dead!

All the same, I do not let go of him. My chest strains against his fall.

I hear the sharp bite of his air. It is the last sound, all of his life given to the rock. Dirk's fingers catch. He wills himself into the bending cliff face. He stops, his face crushed by muscles, spit spattered in front of him. I hear the breath of survival, quick, curt outpourings. He is poised at the final edge.

I let out a breath.

He is not free yet. The shadow gathers beneath him. Dirk cannot wait. He slides his first boot across, fingers crawling. By tiny increments, he moves. Below Dirk is a shelf, no longer or wider than the handle of a spoon. He reaches it and balances there, spreading his arms and hands against the wall. He presses his cheek to the cold rock and breathes. He is a small, scared child clutched to his mother's legs.

I see Dirk's mouth open to the rock, his lower lip wilted, his saliva bright on grains of sandstone. I wait. Dirk looks up to me and nods. Ready to go. There is nothing to say. No moment to waste. We climb across the shield in tandem, him just below. The rock lets us off at the shelf of a canyon, a place that leads down again, perhaps to the second chasm. Dirk shakes out his hands, bottoming out a thermometer's mercury, expelling his fear.

"You okay?"

"Yeah. Yeah. Okay."

"I really thought you were gone."

"Yeah . . . I know."

We look into this next level. The only thing to do now. We've got to get out of here. Our minds scour in front of us, sent ahead immediately like small dogs to scout what we cannot see and return with word of banks and routes. Some questions drift into unforeseen places and do not come back.

Backtracking would be suicidal. Even if we could press back to where we began this morning, to the great Egyptian hallway of a shelter where Dirk and I kept our fire last night, we would be weaker, hungrier. We would sleep too long. There is only this way now.

Within minutes we reach a narrow enclosure of cliffs with a barricade of boulders wedged between. Water lies below. The rope must be used. Leaving my pack behind, I climb down the wall, but it steepens and fear shrinks my blood, contracting into my body again. I am too tired for this. I want a clean route, one with promise and ease, no more challenges. *Please.* But who am I begging? The land lies motionless.

I try climbing face-forward, a foot lowered for my heel to find purchase. This doesn't work. I inch myself around, my face to the wall now, and reach down with a boot toe, then a hand. Not this way either. Like a dog turning on its tail to sit, I circle on the rock, beating down the grass of my doubt. I am unable to find the perfect center of gravity. The water below is murky from the storm: It conceals whatever boulders I might fall into.

Of all the options available, how do we know that this is the way? There are keys, like the boulder-jammed canyon we started with this morning. This gap is filled with boulders in the same way, which means that housecleaning floods are not frequent in here. Which, in turn, means that this canyon is not solely flood-formed, that it is an irregularity within the geology, a fracture that could have some continuity. Continuity means passage, so we follow. Still, I wonder about our decision to come this far. How do we know?

"I don't like this," I call up to Dirk, who stands with our two packs on a ledge, busy with the rope for lowering. "No, this isn't good . . ." I give him my entire litany, the procrastination against what must be done.

But I cannot keep making these dog turns on the wall. I have to find the way. I commit my body. A hand goes down, needing to find something. Right there I reach an invisible hold. Just a divot worn into the rock face. I use it and slide my foot down. Right there, again, is another hold. And then a hold below that, and another.

This is a stairway. These were constructed. Someone carved them. I lean over, seeing a row of hand-formed holds leading down the face. This is where the people before the Diné once came through, chiseling at the rock to make their path.

"Wait a minute," I say, making sure that I do not speak too quickly. But I am certain. This means that people used it as a pathway. If it had been yet another dead end, they would have left no sign of themselves. Instead, they eased their route through here by constructing a passage. Finally, something in this land is made on a human scale.

"I can see steps down here," I say. "There are steps carved into the face."

Dirk stops his rope and looks down at me.

"This is the way!" I exclaim. I stretch my head farther out to examine the entire set of small cavities. "Holy shit. This is it. This is the crossing. There are steps all the way to the floor."

Dirk nods, says, "'Bout fucking time," and returns to the rope.

Like me, he knows exactly what this means. We have reached

an axis point, one used long ago. We are not lost. If this is the axis, then we know we will reach across these two remaining chasms. This is the promised way to the other side.

———

The Protectionway is prophetic. It tells of an ancient path hidden beneath pedestrian walkways. If you slip beyond the guard of roads and trails, so far past ordinary layers of living that you imagine yourself hopelessly lost, there you will find a way. It is a tale that is so old and familiar that it could be easily dismissed as nothing but a charming metaphor, hope for the hopeless, yet in the throat of this canyon, the pathway is suddenly irrefutable. Stone-clawed ladders and steps lead along like a path of bread crumbs. I am traveling this prophecy, reaching ahead for its next grasp, scaling down rung by rung into . . . what?

The steps are old, deeply worn by weather and passage. None is any deeper or rougher than the sidewall of an eggshell, barely wide enough to hold two fingertips at a time. I wipe the sand out of each. There is an order to these steps, a demanding sequence, left hand to right foot to right hand to left foot. They are designed for the exact weight and angle of a human body on this very wall, each placed just so, barely enough to allow a reach to the next. Whoever made these steps, many hundreds or thousands of years ago, understood the art of human movement. Soon I am hanging over the pool of water, and the steps lead to my right, avoiding the water, water that has gathered in this same place for thousands of years.

Hand by foot by hand I reach the floor. From there I call up to Dirk, ranting about beauty and order and the way through, announcing to him that this entire landscape is a prophecy: the foretelling of fault lines, the divining course of ancient humans. Dirk is nodding his head impatiently. He has yet to climb this mystical little route of mine, and to him it still looks questionable.

Dirk shoves the first pack over, and it scratches its way down. Its weight fires up the rope into his arms, straining his back. The rope sends out, and the pack catches on a meager ledge. Dirk snaps and pulls, mumbling at the pack, "Walk, you bitch."

The bitch walks. It steps from the ledge, and Dirk wrenches back so that the pack does not plummet and pull him off. It floats into my hands, and I carry it out of the way, sending the rope back. Same with the next pack. Dirk follows with the anxious stretch of an overexerted climber. He does the same dog turning, afraid to put his weight down, unable to see the first hold.

"Right here?" he asks nervously.

"Right there."

"Right below my hand?"

"I can see it from here."

"Damn it. This is a close fucking cut."

"Trust it, Dirk."

Finally, he commits his weight, leans into the air, and his hand slides down until it finds something. Then he is in. The path becomes him, stairstep dishes leading one to the next. I watch Dirk and think, How many bodies have traveled here? In the last thousand years, perhaps very few. There came the refugee Diné and the singer who hid here from the Indian school. Before them were the Paiutes, who were chased here by the Diné, and before them, the makers of these faintly carved stairs. These first people found themselves in a land so complex and difficult that they had to cut their way out of it . . . or into it.

Dirk touches ground. We carry our packs down the dense canyon interior, again finding trains of carved steps that lead us along walls into the hole of the second chasm.

We reach the bottom. It is very late in the day, and the light is fermented with cherry and dusk blue. I am ready to lay down gear in this dragon's gut of a chasm. I want to rest.

I let down my pack and wander weightlessly along the scoured stone basin. My hands hang like bells at my sides. Dirk watches me go. His posture is uncertain, asking why I have stopped, where I am walking to. He follows.

The chasm deepens ahead of me, so massive and tightly cut that it seems catastrophic, the result of some immeasurable violence. The sky has become overcast. The only way to know this is by the altered color of evening, darker than it should be right now. I walk slowly beneath this gauze of shadow and light — can it even be called light? The chasm skinnies into a fall, a sensuous, female descent of dishes and lips down to the black of nowhere.

In my mind this is the darkest of all three chasms, the impenetrable center. There is one crossing left, one chasm we know nothing about, but there will be no way to reach it tonight. I want to remain here. The route has led to the gloom of this innermost space where the walls twist among one another.

Dirk comes to my side. I recognize the question in his silence as the two of us look over the edge into the velvet blue within blue beneath us.

"I want to sleep in this place," I say.

Dirk is quiet. He doesn't like the idea.

There is an invisible point below us where I can no longer

peel one shadow from the next. One stone wall becomes the other. My eyes are gripped by this chasm's architecture. Yes, I will have to sleep down here. I have walked all this way to find myself at the bottom of the earth, a razor cut through the palm of this landscape. This is the outermost of all edges, the realm where unnamed comets sway beyond the planets. The shapes and layers of darkness are so massive and overwhelming here that I cannot possibly deny them.

"We've never been in a place like this before," I say.

Dirk's hand touches his face. He looks for the sky, then glances behind us. There is no way he is sleeping down here.

"Listen, I don't want to be the one pushing the issue," he says, "but it's late. We're tired. A storm might be coming, and this place is as bald as a cue ball. Doesn't look like a flood kind of storm, but I don't know."

I say nothing as Dirk talks our way out of here. I could sleep alone, but no, not without Dirk. I need my knife.

Dirk looks at me once, then continues his investigation of the space around us, voice vigorous but tired. "I have the energy for one more hard push; then we can stage ourselves for the last crossing. Set a camp up higher, the first place we find. But I'm not sleeping down here. This place is too . . ."

His eyes search.

Too what? I wonder. I wait for the next word, but even Dirk does not know.

"If the sky were clear . . . ," he says, waiting again for me to assist his sentences. "If there was someplace to sleep down here . . ."

Why this place? I know better than to believe I have found the ultimate verge here. The steps I have taken across this land, through my life, have told me that every edge is the farthest. No one place is greater or more influential than another.

Dirk moves closer. "Craig," he says.

This is where you failed, my father. You stopped at this notion. You found yourself in the tortuous bed of the maze. Was it for fear or laziness that you never moved again? Did you believe that you had found the bottom of all possible depths in your life and that that was enough, that you had discovered pure hopelessness and it was too good to abandon? You were frozen in gorgeous, horrible despair as if caught by a snake, your eyes fixed on some dark point. Is this how you died?

I feel my breath. I look at Dirk. "Let's get out of here," I say.

Dirk nods with certainty, motivation. Work to do. Canyons and cliffs to climb before dark. He turns for his gear, and I follow.

We launch packs onto our bodies and scramble against the night, rising up a side canyon that crosscuts this second chasm. This route sends us across massive bridges of stone that arc over smaller canyons, formerets and buttresses holding up the next layers. By dark we have climbed into the highest arms of this chasm. We are both moving slowly, scanning the ground, nearly shoulder to shoulder. We are looking for water and a place to sleep.

Walking just ahead of me, Dirk comes to a leaning boulder and throws his weight on it. His shoulders fall as he sits to rest. The shape of the land is barely visible around us. I round to the side of the same boulder, lean my pack against it, and slide to the ground. We will sleep here. The air is cold on my face, but not yet freezing. By this time of night I usually have my sleeping camp set, my pack contents strewn, and I'm wearing layers of everything I brought. Now, I only have on a single layer, my body hot from the climb.

Rising up from the second chasm, I feel as if I have just walked from the grasp of the predator. Throughout my life I have been performing this dance of predator and prey. I have been honed by it, turned lean and quick in my steps. There are other, less-threatening landscapes to traverse, other ways of life that would keep me warm and not hounded by falling rocks, but I have found this to be my home. I am more certain here than anywhere else, yet I know that a handful of sand is no greater than the blade of a knife.

I want to tell Dirk about these thoughts. I open my mouth, and instead of them coming out in a rational stream of conjecture and conclusion, another story emerges, the only way I have of speaking my truth.

I say, "I was in this altercation with a drunk guy once."

Dirk's head sways slightly toward me.

"I took his car keys away from him so he wouldn't get anyone killed. He pulled a knife on me. It was this big knife with a curve to it."

I show Dirk with my hands and can barely see the acknowledgment of his expression.

"Maybe he was bluffing. He's just waving this thing around, saying he's gonna cut me. I should have backed away, but I leaned right into him. Right into his face until we were breathing on each other. I told him to go ahead. Cut me. He keeps threatening me, and I'm just bizarrely calm, telling him to do it if that's what he's going to do."

Quiet for a moment, I hear Dirk pondering my tale. I add, "You see a knife, you get as close to it as you can. Dealing with a madman? Get so close that you are staring right into his eyes, until the situation is so ripe you can smell it."

Dirk finally responds. "You're a downright foolish boy. That's all there is to it."

"Foolish?" I ask. "I was alive . . . engaged . . . utterly present. Not necessarily foolish."

"Necessarily? No. Foolish? Yes. Getting up in the face of a drunk man who's got a knife?" Dirk asks, and then plants his answer: "Foolish."

"I judged the risk. I was telling him, You can't harm me with that thing. You might cut me open, but you cannot use your knife against me. We are both using it now."

Dirk shakes his head. "I've seen the situation before. I've had to deal with the knife and the drunk man. Stay away from that shit."

"But there it is," I point out. "You didn't stay away from it. That's what you and I do. We get up in the face of it."

Dirk is not looking at me as he rests against the boulder. The night saturates his view. He sees shapes, barely makes out the farthest landmark, the Diné's cliff-stripped Head of the Mother beneath thinly clouded moonlight.

Dirk's left hand claws through his hair, feels his sweat turning cold. He has spent these years pursuing the madman with the knife, shooting at him, running him down in car chases, trusting his life to him in the wilderness. He wonders how he can possibly explain to me his fear, this feeling of his manicured illusions falling away. He survives against his memories by organizing them the way a person might tend a garden, planting in perfect rows, keeping out the weeds, watering exactly when needed. Meanwhile, Dirk is devoted to this country and its disheveled order. He sees the desert in all of its flagrancy and subtlety, captured by the twists of juniper trees and the marvelous, appalling bends of canyons. He remembers that, indeed, he chose to hunt the knife-wielding drunk man, and he still calls himself sane.

Dirk was never the cop who went home easily. Always there was a looseness to his stringent world, a knowledge that if he killed a man out of rage, if his grip failed on me and I tumbled away, he might burst. How can he tell me that beautiful and savage weeds have entered his garden? Their seeds have long waited to split open, and now he feels them growing everywhere.

He asks, "Did the guy cut you?"

"No. A friend came up and grabbed me by the shoulders. He pulled me back, and we called the sheriff."

"Thank god for your friends."

I think for a moment, then say, "Thank god for yours."

I feel Dirk glancing at me, probing my faint shape in the early moonlight. Then I feel him look away.

"Let's find some water," he says. "We can set a camp right around here somewhere."

Agreed. We head in different directions in search of water.

As I walk, moonlight drifts among clouds, rolling across fields of junipers and black soil. It is the first time on this journey I have been able to move without restraint in the dark. The night landscape has been changed by the moon. Even under cloud cover, I see the hazy, dromedary shapes of landmarks around me. I see mounds of blackbrush across the narrow plain, and they look like small creatures waiting patiently, lined up along fractures in the rock where they have been able to set roots.

Even my own shadow is visible, faint but true. There is definition. The drop of a crosscutting canyon in front of me is tiered in gossamer. Blue-gray moonlight spills down the walls, losing strength until I see nothing.

I realize that this plummet in front of me is the final chasm. One last hole in the earth to cross. I walk to its brink, looking down among ledges and shoulders of sandstone. On a level below me is a reflection. It turns to black and then to liquid mercury as the clouds pass overhead. I climb to this space in the ground, dropping to its edge, my knees alert through my pants to the sharp cold of the bedrock. It is a pool of water not yet frozen. The sky is perfectly reflected through its mirror. Looking into it, I see herds of clouds grazing by. I unclip a water container from my belt and slip it in. The mirror transforms into a surface of abalone ripples.

The Only One Alive

If he had fumbled for his keys half a second longer, everything would have been fine, status quo in the city. If he had taken that instant to sling on his seat belt before gunning the engine, perhaps he would have stayed with the police force, although unlikely, for another five years, ten maybe, until retirement even.

But it did not happen that way. The timing was precise. It began with someone's call for backup. Backup is a last-ditch effort, a dire circumstance. If you respond to the call fast enough, maybe no one will be killed.

Dirk swung into his car and soon topped seventy miles

per hour down the barrel of the avenue. Predawn dark enveloped the city; the streets were vacant. He crested a slight hill. Ahead was a freeway overpass and below it a stoplight. Of the thousands of intersections in the city, this one was exactly one block from the mobile home where Ed had been killed, a nexus. A sports car was heading toward Dirk in the turn lane, a man on his hazy, early morning way home from a long night out.

Without pause, the man turned left, stepping on the accelerator. He might have seen the blur of sirens coming toward him. He may have had a flash of thought, a millisecond of electrical memory repeating *oh my god* for eternity.

Dirk tried to miss him, but he didn't quite.

At seventy miles per hour the collision was a simple sound, not multifaceted and full of communication like water, but a single broadside of metal into metal. The patrol car's spinning lights exploded. The sports car wrapped around Dirk's engine like a black glove. The driver's body somehow remained intact, but his brain turned instantly to liquid.

Without a seat belt, Dirk flew into the steering wheel. His head punched a salad-bowl crater into the windshield, and he crumpled back into his seat.

The predawn street then lay open and still like a gutted animal. The only sound was the hiss of hot engine parts. The stoplight overhead went through its motions. Green . . . yellow . . . red . . . green . . .

Only one person was still alive, and barely. Robbed of his identity, the man who had been called Dirk Vaughan slumped bleeding on the rack of a steering wheel. His patrol car was twisted into a new sculpture around him. Eventually, Dirk became aware of sensation. Pain, the first division between him

and the darkness. Elemental, urgent. With this first call to awareness, he now existed.

He knew this. Nothing more.

The next sensation was taste. It gave him imagination, a line
to follow into the world. It offered information, something salty
and acidic, like wine and meat. It was blood. He knew then that
he was a living creature.

He felt the inside of his mouth with his tongue and found
knife blades. The soft flesh of his tongue opened and bled
across his shattered teeth.

Then came the sense of loss. Things were missing. There
had been death before this moment. In his mind, puzzle pieces
separated from one another, and among them he felt emotion.
He became aware of his own heart, of an individual soul. He
was a gathering of elements, a bag of seemingly unrelated seg-
ments. He had memory now. Confusing, disconnected images
entered his head like a feverish, wakeful dream. He saw a man
strapped to an emergency room table, vomiting black sludge.
Out of the man's mouth sprang a whole crawfish, its armored
body limp and shiny as it fell to the floor. He knew this was not
a fictional delusion. The details were too memorable. He had
actually seen such a thing.

He saw a woman seated on a toilet and holding a dead fetus in
her hands, its umbilical cord leading back to her body, her eyes
turning up to him, eyes too vacant and lost to still be human.

None of these sensations seemed particularly relevant, but
each was disconcerting. They came into view like clouds drifting overhead, perennially changing from one to another.

Dirk felt his mouth again, the nest of broken teeth. The
sharp edges drew more blood from his tongue with every pass.

Finally, he opened his eyes. The scene was unreadable. His world was divided into countless tiny fragments — light, shadow, form, distance. He had to find his missing teeth. It seemed suddenly important that he not lose any more than he had already lost.

His first physical movements defined the inside of the vehicle. Its dimensions seemed strangely out of proportion; the dashboard and steering wheel were too close. The frame was bent into odd characters that did not look like a car. Looking around, he thought, Where to start?

A woman jumped out of a patrol car, its red and blue lights oscillating across the carcasses of metal. She found what remained of Dirk's side of the car and looked in, saw him groping on the floorboard with his free hand, looking for his teeth.

His sensations expanded and contracted. He became aware of hands touching him. He was being moved. The responsiveness drifted out of his reach, falling into images: a gun barrel pressed into his stomach but not fired; an old man on the floor among spilled envelopes, his chest opened by the stabs of an ice pick. Dirk was aware of invisible details within this image. He knew that the old man had been stabbed exactly twenty times. He knew the murderer would be caught the next day with the car he had bought using the thousand dollars he stole from the man. He knew that the dead man and the killer had been friends.

Dirk let go of the images when scissors began to cut his clothes away. Was he being robbed? White lights melted through his eyelids, and then came the sound of a helicopter. He was off the ground. Something has gone wrong, he thought. I am being flown to safety.

My wife, where is my wife? Is she okay?

He listened to a conversation between two men very close to him. Medical specialists. They were talking about the handgun strapped beneath Dirk's left arm. They needed to get it off in order to reach his injuries, but one said that the last time he tried to take a backup gun from an unconscious police officer, the body leaped to attention, ready for combat yet still unconscious.

Dirk lifted into their world for a moment. Without opening his eyes, he reached his right hand across his blood-covered chest. He pulled out his backup gun, clicked the safety with a thumb, spun the barrel into his palm, and handed it over butt first.

He heard the astonished silence between the two men. He felt the gun come out of his hand. Again, he fell into his dreams.

Ending on the Bathroom Floor

I sometimes imagine generations of my family as holes cut near each other in the same bedrock. Some holes are water-bearing, some dry most of the year, some carved into unexpected bands of color. Eventually, each might erode too deeply or too wide, like an envelope opened at every seam until it can hold nothing. That is how holes in stone grow old and die.

I come from a family of ravenous men, of water holes drilled insatiably downward. My father, my grandfather, and I used to drink together. We walked forest-mangy creeks fishing for small trout, carrying whiskey in our satchels and packs. In New Mexico we got drunk on the Rio Chama, with its black asteroids of basalt wearing away in the creek bed. We got drunk at Cimarron Creek, nested in its messy hair of willows and cottonwood trees. In Colorado we got drunk along the warm-blooded summer Conejos, which split meadows like a blow to the chest. We also took to the canyon-infested creeks running through Arizona's Mogollon Rim, and the rare sprinklings of water that flow into the Gila in southern New Mexico. We never went to the famous fishing rivers, the Gunnison or the Green cold below Flaming Gorge. Our lives belonged to these complicated, tinkering streams that pour through dry country like spells of magic.

On the final trip for the three of us, I was twenty-two years old. We were in the high country of northern New Mexico landing artificial flies across mirrorlike beaver ponds. We stood especially far back from shore so that the fish would not spook.

The whiskey was Yukon Jack, a square-sided bottle on the ground between us like a translation device, something we could each speak through. My father and grandfather had grown to be enormous Caesars of men, moving with storm-cloud authority and heavy guts. Cigarette smoke tangled around them as they drew their lines off the water, stringing alphabets through the air, weaving the willows unsnagged, tapping ashes to the ground between casts.

After three days we were done fishing, and we came out of the high country to close down a Mexican restaurant in Albuquerque, checking in to a hotel by midnight, our blood venomous with tequila. We sat in a room and argued and accused and talked of death. My grandfather made a point that night, explaining that if it ever came to it, he did not want to be kept alive on some machine. I said that I would pull the plug on him. My father said that death is the only freedom.

By 2:30 AM everyone was asleep, my father with his girlfriend down the hall, my grandfather and I sharing a room. Around dawn I heard my grandfather pacing in front of the imitation-wood drawers.

Jesus Christ, what time is it? My eyes refused to open. A painful, nauseating thirst scraped my gut. I barely cracked a look around, facedown in the revoltingly bleached motel pillow. Tequila was still strong in my blood. The heavy drapes were soaked in a dim blue light. I heard a complaint. Chest pains; heartburn; hand rubbing the spot. All I could do was mumble a warning about whatever he had eaten last night.

A dark thud came from the bathroom. I was out of bed instantly, hopping into pants as I crossed the room. The drapes were just then turning orange with first sunlight.

My grandfather's body occupied the entire bathroom floor. One arm had fallen over his chest. The other had somehow screwed itself behind the toilet fixtures. He was a big man. His mouth draped open in complete abandon.

I dragged him free and was on him like an owl taking prey, checking his throat for a pulse, ear against his mouth to listen into his body. There was no sound. I cradled his head and flooded his lungs with my own air.

Before I could give him a second breath, I reeled my head back. I almost vomited. He was dead. I tasted it on my lips, the foul tang of rotten meat and cigarettes.

Then, elbows bent, fists locked over his sternum, I drove into my grandfather's heart, counting each thrust out loud. Somehow, I hadn't been this close to his body since I was very young. He felt awkward, like an unresponsive horse. Again, I blew air into him, masking the taste from my mind. His body took it like a leather bag, deflating as soon as I leaned away.

Breaking the rhythm, I sprinted to the door, threw it open, and shouted down the hallway, *"Dad! Help!"*

I kicked a shoe into the door's path to keep it from locking closed, then fell back to my grandfather.

Partly dressed, shirt buttoned unevenly, my father reached the bathroom and stood still. I did not look up. I knew he was there, that he was frozen, carried off. His girlfriend ran in. She used my father's body as a stop while her voice carved the air, *"Oh my god, oh my god!"*

I kept my rhythm, counting on my grandfather's chest — *one-and-two-and-three-and-four-and-five-and* — the *and*s turning into open, holy spaces, while the whole numbers were the grunts of raw, body-to-body force. Then, pulling back his head, clamping his nose, my hand under his neck, I stretched my life from my mouth into his. It would not take hold.

I was aware at every second of my father standing there. I could see him in my mind. Do you see me now? I asked him. Do you see that I am as willful and alive as you?

My father's eyes saw a tiny, manufactured room of formfitted plastics, artificially clean, his father loose and absent on the floor like a washed-up jellyfish, his son playing out measured but pointless actions on the dead body.

I looked up at him between one maneuver and the next. A half second. I saw stars in his eyes. Far lights and the writhing blues and oranges of nebulae, brilliant clusters of pinpoints with edges trailing into chaos, crumbs of stars alone near the perimeter. My father seemed ancient and infinitely wise. He seemed like a newborn. He looked straight at me, and we understood each other. His father was dead. The generations welded through us at that moment, linking son to father to grandfather to who knows how far back.

I swayed into my task, the momentum of my body locked like a pendulum, deep heaves into my grandfather's chest.

The paramedics came, and the motel's manager pranced around them. We pulled the body into the hall, where there was more room. Doors opened. People gathered over each other's shoulders, hands on mouths, not stepping past their thresholds.

Allowing me to play out my animal urges of hope, the paramedics left me to do the chest compressions while they worked air and pure oxygen mechanically into his lungs. But it was all for show. My grandfather's heart had left him. Each of us knew this. A stranger finally touched my shoulder. My head fell into my chest.

The next day, we gathered at my grandfather's house in southern New Mexico. Seated in a living-room chair like a vengeful king, my father drank an entire gallon of vodka. He kept clattering the bottle's neck against a glass and edging the glass to his lips. I begged him, saying I did not want him to die, too. *We have seen the stars together, please stop, I don't want to lose you, too.*

"Stars?" My father's incredulous eyes swayed toward me, head following as if towed behind. "You and your goddamned stars. My father is dead."

He could not get up. Cigarette ashes gathered across the rim of his gut. Neighbors brought chicken and pie and baskets of fruit, while my father's eyes simmered and cooled and simmered again from the chair.

That evening, I saw him staring at me, an empty bottle on the floor beside him. His arm suddenly lifted, fingers bracing a cigarette that aimed between my eyes. My father mumbled something I could not hear. Through the dim living-room light and the hanging mist of smoke, the forms coming to his lips were invisible. Whatever he was saying, it was important and angry. He violently stabbed the air with his cigarette. He looked like a judge passing a sentence of death. The last word, whatever it was, ended with a tuft of ash dashed onto the floor between us.

I watched my father's hand return to the armrest; the cigarette remained skillfully in place. His head lost suspension. He vanished into the fog.

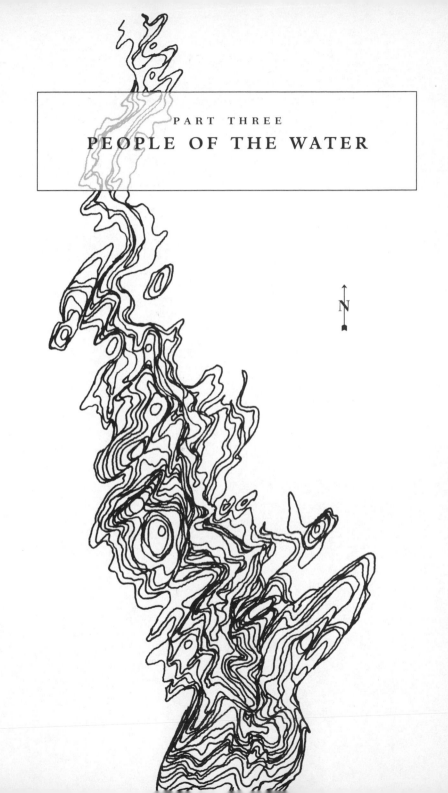

PART THREE

PEOPLE OF THE WATER

N

Black Lightning is put in the body.
Male Rain is there.
Black Water is there.
Crystal Rock is there.
In the Wide Land I walk.
In the Country of Water I walk.

— song from the first three nights of the Coyoteway

DAY THIRTEEN

Stillness. I am alone before sunrise. The air does not move. Canyons stand empty and in them lies a cold silence that even the sun cannot touch. My hands gather heavy as clay beneath my serape. After a long wait, the land holding its breath, the sun cuts the horizon. A line of light extends over my eyes.

I feel not like a man, but like a rhythm, a steady drive. I have the same measure as this land and as the first light coming across, the driving out of some shadows, the deepening of others. I am engraved by erosion this morning, a stone in the desert. I am the cadence followed by anyone who has ever walked here. This is why an infant clings with such satisfaction to its mother, listening for a heartbeat to follow. I remember that infants sometimes die when sleeping away from their mothers, overcome by the lonely silence, unable to recall the beating of their own hearts.

I wonder about the prophecy of my family name, the one that tells how I will die, how my heart will stop. The prophecies of men, I think, are myopic. They serve fear and hope but are maybe not true. The prophecies of the land, the telling of boulders and the inches of morning light, these I can believe. This is why we read tea leaves to tell the future, why we study lines in people's palms, why we build institutions around mathematics. We are looking for a heartbeat that matches our own.

I stand, and the drapes of my serape fall to my knees. Cold is on my skin. I turn back so that I can collect my night's gear. Dirk and I quickly strike our camp as I tell him that I noticed a way around to the west, a bench of stone. He says, "Good, it's about time." We load up and follow this nearby route, sent into gaps of boulders. We lay our hands on the rock, pushing and balancing ourselves.

Ahead of me, Dirk looks up, and I know that he is searching for the source of these freshly broken boulders, all of them taller than most city buildings, their edges cornered by impact. He cranes back, probing the narrowing cliffs. Where was the break? Which face gave way? How long ago? Where will you send me?

The route doubles back high over the chasm we crossed at dusk yesterday, the second chasm, the one that had been filled with so much darkness. Now we are on its opposite side and some distance downstream. Only a narrow ledge is allowed, curving dangerously into the dark below. Our hands spread on the wall to our sides, contact made. *Hold us here, please.*

Every step is frank, given just the right measure of weight and momentum. The chasm inhales below us and we stop, gingerly lowering our packs onto a wider platform, crouching, looking in. I pick up a small rock and toss it. After a few seconds, it springs off the opposite wall, then falls from view, hitting still another wall, then another, finally plucking the still water far below. The stone sinks to the floor unheard. This unfathomable

darkness seems alive to me. It consumes, quietly covering whatever falls in.

My weight taken by my knees, my hands lie on the stone. I
should have slept there last night, I think. I should have proved
that I can keep my heart beating, that it will not come to rest
even in the death of space. Only then would I have known if I
will survive where my father did not.

Dirk pulls me away again. I am caught staring so deeply that
I have trouble looking up at him when he lifts his pack. Time to
keep moving. Another crossing remains ahead.

I shoulder my pack, exaggeratedly careful with my weight,
and look back once. Out of habit. My fingers graze the smooth
stone on my necklace. I feel fragile all of a sudden, a leaf fallen
to the ground and about to be swept up.

I hear Dirk's boots across loose plates of rock. They call my
attention, and I turn from the second chasm, following him
away, the spell broken. We walk through a gap into the light,
and the morning's sunrise returns to me. I recall the earlier sensation of sitting on the rock edge, my life honed to a rhythm in
that first light. The act of remembering is so much more potent
than the act of forgetting.

As we come away, the muscular stone swales of this next
chasm lift around us. We slip through an open basin to the bell-
curve drop of a cliff.

Dirk points suddenly into the air and blurts, *"Tiny bat!"*

I look up and see the same, a dark wing-fluttering creature
that darts against the sky. This means something to both of us.
It suggests the presence of insects — bats being eaters of
insects — and then perhaps a place for them to live, vegetation
somewhere. Birds, maybe. A steady source of water. A few minutes later we come to an edge. Looking directly into the third

chasm, we see far below a silver string of flowing water. Sunlight touches it, dazzling the chasm walls with arcs of green and yellow. The water pours down ledges, the sound of loose change falling from step to step. Upstream the water is enclosed in a tight alley, a narrow swim.

I crouch to relieve the weight from my back. My arms hang across my knees.

"Tiny bat," Dirk says, nodding in agreement with some conclusion he had come to.

I look toward the chasm's head, which does not connect to any higher country. This water cannot be recent snowmelt from a far mountain; for that there would have to be a far mountain. It is not left over from the recent storm. A spring must be feeding it, water from out of the earth.

Dirk and I cut back and forth down the bell of sandstone. Shadow-bolted cliffs and humps of rock gather around one another, pinning down this small creek, holding it to a thin channel. A couple of hundred feet above the water, we are taken across crusts of dark crypto soil interrupted here and there by smooth backs of rock. Crossing these lanes of fragile, steepled substance is like walking summer sea ice in the Arctic, coming to thin spots of meltwater, finding ways around so that we don't have to slog clumsily through.

There is a place where we must cross, no way around. Soil crushes under our step as we waltz across. Here, I stop and come to one knee, my body carefully balanced under my pack. I place a finger in a mark left in the ground. Dirk stops beside me.

I say, "Human."

It is exactly where I was going to step, a faint scuff in the ground, a horseshoe divot left from the toe of a boot. How old? I trace it with my finger. Six months maybe, wind-eroded but rigid enough that it was not beaten apart by late-summer thunderstorms.

While I ponder this mark with my finger, Dirk walks this print to the next and to the next. A short distance away, he turns and says, "This person knew how to move out here." He follows the tracks back to me, doubling back in his own prints.

"Two of them," he says. "Walking just off from each other. They got this walking thing down. Kindred monkeys, I'd say, same tribe as us."

I rise to a half crouch and slowly pace out the footprints. Might we know them? Dirk is right. Instead of walking straight across, point A to point B, with an open, regular gait, these two had moved left and right, a hunting kind of walk acquired by knowing this kind of country. It is why maintained trails are such puzzling things to me, indifferent to the ground, serving a sole purpose unlike the fractures that pop out of the earth, canyon floors that command both water and footsteps. The trails out here are hardly visible at all. They are the lanes of juncos in flight, droppings of bighorn sheep cracked in drought, a footstep remembered of a partner thirty seconds ahead. These two travelers six months before us have this way of walking.

Their steps gravitate toward a bit of wash sand, where they vanish, aiming for solid rock crossings. Thin slabs of stone had been avoided lest they break underfoot. I look at Dirk, who is lining his stride with them, determining who they might have been, how quickly they were walking. He is scenting with his motions, picking up their trail, losing it, picking it up again.

I wonder at the travelers' knowledge of this place. Do they know it the way Dirk and I know other parts of this desert, moving freely without thought of folded maps, recognizing certain boulders from years before? If this is true, then in a single day they would be able to cross the entire distance that Dirk and I have walked in nearly two weeks. In our own familiar landscapes Dirk and I know the routes that can speed us across terrain in days, where others would take months, and where some would surrender, claiming the place as absolutely impossible.

I know what these two will do when they see our infrequent footprints months or weeks from now. They will examine us, riveted. Their fingers will scrape the inside of my toe. They will blow away loose sand that has gathered around Dirk's heel. They will follow us even if we are out of their way, tracking us across bare stone where we leave no prints, reading our minds by the directions we choose, seeking a small rock that only a boot will break, searching for even the scatter of that same broken rock when I stopped and turned around to erase the mark of my passage. This is how they will know us.

Dirk and I walk down a belt of sandstone with this new knowledge of human presence. I think of these other travelers as I move, watching them in front of me, behind me. Other people, strange animals like myself. They appear beneath my next step, a dead gray branch of juniper partly snapped on the ground, right with me, the same move. I become curious when I do not find a track in hardpack sand where someone should have stepped, where there should still be a faint impression. I stop and look for another possibility, spotting a way not far to my left. I walk in that direction, assuming that these two people came through here and dropped into this funnel of a short canyon. Eventually I hear Dirk descending behind me.

Dirk passes me and is the first to reach the chasm floor. I stop above him, just at the margin of marbled light reflected up the walls. I resist going down. Although as immense as the two others, this third chasm seems strangely serene. The water sings down the passage. It gives an illusion of meaning to this landscape, elucidating the form and function of this chasm's every bend. It feels good. But it is alien. We could actually walk along it, where the other chasms had been impassable. I feel like a raven hesitating over some unfamiliar object on the ground, strutting near to it, ready at any moment to startle away, opening my black wings, accusing it with a voice of gravel and stone. What is this thing below me, this beautiful creature of clear, sunlit water and carved earth?

I drop my pack, pull out the map, and study the place from an overhead perspective. The chasm appears long and fairly straight between topographic lines. Straight? Out here? This is nonsense. It should be wrapped inside out and backward. And when have I ever seen water flow like this through an unknown desert?

With the map flagging from my hand, I speak down to Dirk, who is at the edge of the water. "Let's get a camp set somewhere. We have enough food, plenty of water. Keep it light and go back, check out those last chasms we crossed."

Dirk looks at me as if I were insane. "What are you talking about, going back?"

"Just drop back into the last two crossings. Poke around a little. We were moving too fast for me to get a good look."

"They were dead ends."

"I'm sure there are other routes. Must be."

"Listen, this is the promised land. I'm not going back into Satan's eternal glory hole when I'm here in the land a god-damned milk and honey. That place damn near killed me."

Dirk disregards my deliberation and comes to one knee. He puts his hand into the water, then feathers it with his fingers the way a merchant might examine a sack of beans. He looks upstream, sees the gathering walls of sandstone, huge and pale. He judges the chasm's dimensions. From what he learns in this instant, he can assess the water's quality. He knows its history, how there is very little mud, mostly sand, telling him that it flows mostly across stone. It does not come from far away. It is good water, drinkable. Springwater. Planting both hands in the stream bed, he lowers his mouth and drinks.

Even with the way the country we just crossed lures me back, I share Dirk's curiosity. This unexpected stream is full of diamonds. Bubbles gather and spread below each short water-fall. I drop down behind Dirk. The stream floor is a coral-reef waterscape: sand ripples and ghostly, decaying cottonwood leaves that have drifted down from far off. I drink. The water tastes nothing like that of a water hole, no greenish flavor of rampant life, no dark putrefaction. It is water that runs year-round, host to beetles and threads of algae making their way unhurried through their life cycles. It tastes like nothing at all in my mouth, yet there is a flavor. It is the taste of presence.

Among the aquatic life below me are zips and spins of nearly invisible insects and crustaceans eating back chlorophyll hay-fields of greenery. From my knees, I watch the cowlike grazing of caddis fly larvae in their cases made of twigs and sand grains. Patrols of waterborne predators loom over these herbivores.

I realize that my sense of scale has been ruled by hugeness over the past several days of walking. I have been in an enor-mous landscape, my eye constantly drawn to infinitely distant points. For the first time in days I am taken by smallness, chevrons of ripples leading into a chute of water, the darting of coffee-stained beetles into groves of algae.

My eyes drift away. I study the curve of ridgelines that Dirk and I have just come through, figuring out the best way to return beyond last night's camp into the deep fissures that lie behind us. Dirk sees my gaze and follows it.

"I'm not going back there," he says.

I draw my lips together. "Aren't you even curious?"

"Listen, this is the winter ass end of nowhere. It's not like we just pulled into the Hilton parking lot and we've got mints waiting on our pillows. We don't even know what's up ahead. We still have to find the way out. Mister Toad's Wild Ride ain't over yet."

But I do not want to back away. I don't believe Dirk. The wild ride is behind us. I'm afraid that I have not finished my business here. I still nervously tinker with my necklace, eyes tracking the land we have just come down. I leave Dirk and stroll along the smooth, round floor of the chasm to sort out my feelings.

I stop at a scent, my head jarring to grab it. It smells like fur, like an animal, musky and dark.

Immediately the scent is gone, passed by as soon as I move. I step backward to try to walk through it again. It is no longer there. I trace the air, lifting my nose. What animal was that? I wonder, reaching down, wetting my fingers, then dampening the rings of my nostrils. I can smell the sandstone's slow rusting and the dry wood of dead junipers. But no animal. I walk nearly in a circle, crossing the stream with a leap, then crossing back.

It had been the musty smell of a large animal. Bighorn sheep. Mountain lion, maybe. Something nearby, up one of these shaded canyons closing in from every side. It's too close for a coyote. Coyotes tend to keep their distance. I remember my father and his coyote hunts, how he was able to draw them to us. Maybe I should not be so certain of what I believe about coyotes.

I cannot recapture the scent. My memory does not have

enough of it to grab. Mountain lion, I believe, just because it is a pleasing thing to think. It is the only animal of size that would allow us to come so near to it, trusting its stealth not to be seen.

This talisman necklace I wear is a gift from a mountain lion. A full-grown male once approached me at a water hole. I was alone. The lion circled me from ten feet away, green, calm eyes hunting my strengths and weaknesses. Never once did I break eye contact. When it was done, when it decided whatever it needed to about me, it left, and I stood there frozen. I was wearing this pendant at the time, but low, out of sight on a long cord. The necklace that I kept tight at my throat in those days — my protection — was the image of a raven, something I had worn for years. After the lion left, I reached to touch the raven pendant and found it gone. It had fallen off, and even though I searched the ground, I could not find it. I then tightened this claw of greenstone to my throat, a new reminder, the sharpness of a predator hanging as protection in the delicate cup at the base of my throat.

My fingers trace the pendant as I settle on this thought, that a mountain lion has been watching Dirk and me.

I look up.

No one there. I check my back, my front. I look across the high benches around me where the animal would be so easily camouflaged.

There is a mountain lion in this chasm, I think. I turn back toward Dirk. I am ready to walk with him. This ride is not over.

———

Elephant heads and mosque domes, hieroglyphics two hundred feet tall. We walk under a clear night sky, the land raging with the chill fire of moonlight, dust grays and cream shades, no true colors at all here on the ground. No reds, no oranges, no yellows. Stars float around the near-full moon, turning the sky into the only color visible, a royal, ink-saturated blue. Dirk and I cross the stream back and forth, jumping, scrambling as we follow the third chasm. Our packs grind as they touch the walls. Footsteps echo in this darkly lit space.

Every once in a while we have to use our lamps as we cross through gulps of shadow. My light swings down and meets moving water. The sight reminds me of times when I have been deep inside caves and have turned my headlamp onto some small, subterranean stream. The skeleton of the water's movement becomes visible, a thing that cannot be seen in sunlight. I see the glacial rippling of shadows, patterns and pathways revealed as if looking through the planes of a crystal. I do not keep my light on the water for long. It seems to me to be an intrusion. But just for a moment, I crouch at the water and stare into it.

Dirk and I reach the dry cove of a side canyon. We pass between its gateway walls. It is one of those canyons that could go on for miles, but it ends as soon as we enter, a giant, egg-shaped hollow, the plunge point of a flood's waterfall. Even in the moon's brightness, the walls of this canyon have no edges. It is as if this strange light is water, a solution, an agent that dissolves solids. Milk sand lies in a circular plain in this side canyon, and in the very center stands a solitary redbud tree. We are both drawn to the tree, pure caution in our movements, even more care than when we catwalked the second chasm earlier today. The tree gives off rays of spidery, leafless shadows. We do not walk in these shadows. We walk around them, as if reading the script on some monolith.

In the shape of this room is the roundness of an enormous flood, a whirlpool that has shaved away the bedrock and filled the floor with sand. The eye of the flood must have been here, the only place lacking in turbulence. The redbud tree is the single seed kept safe in the center. There is nothing else alive in here.

The tree is not tall. Its head is pressed down by floods, forcing the branches to swirl around one another. Its branches have taken the floods into their shapes, obeying the twist of water, becoming the flood. I have seen this same phenomenon, a mirror to the environment, in the way junipers take on drought, distorted as if in some elegant and painful dance. It is the fluid curvature of defiance and acceptance.

The tree's shadows cross in and out of its branches. One moment it looks as faint as lace, and I can imagine that the tree is not even here, that we will wake in the morning and find that we had seen only a ghost, an anagrammatic memory of a living thing. The next moment I touch it, and the rattle-bone branches clack against one another like a skeleton shrugging its shoulders.

Dead branches have fallen to the ground. Dirk and I reach down and gather them. Not far away, we build a small fire. So cold tonight. Dry cold, every motion flushing out pockets of meager warmth in our clothing. Our breath does not show in the air. The idea of sleep, of laying our bodies on this dry-ice sand, is chilling. We hug the fire, eyes carried down into it.

Eventually we use the last of our wood. The flame tapers. Coals tick and crack as the air shifts. Mostly, it is a still night, silent but for the stream's distant talking. We turn away to sleep on the sand. A cone of moonlight stretches through our canyon.

When it passes, we are shut into the dark and the redbud vanishes.

All-Night Refuge

Surgeons stitched Dirk closed after the accident. When he was again fit, the police department gave him his guns, sat him in a new patrol car, and sent him back to the streets, where he did nothing at all.

He now preferred parking lots. He clocked barely enough miles each night to account for driving from one parking lot to the next. He told headquarters that he would still shoot, he would still scramble faster than anyone on the team, but until that moment came he would be here, waiting in the predawn quiet of his patrol car. He would position himself in the driver's seat, taking refuge behind Johnny's Diner ("Breakfast, Burgers & Shakes") and just sit in the late-night radio silence, surrounded by a fortress of strip malls. The parking lot was empty and clear on all sides, so no one could walk up without warning.

Another patrol car sidled up, parking mirror to mirror, the way horses sometimes do, swatting each other's flies with their tails.

Dirk rolled down his window and after calm greetings said, "I'm losing touch with this menagerie."

The guy in the other car nodded slowly and said, "Don't worry, it'll come back."

"No, I don't think it will," Dirk said, gazing out the window at the featureless blacktop. "There's always been this part of me watching in horror. I don't think I can look at it anymore."

The other officer listened patiently. He knew Dirk's fear. One day you wake up and there is nothing but a meaningless shroud of violence, when yesterday there had been tapestries of crimes, a delicately woven fabric of danger and resolution. You weaken. You become cruel, unnecessarily violent. You kill. You die. He does not know how to help. He figures Dirk will snap out of it.

Dirk moved from there to another refuge, in the streetlights and tree shadows a block down from a convenience store. His radio was tuned to a local rock station. The car thumped lightly with the music. Dirk's eyes barely reflected the radioactive computer glow off the dash. He saw a teenage girl walking by. He drove over, rolled down the window, asked a few questions.

Typical response. Girl out after a fight with her friend, walking home before sunrise. Teenage theatrics.

Dirk told her to get in, he'd give her a ride home. She did not have a choice. He went through the routine, calling the station, taking her address, recording the data, the mileage, the destination, the cause and the proposed effect. The girl lived in a fairly wealthy part of the city, houses ringed with moats of lawns. At that hour, each one seemed like a sleeping beast. The girl was unaffected, answering questions without care as they parked.

Dirk escorted her to the door, rang the doorbell, and the porch light came on. Everything was procedural. Parents, early forties, stood there gaping. Dirk asked if he could step inside, just make sure everything was fine before he left. The parents stepped back, stunned, father saying, "Of course, of course."

As Dirk entered, the mother seemed overly excited. "Oh

god, not the police. Not the police." She began pointing at Dirk's patrol car, demanding that he move it. Dirk explained that he would be gone in a moment, that he just wanted to make sure that everything was all right.

The mother's voice began ringing like a struck piece of metal. She fired accusations at the girl, who ran up the stairs crying, while the husband smiled sheepishly. The mother ordered Dirk to leave.

In a moment, just give me a second.

The husband kept smiling as if he had something very painful in his rectum. He said to Dirk, "Really, you should go. Thank you for being so patient."

But the mother's voice continued its ascent. "Why did this need to happen? You parked right in front of our house. Do you have any idea what this looks like?"

"Please, lady. I'll be gone in a moment, I just . . ."

"I can't believe this," she belted, her pitch rising like a steam kettle. *"You just park here? You just think you can do that? People can see!"*

The woman started screaming as if Dirk had broken through the membrane of her mind. He tried to explain what needed to happen, that she should remain calm, but she began upending the furniture, throwing objects like a small dog furious in the trash. She caught Dirk's instincts, her movements too swift and uncontrolled. His body widened, fingers extending in preparation: reaching for his gun; deflecting a blow; restraining and handcuffing; protecting his face.

The woman shrieked at Dirk that he had to move his car, that he could not imagine her agony. She ran into the kitchen, and plates began to shatter against the floor.

The husband turned to Dirk and for the first time dropped his smile, replacing it with a timid, ghostly sternness. "You should leave now."

"Fuck no, I'm not leaving. What the hell is going on here?"

"She's just upset."

Dirk looked at him for half a second in disbelief, thinking, You, little man, are very frightening. Dirk paced directly into the kitchen, where an amazing array of dishware was being destroyed. The woman rampaged through the coffee cups and on to the drinking glasses. With hair lashing her face, she pointed straight at Dirk.

"YOU WILL LEAVE! YOU ARE NOT HERE! YOU MUST GO!"

More than anything, Dirk wanted to flee. But the paperwork and the explanation of what he saw and why he left a problem unresolved must be filed. If he walked away and the next day this house became the investigation scene of a suicide/double homicide, he would have no recourse. Yet this was none of his business. He did not belong here.

While the woman crashed and screamed, commands launched through Dirk's head. *Solve the problem. Find the solution. Kill this animal!* His fingers twitched. His gun was there, in its holster. The wisdom he had once found, that he had when he'd walked through a street-side crowd to shoot a badly suffering horse, was no longer available. He felt the urge. Pull your gun and silence this woman. *There must be peace.*

As glass shattered and the screaming continued, Dirk pulled his radio and called for backup.

Five minutes later, the woman was handcuffed and still screeching. Every house on the block basked in overlapping waves of blue and red police lights as the other officers dragged the woman across the lawn and shut her into one of the cars.

There must be peace.

Dirk could still hear her, muffled now, but screaming all the same.

He ducked into his patrol car and sat there for a moment. A moment of quiet before driving to headquarters to file yet another blueprint of human madness. Dirk felt the sag of his shoulders. Every answer he might call upon seemed false.

DAY FOURTEEN

In the first mushroom-blue light of morning, Dirk and I gather our things and go, leaving the redbud tree behind. Travel has changed for us. The demands now revolve around moving water and sheer rock to which we cling like spiders. We are bottom-walking, an entirely different experience from these past days of poising among scaffold platforms and benches hung midway up the chasms. Now, the palm of the land holds us. We are in the focal point, the lowermost of places, our course defined by the lay of this single chasm.

Rumors of side canyons appear from above, their shadows lifting away like laughter. Eventually, there are no other canyons at all. The chasm becomes its own, conferring with no one else. Round cliffs bully over us until in places the sky is gone for good.

In the faintness of inner morning shadows, far below sky-scraper streaks of sunlight, our route becomes too narrow. There is no place to climb so as to avoid the stream. Ice lines the edges of the water. Damp sand is splintered and heaved by frost. Dirk and I pull off our pants and our boots, hoisting our packs high onto our shoulders. Dirk goes first. He slides into the water.

I am behind him, skin flayed inch by inch as the water deepens. I pass the terminal depth, my testicles pierced by bee-sting cold. My feet test the stone floor and turn awkwardly sideways for support along the crack. My hands brush walls on both sides to hold me up. Water slaps and hushes around me. The cold does not truly come, though, until we crawl out of the water. My skin blisters red in the air as I sit on a boulder. I have been dipped in acid. I pull on socks, pants, boots, and keep moving.

Now the chasm bends open and closed. I imagine a snake, the way it breathes, each of its hundred ribs swelling and falling back, swelling again. I recognize the architecture. This is the same orderly back-and-forth I saw in the clockwise and counter-clockwise water holes we watched during the snowstorm. This is the vortex street, the fluid mechanics of resistance and motion. I see now why this chasm appears straight on the map. Seen from an airplane, it would be only a linear passage, a generally direct line cut through the floor of this land. But that is only a roof over a still-deeper level. Down here the chasm's true course sweeps wildly back and forth, digging under the earth, hiding itself from view. Ceilings of solid stone hang immensely tall over us as we are slung into the bends. Every word spoken between us swells, deepening and booming.

Gulfs of chasm walls rise over us as we follow the stream down into the planet. We are walking upstream, heading for the source, yet we are burrowing deeper, cutting into solid rock. The encircling shadows are touched with a faint light, a warm remnant of the now midday sun.

Dirk and I both stop, heads craned. This chasm is larger and more confined than any I have ever seen. The proportions do not register easily in my head. This is what it is like looking through astronomical photographs of galaxies, the vastness meaning nothing and at the same time seeming eerily familiar. The structural design is preposterous, sweeps of continuous stone pulled back like a woman's long hair.

We set an early camp inside these bowls of shadow, laying our gear on a flood terrace, its high ground covered with glossy gems of water-rounded stones. We sit with them as we eat from bags of nuts. We pass back and forth the last of our pulverized dates, scraping them out with a spoon.

With our day packs Dirk and I walk farther up the chasm, checking the few narrow side canyons for escape, and find ourselves pushed back to the center every time, as if a hand were nudging us, insisting that we stay in the chasm floor. Water runs in the very back of a bend, curving around the outside stretch. Water sounds wrinkle and lift. They are small tones, privately elaborate. Thickets of maidenhair ferns are suspended over this water, growing right out of the rock. Our map does not describe this. The maps we make in our heads are little better. We register the light movement of a breeze through the ferns, their coral-black stalks trembling.

Dirk turns his head up to see the ceiling, chest rising to take in the air.

Man, you might say, is nature dreaming, but rock
And water and sky are constant —

His voice rains back on him word by word, growing, changing, drifting away.

I stand still, knowing he said this only to hear himself
echoed back, to hear the way this place bends the poetry.

We walk farther, following the water through its cave. The
floor greens with moss. Even the loose rocks fallen two hundred
feet from the ceiling have been blanketed, hands of moss feeling over whatever rests too long. Ferns crouch as if drinking at
the trickle.

Dirk and I come to the print of an animal. It is impressed
like a fist into stars of moss. Both of us bend to it, neither touching. There is no doubt: rounded, claws retracted, toes pushed
away from each other. Mountain lion.

How fresh? Can't say, not in this exotic medium of moss. But
that is not the question. There is, in fact, no question. A lion has
been here. The control of its step is visible, head down as it
glided through, tail carried like a weapon in a sheath of velvet. It
is all we need to know.

There are things that most of us have been led to believe
about animals. The proliferations of glossy nature photography
and staged wildlife footage on television have censored their
lives, restricting each to its own popular image — the eagle is
sweeping and stoic, the mountain lion watchful and relentless,
the pronghorn ceaselessly alert. In many of our stories, includ-
ing ones that I have told, we have stripped animals of much of
the personal ingenuity that we ascribe to ourselves. This track
before us now is from an animal's real life. It tells something
personal about a creature moving alone and with sincerity. I
know that the lion craves the quickness and flush of the kill,
that it is an unparalleled predator in this desert, but I can also

see in this single print that it is not just a ravenous beast. It did not come through here pressed deep in a run. It was not turned slightly away from the axis of the chasm, warily listening ahead. Like us, it came through on its way.

Neither Dirk nor I lay a finger into this track. We crouch around it and imagine ourselves as animals living here, following the path.

The Sportspal Rides Again

Sitting among porch furniture at my father's house, I watched skeptically as he flurried around his canoe with tools in hand. Lights were hung and propped here and there so that even at night he could keep working. His ashtray overflowed like a backed-up toilet. Two cigarettes going at once. He put one down, moved to another side of the canoe, picked up the second, and took a drag.

The Sportspal was made of aluminum so light that it required a spread of ribs to keep a person from falling through. My father had pulled the canoe up on top of a metal outdoor dining table like a submarine dry-docked for repairs.

When I was a child my father would take me to desert reservoirs with the Sportspal, and we would fish all day. We would rest our paddles and rods to sit silently in the dusk. I remembered so many evenings that we waited until phosphorescent bands of skylight finally relinquished the stars. Every movement caused the canoe to nearly tip, so we did not move. When we paddled it was slow, as if sneaking up on an enemy, as if deep in a meditation.

The canoe's useful life ceased when my father drove into the garage with it still strapped to the top of his truck. With a loud grinding sound and an avalanche of metal pieces and bits of ceiling, the canoe became one of my father's many unkempt items. It joined the spiderwebbed, blocked-up cars parked around the front yard and the cupboards overloaded with broken kitchen appliances. The canoe remained in this state, leaning hopelessly against the garage wall, cared for by black widows, until my father decided that the Sportspal would float again.

He went at it with a blowtorch, masking the bow in fiberglass, adding the tiniest of screws to the gunwales. He pointed out to me the genius of his repairs, how he had dismantled parts of one of his front-yard vehicles and spliced them into the canoe's chine. He asked my opinion a couple of times. I sat back, a cynic on the sidelines. I told my father that this was nothing but a low-walled lake canoe. I was accustomed to expertly finished wooden dories and deeply rockered white-water canoes. I told him that I wouldn't trust it on even flat water. Too unwieldy, I said. Poorly built for the demands of water.

My father went on undaunted, his hands toiling inside the canoe like a surgeon unscrewing someone's lungs. He said that tonight it would float. It would be majestic. We would test it together. When was the last time we were in this thing? I had been twelve? thirteen?

I was thirty-one now.

Was my father drunk? Hard to tell, the way he busied himself in this task of repair. Maybe it did not matter. I watched him dart around the canoe, cigarette hanging from his lips, caught up by his words as he mumbled about the strength of epoxy and the need for screws of a certain size. I could not remember the last time he was like this, when he was not stalking through the house, his eyes narrow with attack, doors slamming. These last years of his life had been filled with rage. When his wife left him, he smashed in through her apartment window to get her back. He ripped the phone out of her wall when she tried to call the police, only then realizing that he had slashed open one of his wrists on the window and needed to go to the hospital. But there was no longer a phone to call for help, so his wife had to drive him. This was the environment he lived in.

But on this night, I realized that I was looking at an ordinary man, a man with hobbies, interests, with honest questions riding on his tongue. His more customary wizardry and aimless ferocity knotted suddenly into a single person, not a god and not a demon. An everyday human being.

My father asked if I wanted anything to eat, and when I said maybe later, he continued milling with the screwdriver, telling me that there were leftovers in the fridge. He'd heat them up for me. At that, I wanted to rise from my seat and touch his face. I wanted to cry against his chest, feeling his arms pull me in. Talk of such simple things was something that I had not heard in years.

After my father had refastened the last of the twenty-odd ribs, he said, "Done. Let's get this thing into the water."

We carried it together, lowering it into my father's swimming pool — a kidney-shaped basin that every other year he let lapse into an aquatic biology experiment because he did not have the heart to introduce chlorine and interrupt the life cycles he had allowed to begin.

My father handed me a stubby wooden paddle, the only one.

"You are the master of rivers," he said. "Tell me if this is a good boat."

I carefully studied his voice, the precise intonation, and I found no sarcasm in it. He wanted me to approve of his creation. He believed that I was a master of rivers. I gathered up these words of his and stored them for whenever this would end.

In the pool, I lowered myself into the stern and braced my knees against the canoe hull instead of taking the seat. This gave me a better position to ward off capsize. My father came in awkwardly with his body weight. I balanced the canoe as he situated himself onto the seat at the bow. Every sway and shift of my father's body was communicated to me through the canoe's tugs and dips. This was an old skill of mine, from years of guiding and reading people's fears and demands as they stepped into my boat.

Through the gunwales and the hull, I felt something from my father that I had not expected. He trusted me.

With both of us in, I could feel the weight of water pressing in on the canoe. But it held. The Sportspal floated. With the most practiced of drawstrokes and sculls, I spun the canoe to and fro, never once tapping the tile decking. My father reclined, enjoying the fluid motions that I gave to him.

Finally I set the paddle down so that it rested on the gunwales. The canoe did not move.

"Your boat is good," I told him.

"Thank you," he said.

Then he said nothing, his body still and dark in front of me. The canoe floated, and we were silent together, the city sky overhead offering its few stars.

DAY FIFTEEN

Walking through this final chasm, I keep my eyes lowered, not so much out of gratitude or awe, but so I can keep moving. I do not want to be scrambling for my journal every second, gawking and recording. Even so, my head turns up and I stop.

The ceiling of this bending chasm is a planetarium. With fingers ticking into my pocket, I fish out my journal. It is difficult to move down here not because of obstacles and impasses, but because my eyes drift and I have to write things down. I have never been good at saga crossings of the desert. I get caught in the middle of places like this, trapped by spaghetti canyons, frozen beneath the back-bending curve of a cliff because I do not want to walk away.

Dirk and I have been uselessly scouting for routes out of this third chasm this morning. We have left our camp behind for the day. I am alone now. The very back of this bend glows with the underwater jade of whittled sunlight. My head tilts up as if I might rise out of my own skeleton. The stream's ventriloquist voice curves into the rounded ceiling, and I am looking for it, expecting somehow to see a mirror of water running high overhead. I originally had a question about this landscape, looking left and right, wondering where in the terrain of his life my father had first made his fatal error, where he turned and got lost, and lost again, until he could never get out. Now there is only one way. The route is unavoidable. The chasm is no longer giving choices. This is the part of the maze where I walk ahead as if falling down the yawn of a well, the final corridor pushing at my heels, leading me along.

Dirk is somewhere ahead. He left me here to my musings, tired of waiting for my journal scribblings to end. It is not possible to lose each other in this sole passage. I stay for a while and admire the formations high above, the pieces of boulder soon to divide and fall. I am in a bomb zone. Javelins of rock fallen from above stand nose-first in the ground, hard obelisks everywhere. Stream water winds among this breakage, sheltering itself as far back as it can reach. I pocket the journal and walk on from here, stepping through this red-rock dust of Mars.

I find Dirk lying on his back in a tiger stripe of light, eyes closed to the morning warmth. He is in the single thin space between stone faces where sunlight is allowed through. It stabs its way down, most of the light lost against higher walls. I stop beside him, and he opens his eyes. He talks to me, using the gentle voice of a cloistered monk.

"The strange place where my spirit goes . . ."

I can hear that he has been waiting for me, that he has been gathering his words for my arrival, each one planted like a seed into soil.

His meters go on. "Where ravens rip away the flesh and collect bones for the pile they dance around."

This is not someone else's poetry, not something gleaned from the big book we brought along. These are his own words.

Dirk sits up and stretches his back, making way for a story with his body. He tells me about an event from his childhood, a story I'd never heard. He once made a fish trap out of chicken wire and tossed it into a city canal where, for amusement, he would catch a perch, maybe a bass, then let it go. After giving the trap some time, he pulled it from the water and found inside of it a fish as big as a table dictionary. It was streaked and painted in colors, startlingly thin when viewed edge-on, like a plate. This was a fish of the tropics, he figured, like the legendary crocodile babies flushed down toilets, grown monstrous in the sewers. Stripes and bands leaped across the fish's body as it struggled. The fish seemed to Dirk as jigsawed and brightly colored as classroom maps of the world. The trap was nearly too small. It was a miracle that he had caught this fish at all, that it was able to fit through the one-way opening.

Without hesitation, Dirk slid the trap back into the murky soup of the urban canal. He ran and gathered friend after friend, knocked on doors, called into backyards, told everyone that he had caught a sunfish, whatever a sunfish was. He escorted his friends to the canal, and they were ready for a performance, for the stunning King Kong of fish to be revealed. Dirk was prepared to marvel at the emblazonry, giving to his friends what they had never before imagined coming out of this scrawny canal. Boys stood at the edge staring at the line that led into dark water. Dirk reached in, driven by seriousness, as if partaking in important scientific work, bringing a new species into the light of day. He lifted out the chicken-wire contraption. It was empty.

Dirk held the trap for a long moment. There was no embarrassment, even at the laughing and scornful words of the boys. Dirk only stared in disbelief. The trap seemed uninspired, vacant. He could not speak.

He still holds that empty cage in his hands. Even now he marvels at the impossibility of the fish's escape. The fish had been so large, and the cage so small, and it happened so long ago to carry such weight in his memory.

Suddenly, Dirk sweeps himself up, grabs his day gear, and slips the climbing rope around his shoulder.

"Gotta move," he says.

I remain still for a moment. I stay with Dirk's magical fish, imagining its escape, imagining young Dirk Vaughan enthralled by both its appearance and its disappearance, remembering, This is why I am with you; you are also pursuing the Great Carp. Then I quicken to catch up.

The chasm will come to an end soon. There is a wall in the back, a stopping point that eclipses the chasm below. It is a clean slab rising far beyond reach through striations of claret colors, a thousand feet up to nowhere. But as Dirk and I walk, the chasm does not come to an end. It tightens. The bends collapse into each other, an accordion passageway, gathering on themselves the way a snake bunches against a warm rock, the clear blood of its stream pooling and falling down the center.

For a short length, the chasm widens. We enter the thick of marshy vegetation on the floor. Horsetails shudder and grind like dry wheat. Whipping limbs of willows snap at our cheeks and earlobes, bringing tangs of pain. The floor is broad and soaked wall to wall, the watery bed invisible beneath rugs of dead plants, willows and reeds jutting upward. Dirk and I walk as if stepping through a bog: heel in first, then a jump and the dark soak of pants to just above the boot leather, next foot down through the sparkling floor of dead reeds into the unknown. Vengeful stalks of poison ivy are leafless and difficult to pick out in the winter. I walk with two hands in front of me, slipping open a passage.

We narrow into a pen of low cliffs and minefields of cattails. We move carefully, not budging the cattail seed heads lest we be vomited upon by billows of floating down. The vegetation here is a jail, bars and crossbars blocking our movements. I stop in this cattail thicket. The pods are dry as punk, ripe and ready to explode. I cannot help myself. With the back of my hand I slap one of them, and thousands of starlike seeds burst into the air. They are immediately everywhere, and Dirk flashes me a quick scowl. *What the hell?*

As soon as he looks at me that way I thrash through several other stalks to prove my point. Dirk gives me even more of a look, but then is distracted by the way the clouds of seeds float around him, rising over his head, passing between his fingers. He lifts his hands, not to shield himself, but to give context to the passage.

There is an easy breeze not far above us, and the seeds loft into it. The chaos of this pillow fight is suddenly channeled into the air. Cattail vapors corkscrew upward. Drafts curl up through the chasm, drawing the seeds into order.

I crash through more and more cattails to watch the seeds fly. At first they hang in the befouled air at the chasm floor, clogging my nostrils, feathering my lips. Then they are snatched into the wind up higher, a pale, ivory dye turned sheer as clouds. Level after level, these tracers rise into different winds, spiral galaxies, and down-welling sinks, turning the sky into a map of wringing hands. I have never seen such a thing. I have seen cigarette smoke worried into question marks, and I have seen blood swirling through a clear stream, but never a chasm sky overflowing with arteries of wind and seed.

Between the two worlds that my father spoke of lies this dust. Between Dirk and me, between the known and the unknown, is a fine mist that holds us together the way electrons are kept in each other's company even as they threaten to speed away. It is the binding that I feel surrounding me. The order of the land is my reflection, my vision into my own life. It is a happenstance of arrangement, a native compulsion for structure in this universe. My eye is so easily caught by the extravagant flash of entropy and of gestation that I forget that between these two is inestimable dust, the floating seeds that trace for us the greater paths. Moments ago patterns had lain invisible in the wind, meaning nothing to me. Only this sudden passage of thousands upon thousands of cattail seeds exposes the implication.

The seeds fly into an even higher wind, where they finally burst apart, grabbed and shoved by a mad, high gust that Dirk and I cannot hear from this far below. Some ribbons of seeds slide into still-higher winds that cross one atop the next. Overhand knots of wind and seed spread away to nothing, missionaries of cattails sent to far nations where some will plant and most will die. This is why children watch their lost balloons float away. It is why they accidentally let go of them in the first place. They stare up at the accelerated back-and-forth of their cherished balloon, the string dangling as it lifts away, hand open on the ground in astonished surrender.

Dirk opens both of his hands to the air. "Life moves," he says, turning slowly to watch the seeds. "Go into the world. Find your place. Set roots. Die."

Ashes

Only a matter of months after my father died, I gathered some of his ashes in a pouch and walked with Dirk for a month across the desert in Utah. We used a series of stashed canoes to ferry the Colorado River and, days later, the Green River. We walked toward a specific place, a devouring land of steeples. We traveled between columns of rock, down in the snug spaces, the enclosures and cavernous passageways between. At dawn on the twenty-seventh day of our journey, Dirk and I planned to walk across a great bridge of stone. There, standing beside Dirk in the calm of a winter's dawn, I would let my father go.

But this was not how it happened.

The night before there was a windstorm. In the dark, rocks screamed like animals. We sank our gear into boulders and meager overhangs, making sure not to bring out journals or anything small. Rock dust lashed our eyes. Dinner was abandoned in the hail of wind. We instead relied on sacks of dry, hand-snatched food. Both of us withdrew into cracks like crabs against the shadow of a hunter, bodies drawn tightly. Nothing could be spoken between us.

I suddenly grabbed the pouch that held my father's ashes and lurched into the open. He and I had not lived the way I had wished. We had not floated in peaceful air. The storm had often been upon us. This wind pulled fiercely at me.

My body, everything I sensed and imagined, was a fabric of chromosomes, a walking, breathing phantom, a recollection of countless generations extending ceaselessly back. I was the utter improbability of survival. My bones were nothing but stories ready for the telling.

Into the night-black of the storm, I staggered. I opened the pouch, standing hard in the wind, feet apart so that I would not be thrown to the ground. My father swiftly billowed into the gale. Fragments of his burned bones sounded like shells clattering away in the boulders.

Still louder than my father's bones, more deafening than his memories, was this wind. I no longer heard my rattle-bone father. I heard only wind.

Take me, wind. Bury my stories in your howling. Turn me into your dunes, your incalculable grains.

I could no longer stand against the force. I bunched the pouch into my fist and stumbled back to shelter.

DAY FIFTEEN

I stop for an instant in the quiet trickling of water. I turn once to see if Dirk is behind me. He is not. I continue, moving quickly, knowing that within minutes I will find the source of this stream, the upper end of the third chasm. The high wall I can see at the back is clean and parched, so I know that the water is coming straight from the rock face. I also know that I will reach a dead end, no way out. But I move toward it anyway.

I have long been drawn to springs, emergence points where water comes to its first sun and shade. The Diné singer had mentioned the importance of the springs, how they stand as major intersections along the Protectionway ceremony. I have heard many stories of springs from numerous cultures. Even fountains in cities are gathering points, moments of grace within bedlam.

I move swiftly, nearly running, dropping under the smacking limbs of sinewy willows, leaping from one side of the narrow stream to the other. A confluence of two canyons passes by. I glance once into the dry canyon at my right. It rises more steeply than does the watercourse. Its floor is made of dry sand. I file this impression without slowing: a swift twist of drainage, little hope of a way out. I pass on.

Were the Diné here? Was this the sacred spring they came to? I have long been interested in such refugee ceremonies as the Protectionway, reading ethnographic reports on them as if the reports themselves were omens. At home I have a heavy antiquarian book on the Ghost Dance, a performance once meant to banish the Anglo invasion, to dissolve bullets in midair. I've come to wonder if those who died during the Ghost Dance, those cut down by rapid-fire weaponry during trances, were nothing but links in the prophecy. They were prophets themselves, opening the path for the next generation, ensuring that this ancient passage does not slip from memory.

I am on the final track of this prophecy, following it through the centuries. Boulders lie along the main passage, nursing the small stream. I move through them, pushing off one, landing at the base of the next, hand on its face for a half second, registering the surface grain. My touch defines for me how the boulder is wearing, how different this angle is from the native layering of the bedrock. The boulder's bedding of cemented sand will soon enough be thrown wide open by floods. I touch the next boulder, landing swiftly in a crouch on its roof, sensing how it resists my passing, how it endures crosion. This one will persevere, I think, its shoulder pushed into the floods, polishing rather than breaking apart.

The water guides me upward as boulders grow far taller than my head and I no longer climb over their tops. I make the last bend, and the chasm swings open into the enormously round hall of a cul-de-sac. Curved like the rings of Saturn, ledges circle up the back wall of this final chamber. No route from here. This is the end. I expected as much.

Instead of a crack to climb, I see groves of maidenhair ferns hovering about a shallow lens of water. The spring emerges not from below, but from all around. It spills in rivulets and seeps, an aria of drips dabbing into the greenery, spattering on fresh rock, filling the lens. My day pack slips off and falls to the ground.

I remember what the singer had said, that the springs are places to leave your offerings.

What do I have with me that I can leave here? I didn't come prepared. A favorite lighter . . . my knife . . . a broken pencil . . . a sharpening stone. I mentally inventory my belongings. I have come here like a desert merchant, carrying across my shoulders the jangle and sway of curiosities. I have strings of glass beads marking times with my father. I carry textiles imprinted with journeys, bits of metal and shell jewelry murmuring as they mingle with my pace, each plucked from a corpse or traded with others I have encountered in the wilderness.

My fingers habitually touch the smooth greenstone of my necklace.

This is the offering that I have carried.

I stop at the thought. I have not had this necklace off since . . . when? Eight years ago, at least. It was carved by a

Maori man in New Zealand, a sweet, effortless curve of stone that a friend brought back to this continent for me.

The singer had said what should be done at this point, the offering. Rituals of sacred travel sometimes call for exact moves. What if the laws are not obeyed? I wonder. What if I left here without dropping any of these precious remnants of mine, without offering my green pendant? The singer will of course never know, not an old sheepherder who hasn't visited for many years this thickness of sandstone labyrinths, layers upon layers, in which lies a single spring. Or will the weight shift in this place, like a boulder budging underfoot? There are ways to live, I think. Rituals of half-blind men speak to an oldness sometimes difficult to recall. They instruct the hands, bringing up memory.

I lift my knife, reach to my throat, and with one stroke cut free the necklace. The stone falls into my hand.

I run it back and forth between my fingers, feeling for the first time how worn it is. The eyehole has been fretted by its cord the same way the earth is trenched by water and wind. The swipe of my chest and the frequent dance of my fingers have been this stone's weather. I slip it from its cord and step forward into the thicket of ferns. The pendant falls into its dampness.

My breath feels cold. I am utterly exposed. I back away from the ferns, hands in front of me as if I have touched something that might tip, as if the canyon could capsize if I am not careful.

I am in the eye of a mountain lion with no knife in my hand. I turn my head, looking up through the vaults of sunlight and shadow. This is what is meant by a landscape of protection. This place does not outfit me in heavy armor impervious to spears and bullets. It pulls me into the open where I can no longer hide. I stand unflinching and unadorned, as curved and knotted as some primeval tree.

This is where I leave you, fathers, grandfathers, briars of ancients so far back that you seem like a single stone that I have carried for centuries. This is where I have brought you, where I leave you.

I peer back along the chasm. Dirk should have been here by now. I have not been away from him for this long in weeks. It would be reassuring to hear the strike of his voice. Something must have happened to him. Leaving the fern grove, I go back into the lower shadows. The water sends me down as I duck and crawl, grabbing arms of scrub oaks and jumping across still pools.

———

Dirk listens for me. I am not there. Last he saw I had picked up speed, moving quickly along the stream ahead of him, now gone. Off hunting the Giant Carp, no doubt. Dirk thinks that the chasm must end very near to here. A minute or two away and this floor should go off like fireworks, straight up, leaving him on the ground, agape. But he has been thinking this for the last hour. The final wall takes up most of what little sky might otherwise be visible. Dirk listens closely for me, for a crack of rock, a splash. There is only the garble of water. He moves on.

The chasm splits in two. The larger of these two incoming canyons is the source of the stream. The smaller is dry. *Rock, paper, scissors.* Where to from here?

Fresh sand lies in the floor of the barren one, easier to read than the other. Dirk walks almost into its mouth and then sees the tracks of a cat. They are fresh in the sand. Hours maybe. A day at the most. The gait had been easy.

Once more Dirk looks in my direction, listening. He does not see my tracks anywhere, so he knows that I followed the water and did not come this way. He imagines me toiling through the thickness of willows into the Carp's mouth about now.

Dirk goes along the dry canyon to follow the cat.

Arms and roots of scrub oak block his path, and he ducks through, hands taking hold, head lowered, watching how this animal ahead of him had dodged the same obstacles, how it moved unencumbered. The floor steepens slightly into plots of boulders. There will soon be a reckoning, he thinks. The end of this is just ahead. He sees the cat tracks going in but not coming out. There will be a cat or there will be a route. He imagines there is no mountain lion cornered in the back of this chasm, not with such a familiar gait as this. There must be a way out. This is hard, tangible proof. The earth is defined, always leading to an incontestable response. Live or die. Route or no route. Yes or no. Shoot or don't shoot. Still, there is something else, a sense Dirk has of flow, of one thing leading seamlessly to the next, even in this disarray of cliffs and boulders. He is able to read these cat tracks as if they were written in English. The choreography of instinct and knowledge becomes uncanny as he moves: the ability to know where an animal is; the skill of walking through canyons and flanks of palisades that should be impenetrable. The sensation is familiar. Dirk has spent many quickened moments with it.

He remembers one night patrolling a dance club parking lot. On the surface of his mind is the quality of light, how asphalt can seem as dark as the ocean no matter how many streetlights are around. Especially between cars, where it is so hard to see, places all over for people to hide. Dirk came upon a kid sitting in a passenger seat with the door open, his legs casually extended, tennis shoes planted on the ground. The kid had a .38 Special revolver stuck into his belt. When Dirk stopped, the kid panicked and pulled the gun, leveling it at Dirk, who was five feet away.

He had known it would happen this way. His muscles were trained to slip this trap: Feint to the side in an unflinching draw; the first and second shots go to the chest, the clearest target; two hollow-point bullets explode inside the rib cage, knocking the kid back into the car with a burst of blood; and since people are known to fire back even after being hit in the chest, a third shot is steadied on the forehead; the bullet enters the skull and blossoms inside.

Quick as wind, Dirk abandoned his training. Time stretched wide, and he felt his body moving. He did not reach for his gun. Instead, he plowed through the open car door and clobbered the kid with his full weight, pinning him into the seat. He felt the revolver's barrel dig into his stomach.

Dirk knew that he would not feel the bullet. He would feel only the surge of the gun's recoil, the shot barely muffled by his abdomen. The bullet would flee through his body like a whisper, cutting his spinal cord at eight hundred feet per second. But the kid's gun had no bullets. It was just for show. There was no sound, no shiver of explosion. Dirk knocked the gun away and wrestled the kid onto the oily asphalt, thrusting cuffs onto his wrists.

Dirk thinks now that there is something about walking in this chasm that has no name. It leaves him clean of illusions, if only for a moment, for just a breath. Swifter than the reason Dirk had chosen not to shoot the kid. The kid's face had been too scared, flushed with uncertainty — an expression that said,

There are no bullets in my gun. With unmarred clarity, Dirk knows that this mountain lion is at the river gorge by now. The thing without a name lies in the water paths, in the carve of chasms, in the strange erosion of boulders. It lies in his vision as much as it lies in the world surrounding him. He senses it in the motion of the lion ahead of him. He sees beyond his eyes, a skill that has saved him in this desert wilderness, in his cop landscape, in the interior country of his life. People so easily abandon the ability to see, to assess, and to know, lingering half asleep and half awake. Too dangerous a life, he thinks. Too dangerous to live so unaware.

The boulders become larger as Dirk nears the wall: big, freshly broken chunks of cliff standing about, a sign that he is almost there. The cat moves elegantly in front of him. The canyon sinks into the face of the cliff, and the floor ends here.

Dirk sees the jump, the paw-press of sand where the cat sprang upward, glancing against a rock surface, leaping to the next tier. He starts up to follow where it had been maybe only hours ago, stemming through narrow spaces where boulders hang. He imagines the moves of the cat. Like an alchemist, he transforms these moves into his own.

Dirk stops, hearing my approach below.

I am coming up the sandy floor, looking up the slender cut of the canyon. Up, up, up. I cannot see where it ends. I had already seen the cat prints like round hands in the sand. I follow them up with my eyes, finding not a mountain lion in the cliff crack, but Dirk Vaughan looking down his shoulder at me.

Dirk shouts that this route goes out. I study him, then look behind to the rest of the way we are going to have to walk today, retreating to camp to reach our packs.

"It's hours back to camp," I complain.

Dirk pulls himself to a ledge and looks down at me. "It's a perfect route," he says.

I truly do not want to climb this thing. Perfect, yes, but the day is far from over. As it is we will not reach our packs until dusk. There has to be a route out of here somewhere closer to our last camp.

"I'm tired, Dirk."

He nods his head, then stands, turning to face the wall, the mountain lion's route extending high above him. He lifts his arms as if cradling the passageway. I hear him whisper, "Good-bye."

Shamu

Dirk began with a letter to the family of the man who died in the car accident. He wrote,

> *Do I wish I had been driving slower? Absolutely yes. I wish I had gone slower. I wish the car engine had blown up and stopped. I wish I had called in sick that night. I wish I had chosen a career as a mailman or insurance salesman or park ranger. I wish many things. It was an accident in the true meaning of the word. A terrible set of coincidental circumstances that can never be fully understood or accepted.*

Then he resigned from the police force and made his last move with Linda to Moab. This time, they lived differently, settling into a pop-up tent trailer anchored in the parking lot of a river outfit. He avoided any notion of working in law enforcement. Instead he bought into a company that hauled equipment out to the wilderness rivers.

With his last paycheck he purchased two plane tickets to Florida. Sea World was the destination, a completely unfamiliar ceremonial ground where he could relinquish the last fifteen years of police work. Dirk wanted to mingle with oddities of marine life, to stroll the bizarre circuses of aquariums and hot dog stands. He wanted to gawk at the world with no gun on his hip and vanish into the press of aimless and vaguely blissful citizens.

Dirk told this Sea World story to me only once, the night we were camped together in a winter canyon north of here. I remember how his body jetted into the air, how his voice lifted away from everything around him as he talked.

"Linda kept trying to get me to go see Shamu," he told me. "The captured, tormented killer whale. I said no way, this is where I'm drawing the line. Give me the lower sea creatures, invertebrates, anemones, crabs, sea horses, the things that can't tell if they're living in the wild or in a toilet bowl. But a gargantuan mammalian predator stored in a closet, probably berserk from claustrophobia and eating buckets of dead fish? Not happening. I've seen enough horror, thank you. But you know Linda. She finally dragged me out to these bleachers in front of a glorified swimming pool, and I couldn't stop thinking: This is just barbaric.

"Then the pool gates opened, and this enormous underwater shape moved in, circling the edges. I shut up right then. It started going faster and faster, and this ominous music was piped in through speakers while a deep voice announced: *This*

*is the largest predator in the world that hunts like a wolf. It con-
sumes however many tons of fish in a week, weighs this much, jaw
strength of however many ridiculous pounds per square inch.* And
this thing was racing with increasing agility right in front of me,
totally mad with speed, a shield of water slipping over its back.
The music was booming, and the voice crescendoed to a tri-
umphant cry: *IT'S SHAMU! THE KILLER WHALE!*

"Right then this thing exploded straight into the air. Sleek as
fucking death. All these kids in the bleachers were up on their
feet screaming. Man, I was right with them, up on my feet,
howling like a madman. You're in the water and this thing
decides to eat you? You're nothing but a mosquito. I was going
absolutely wild.

"Linda was tugging at me, begging me to sit down. Please,
please, please. But there was no way I was sitting down. I'm
looking at the kids. They're looking at me. This killer whale is on
the same planet with us! I was goddamned born again!"

DAY SIXTEEN

We have been walking for only two weeks. The maps tell us that
since this journey began we have covered no more than five
miles. How much actual wear? Maybe a hundred miles on our
feet. Ten thousand handholds.

In our packs only the sparest food remains, sandy bags of
nuts, raisins wrinkled and hidden among folded clothes. We
will soon find a food cache that we had set near the river in

anticipation of this day. It is a metal ammunition box lodged in sand, its contents difficult to recall. Rice, perhaps. Chocolate if we had the foresight.

Dirk and I climb from the third chasm. Our route turns out not to be the vexing gallows of ledges and cliffs we had anticipated. It is an opening in the land, a falling away of wings. It is not the long walk from camp we had expected, either, just a notch a surprisingly short distance from where we slept last night. The stone walls spread apart as we walk through them. The walking is steady as we scan for the next step, the next shape of rock that will take our hands. We come into a land of stone wells and domes. The chasm drifts behind us, losing form, hidden by distance, finally gone.

When I leave this desert, I will forget these stories, the details of sand and entrancement. I will forget, in the act of opening a letter in front of the post office, of waking up late in a bed of cotton sheets. Then I will remember. I will notice three snail shells on my desk. I will look at them as if I had not been the one who placed them there, and I will remember everything. I will pluck a pebble from my shoe, and the desert will fall back into me.

Now I am here. An image of a horse is engraved into one of the curving walls ahead of us, a big Diné horse with a draping tail, egg-sized nostrils. Beside each other, Dirk and I step up to it, hands against its warm south-facing wall. Someone, probably a sheepherder with a camp nearby, spent days carving it. Perhaps he was dreaming of a mythical horse to carry him across this country. Our fingers follow its outlandishly intentional lines. It might as well be a billboard. We have returned to the human world, a place where stories are not only told, but yearned for, chiseled into stone blow by blow in a wonderful race against erosion. I walk along the wall and find on the ground the grayed sand of campfires and a rusty scatter of tin cans as foreign as Sputniks fallen from the sky.

Dirk and I stand now in the country of a domestic horse, of fifty-year-old rubbish, a land of people with hands and eyes like our own, a land marked by our longing. We keep moving, finding more and more of this. A stairway has been chiseled into stone using metal wedges and hammers, a passage built for sparse herds of livestock that nibble at dead ricegrass and juniper branches. We use their stairs as we descend a great nose of sandstone.

No talking. The sound of boots working the stone. Gear shifting on our backs. I never should have been a man, a human being. All along I was this thing tumbling, a leaf, a wind-delivered sand grain. And all along Dirk was a hawk at the side of the road. It has taken us this long to become familiar with each other. I hardly see him as we walk down this prominence, yet I can see the ground that he sees. No longer are we alone. We have been rinsed in each other's memories. We are two forces of nature forever and irresistibly married, miraculously poised like a needle balanced on its tip. We sleep with infinity. We wake, if there is such a thing as waking, to a world shattered into water holes, X's, and vortex streets.

Finally, Dirk and I reach a drab olive ammunition box in the sand. The water is a few hundred feet below, sun-sparkled at the bend where tomorrow our companions will arrive in a boat. They will toss their bowline to a ledge, where our hands will catch it.

We dig free this military surplus canister and haul it over to bare rock, where it makes amazing sounds. The clack of metal! The pop of air as we break the seal! Inside we find a store of food that could last — how long? We sort it out: rice, pasta, curry, beans, chocolate, foil-wrapped bars of food, dried figs, and apples. Ten days of food, we figure. If we had arrived earlier, this bulk would have been useful, but only one night's worth is needed. Tomorrow we will float away from here.

Passing a bag back and forth, we sit eating figs, their insides jellied and grained with seeds. They are sweet, and they pop open in our mouths. In the quiet of eating, we see a raven a mile in the distance. The first raven. Dirk thrusts his chin toward it. Yes, I see it, too. We have truly returned to accustomed land. The shape of the raven's flight, effortless without a single budge of wings, is so filled with grace, so familiar, that I swallow and do not take another fig.

"Does it see us?" Dirk asks, a question to nobody.

I say nothing.

The raven rides above a cliff edge, its wings held by the rising warmth of the day. Even from here, I can see how it cups its talons, fists tucked into its body. I can see the observant movement of its head, the world that it sees below. We have both loved ravens. They are our clever tricksters. They have clutched pebbles and twigs, then dropped them from the air onto us. They have flown in close from behind and suddenly called, causing us to jump with surprise. We have imagined ourselves in their eyes, creatures restricted to the ground, but curious, looking up, following them as they follow us. We have longed for ravens in these days of walking.

The raven swings into a turn.

Dirk says, "Now it sees us."

If we are lucky, I think, if we are blessed, the raven will come.

The raven drifts across the gorge, making a straight line

toward us. Within half a minute it is here, its black feathers fingering the air as it turns just above our heads, spiraling down to us, wondering who, what, we might be. Its eyes are wet with reflection. It is so close to us. So close that if I were standing, holding up my hand, I would graze its wings. But neither of us moves. We savor this bird as it turns steep on a wing, puzzled.

As the raven touches the sun, blackness illuminates to a blinding white. Its shadow cuts Dirk's face, then mine. So rare is this alignment that I hardly remember if it's happened to us before. We have been found by a raven's shadow.

Dirk and I both lift our hands to shade our eyes. The raven bats the air at our sudden movement, jerking away from us with an astonished, gritty cry. It was expecting maybe two boulders, two carcasses to perch upon. Three strokes of its wings and it is gone from us, sailing into the gorge. Our hands fall back to our knees.

We both want to speak, but finally there is nothing we can say to each other. We sit mute, forever marked by the passing wings of a raven.

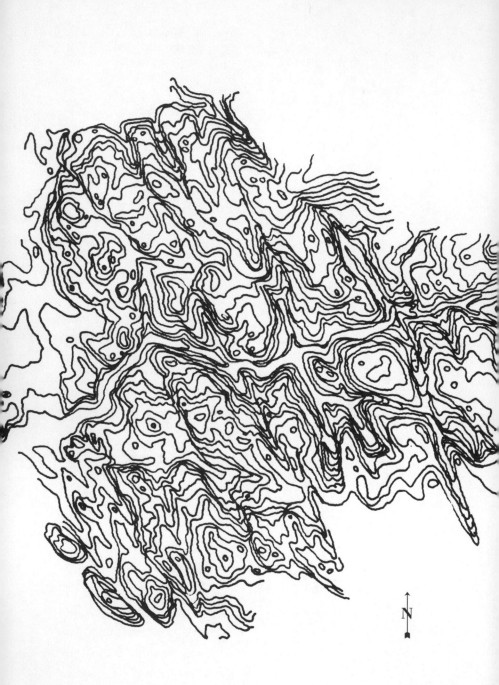

N

EPILOGUE

Summer. I sit on a Utah ledge not far from the dead man, watching Dirk, who is small in the distance. He is approaching, crossing a bench of rock, turning for a nearby canyon. He stops a mile off. We see each other. He moves on from there, coming toward me. The heat is incredible, even as the day is ending.

I shoulder my pack and go to him, the dead man who waits. Evening is coming. I walk across spans of open rock as thunderstorms roam in the south. Bursts of amber light show me the lay of my home country, buttes weeks away standing as sharp and remote silhouettes. I climb down through leaning boulders and enter his shelter, a slight cave formed in the benches of the cliff where he died, where he was buried, rock dust now where the Turin shroud of his skin once rested. His skull is on its side, eyes decorated, jaw fallen open.

Here you are, my desert saint. I tip my head, a gesture of surrender. This is your world. I am only briefly alive in it. Your bones have been relinquished, yet after hundreds of years, they hold their shapes. They are the limbs and trunks of bonsai junipers standing against the wind, your shoulder blades praying in blow sand. This is what has become of your stories, worn down word by word until they are as elegant as polished ivory. I look in on you with my gifts of inconsistencies and longing. You are my dead man in the desert, my clarity, and I am the man who still walks among stories.

ACKNOWLEDGMENTS

I am indebted to Colin Wann and the Brothers V for the journeys (to the eldest, Dirk, for — willing or not — ripping open his heart for this book), to Kathy Anderson for snatching me off the subway and setting fire to my pages, to Terry Adams for combing through the literary wilderness and finding me, and, utmost, to Regan Choi for her elegance, insight, and patient hunger.

ABOUT THE AUTHOR

Craig Childs contributes regularly to National Public Radio's *Morning Edition*. He is also a field instructor in natural history, an adventurer, and a writer. His other books include, most recently, *Soul of Nowhere* and *The Secret Knowledge of Water* (Back Bay Books), and *Crossing Paths: Uncommon Encounters with Animals in the Wild* (Sasquatch). He, his wife, and their two-year-old son live part time in a solar-powered cabin in western Colorado. The rest of the year they are in the field, where little is known of their lives.

READING GROUP GUIDE

THE WAY OUT

A TRUE STORY
OF RUIN AND SURVIVAL

by
CRAIG CHILDS

A conversation with Craig Childs

What does the title of the book mean?

From my perspective, "the way out" does not mean what it sounds like. For those who might catch a glimpse of the title in a bookstore or a library, it means finding your way out of something, a deep hole maybe. Certainly the book is about that, and in that sense the title is apt.

But for me and those in the desert with whom I journey, "the way out" is a place where you go walking and you disappear. It can be damn near anywhere, in any kind of environment. It lies beyond certain obligations — no phone, no emergency plan left with anyone, sometimes no map or compass even. It is best when going to this place not to leave a vehicle behind that marks where you went in. I don't know why exactly. It's better to cut your tethers, maybe hitchhike in on the nearest road or have a friend drop you off. There is no knowledge of dates or hours in a day here, just a sense of how much water and supplies one is carrying, and what kind of terrain lies both ahead and behind. Political boundaries are hazy in this place as I have often wandered back and forth between Mexico and the United States, on federal land and Navajo Reservation territory, without being aware of any transition. "The way out" is composed of wilderness in a true sense, not defined by an act of Congress or marked by a trailhead sign. The topography is complex, maddening even. Waterless sand dunes to the horizon; or blinding, snow-blasted basins above timberline; or, in the case of this book, a sandstone labyrinth packed with cliffs.

Walking around way out there, for me, is a razor blade sort of meditation, usually an easy place to get killed as a result of small mistakes. But with a good eye it becomes more or less safe as a sidewalk, maybe like standing real close to a subway clipping by your nose in the station. Safe, but potentially fatal. This kind of environment rivets my senses of observation every moment I am there. Any extraneous notions in my head tend to dissolve rapidly, leaving me moving around like a skeleton, someone sharpened down to the bone. When you need to get clean, it is a good place to go. I don't recommend it for your first time out, unless you want to get cleaner than you had wished.

When you were passing over the canyons in an airplane on the way to your father's funeral, what thought or impulse dug itself so deeply into your mind that you decided you must return to explore this landscape? Was it something particular about those canyons?

At that moment I was looking for stability, for safety. The view from the airplane revealed a whole landscape that represents protection and liberation to me, a country veritably empty of humans and eroded down to its geological bones. In a sense it is a place to hide, but it is far more than that. It is a treasure vault, a place where I can roam unseen through inexplicable natural wonders.

During the flight the plane passed over what looked like the heart of this country, a maze of canyons that I saw as my own heart, the geographic center of my life. The impulse I felt was to leap out of the plane. I wanted to be down there at any cost. I could have torn that window out with my bare fingers. The canyons were so deeply entrenched and interwoven that I knew what kind of navigational madness lay down there. I could taste what it would be like to move in that kind of world. The next best thing to actually departing the airplane at 15,000 feet was to return with Dirk and physically find our way inside of this labyrinth. There I knew I would find my sanctuary.

One of the most vividly memorable scenes in the book is when you take your father's canoe out in a flash flood and soon find yourself trapped in a storm drain. What made you do this? Had you ever felt that perilously close to death before?

It was probably the most ridiculous and dangerously unplanned thing I had ever done. But I do things like that. I dive in. It is a habit of mine: get into a situation that tests every possible aspect of my life by leaping first and then dealing with the repercussions seconds later. If I did not have such an urge to jump, I imagine I would rarely face the kinds of physical and emotional difficulty that I so often find myself dealing with. The canoe ride into the storm drain was a pinnacle of this sort of behavior.

Yes, I have been perilously close to death many times. Careening through fire smoke in a British Columbian bush plane, standing stock still as a mountain lion circles me at ten feet, slipping down the clean face of a rock spine hundreds of feet above solid ground. Too many of these experiences, really. I've really got to be more careful. I am not an adrenaline junkie, though. I dread the next time I rub so hard against death's shoulder. The canoe in the storm drain was going too far. I usually weigh my options very carefully. What many see as reckless acts of hazard in the wilderness are to me carefully timed and executed maneuvers in a world where I feel very safe. But not that time. I was out of my element in that urban flood. It was a stupid thing to do, but it made more sense to me than anything at the moment.

Your relationship with Dirk is deeply loving, despite being so different from each other. What attracts you to him and vice versa? Did your friendship evolve over the course of your trip? Over the course of the book's publication? Did Dirk have any misgivings about the way you portrayed him?

I worked with Dirk closely through the writing of this book to make sure he knew exactly what I was doing. He had to take a deep breath and let everything go. Certainly he was laid bare in this book and he knew it all along. But so was I. It stripped us both down to our core. That was my intention: write a book that does to us exactly what the desert does. We were revealed.

Dirk did not have any misgivings because the book was utterly honest and there was no other way to tell this story. We talked about making it a fiction, changing the names, but it was real, it happened just as it was written.

How did our relationship evolve over the length of the trip? You must understand that there have been many trips, each one the next step in our evolution. I could have written a book about any one of these journeys (in fact, *The Way Out* was to be about another trip entirely and I just wanted to head out with Dirk for a couple weeks to feel him out a little more . . . those couple weeks became the book). Every time we left for the wilderness together we grew into each other, grafted in a way. Opposites attract. But it is more than that. It is the classic yin and yang. Dirk is vastly different from me, but inside of him I see a secret seed of myself, and vice versa.

Dirk once told me that while we were traveling in a Utah canyon — not one in the book — he looked at me and thought our friendship felt like falling in love. That, he said, was the moment he realized we were inseparable, that the mere thought he was falling in love was something that would more likely come out of my mouth. When he told me this I laughed, because at that same moment in that same canyon I had come to the same realization that we were forever bound. But for me it happened in a different way. For the first time I looked into his eyes and thought, almost giddily, Dirk could actually kill me.

It is obvious from your books — Soul of Nowhere, The Desert Cries, The Secret Knowledge of Water, Crossing Paths, *and* The Way Out — *that you're devoted to the natural world as it exists in the wild. What about cities? Do they keep any kind of hold over you? Can you imagine yourself ever writing about the city?*

In some ways cities are no different for me. I am drawn to their alleys, the oily shadows of subway rails, the press of pedestrians and traffic that looks so much like water swirling inviolably along its path. Humans are boulders. Buildings are cliffs. Every door leads into a cave, a canyon. And no one knows you're there. I lurk through Manhattan and Seattle like a thief. I'm the one with the journal open, leaning against a lamppost. I'm the one in the back of the café alone, the one standing in the shadow. Cities are an explosion of exotic scents and languages for me, absolutely enthralling. Yes, I could write about the city, and my words would be indistinguishable from words about the desert.

What is your writing process like? Do you write while you are out on expeditions (i.e., keep a journal), or do you write from memory once you're home?

I fill journals in the field with tiny, antlike handwriting. It is almost a bad habit, like smoking, tapping a journal out of my pocket and folding my body over it. These journals go home and I read them to spark memories. In ways they are all written in code — all caps meaning one thing, handwriting set at an angle to the page meaning another. These codes are the seeds of my experience. I write from memory once I am home, memory ignited by these chicken-scratch journals.

As a parallel storyline to the adventure narrative, The Way Out *offers a very personal look at the violent relationship you had with your father, and Dirk's equally violent career as a cop. Was it difficult to write these scenes, either emotionally or structurally?*

My heart physically hurt the whole time I wrote this book. I truly thought I would die, that my heart would explode. Yes, it was difficult. My father appeared in dreams that I was certain were real, and I struggled with the thought that he was supposed to be dead, yet was right there in front of me. Dream by dream I began to explain to him that I had written a book that dealt with our relationship, with secrets between us. The dreams are still there, more powerful than ever.

Structurally this was a complex book to put together, but nothing compared to the emotional complications. Dirk knew what I was doing from the beginning. And I knew, too. I was peeling the flesh off our lives. Beneath the flesh were stories of violence. And beneath that was a deep fear. I remember sitting with my father in the front of my truck during a rainstorm, our campfire having gone out. Under the percussion of rain on the roof my father said something to this effect: "You are a small rabbit out in the open." When he said this he lifted the cigarette, drew from it, and returned it to his knee. Then he said, "I am only the hawk's shadow. I am not the hawk. It is the hawk you need to be aware of, not me."

It is the hawk that I found when I wrote about Dirk, my father, and me. It was a dreamlike predator stalking us, driving us through our lives, sending us into canyons where people rarely go.

I know that you have a wife and young son. How do they deal with your itinerant lifestyle?

My wife lives a similar life. When we first got together she was living in a ten-by-ten cabin she had built herself in the Sangre de Cristo mountains of southern Colorado. She is no stranger to this itinerant world. Nor is our son, Jasper. We spend half the year at home. We often enter the wilderness together. When Jasper was seven weeks old the three of us ran the Colorado River together. Jasper has already been deep in the country, weeks with no contact with phones or pavement. And sometimes, as on the trip in *The Way Out,* I have my own, private business to attend to in the desert and it is time for me to go alone.

What are you working on next?

The gist of the next book is a journey of more than a thousand miles, from the Four Corners into Mexico, following the supposed disappearance of the Anasazi. This book, thank goodness, avoids many of the emotional hazards *The Way Out* took me through. It deals with archaeologists, excavations, and deep wilderness where ancient ruins exist that are rarely ever seen.

Questions and topics for discussion

1. Craig Childs and Dirk Vaughn are lost. Frustrated, scared, tired, and angry, they are trapped in a maze of canyons. Have you ever been so lost that, like Craig and Dirk, you felt your sanity being tested?

2. Before Craig and Dirk can embark on their journey into the sacred Protectionway land, they must receive permission from an old Dine singer. Given the cultural differences between Craig and Dirk, and the Dine tribesman, were you surprised that they were granted permission? Why do you think the singer allowed the men to explore his tribe's sacred country?

3. The "endless routes" of the canyons that the men travel through are, as Dirk describes them, places for "completely undistracted internal dialogue." Have you ever visited a place that forced you into thinking and/or talking to yourself? What did you say?

4. The book is subtitled *A True Story of Ruin and Survival*. Where, when, and in what way do Craig and Dirk experience ruin? What about survival?

5. How would you describe the relationship between Craig and Dirk? How are they different? How are they similar? Did you identify more closely with one man than the other? Of your friends and family, whom would you take on a trip like this? Why?

6. Flashbacks are employed throughout the book: memories of the author's difficult, often violent relationship with his father, and memories of Dirk's difficult, often violent career as a cop. How do these flashback scenes enhance the present-day Protectionway journey narrative? How does each man's history affect his present?

7. At one point Craig thinks Dirk sees him as "a reckless person, someone willing to risk death just so I can validate my being alive" (page 131). Do you see the author this way? Do you think the author sees himself this way?

8. The two men come across a set of human footprints and determine they belong to people who "knew how to move out here. . . . Kindred monkeys" (pages 224–225). Have you followed — physically or metaphorically — in anyone's footprints? Where did they lead you? Were you kindred spirits with the person? If someone came across your footprints, what could they infer about you?

9. Throughout the book, Craig grapples with reckoning the different sides of his father — a violent, abusive alcoholic, but also the man who instilled in him a love and respect for the wilderness. By the end of his journey, what conclusions, if any, has Craig reached about the nature of his relationship with his father? How do you think children should deal with a parent who is difficult to love?

10. Reread the epilogue. What do you make of it? Is what the author describes — Dirk in the distance, the skull of the dead man — real? imagined? a dream? a hallucination?

Craig Childs's suggestions for further reading

Arctic Dreams by Barry Lopez

The Collected Poetry of Robinson Jeffers

Everything Mary Oliver has ever written

The Meadow by James Galvin

The Solace of Open Spaces by Gretel Ehrlich

The Songlines by Bruce Chatwin

Dune by Frank Herbert

Bonelight: Ruin and Grace in the New Southwest by Mary Sojourner

The Monkey Wrench Gang by Edward Abbey

Also by Craig Childs

The Secret Knowledge of Water

"Utterly memorable and fantastic. . . . Certainly no reader will ever see the desert in the same way again."
— Suzannah Lessard, *Washington Post*

"Sometimes a book comes along that is pure oxygen. . . . *The Secret Knowledge of Water* stings like a slap in the face."
— Susan Salter Reynolds, *Los Angeles Times Book Review*

"Childs's tales of rain in canyonlands are narratives of suspense and tragic chance that transform his lyrical, meandering work into a sudden page-turner."
— Heather Mackey, *San Francisco Bay Guardian*

"Childs takes delight in continually surprising the reader."
— Martin Napersteck, *Salt Lake Tribune*

"Childs's narrative ripples with adventure. . . . His highly personal odyssey combines John McPhee's gift for compressing scientific knowledge and Barry Lopez's spiritual questing."
— *Publishers Weekly*

Back Bay Books • Available wherever paperbacks are sold

Also by Craig Childs

Soul of Nowhere

"Awe-inspiring. . . . Childs uses the desolate places he writes about as an existential testing ground where, in facing the prospect of his extinction, he discovers an abiding will to live."
— Rand Richards Cooper, *New York Times Book Review*

"Craig Childs helps us understand that it is neither the journey nor the destination that is most important but rather what it is you are willing to find. Those most open, like Childs, find their souls." — Martin Naparsteck, *Salt Lake Tribune*

"Nature itself, as it turns out, is way trippier than peyote. . . . Childs's sincerity and (literally) cliff-hanging narrative make a compelling case." — Richard Speer, *Willamette Week*

"Where his language is as taut as the lands he chronicles, Childs achieves the spare elegance of these Southwestern landscapes." — Rachel Elson, *San Francisco Chronicle*

Back Bay Books • Available wherever paperbacks are sold